Jean Conil's
FRENCH FISH CUISINE

Cuisine Marinière Francaise
Gourmet Recipes from a Master Chef

Jean Conil's
FRENCH
FISH
CUISINE

Gourmet French Fish Recipes
from Master Chef
Jean Conil
with Fay Franklin

Colour photography and styling by Paul Turner and Sue Pressley, Stonecastle Graphics
Illustrations by Paul Turner

THORSONS PUBLISHING GROUP
Wellingborough, Northamptonshire
————— · —————
Rochester, Vermont

First published 1986

Page 8: A reconstruction of a typical menu from the Buffet de la Halle, Boulogne-sur-mer.

British Library Cataloguing in Publication Data

Conil, Jean
    Jean Conil's french fish cuisine: cuisine
marinière française.
    1. Cookery (Seafood)   2. Cookery, French
    I. Title   II. Franklin, Fay
    641.6'9'0944   TX747

    ISBN 0-7225-1252-X

Printed and bound in Singapore.

Contents

Acknowledgements

The authors would like to express their gratitude to the following people and companies for their help, advice or support in the testing of recipes and the preparation of food for photography: Mr James Pringle, Editor, *Fish Trader*, Queensway House, 2 Queensway, Redhill, Surrey; Mr Brian Ehmes, Sea Fish Authority, 144 Cromwell Road, London SW7; Ms Amanda Courtney, British Trout Association, 22 Ringmer Avenue, London SW6; Miss Linda Lane, Headway Public Relations, 28 Southampton Street, London WC2 (on behalf of Martini and Noilly Prat Ltd.); Mr W.H.C. Bayliss, Bayliss and Sons Ltd., (Wholesale Food Distributors), 99 Plough Way, London SE16; Mr David James, Scottish Salmon Information Bureau, Richmond Towers, 26 Fitzroy Square, London W1; Gwynne Hart and Associates, Uncle Ben's Rice, Walter House, 418 Strand, London WC2; Mrs Diana Fleming, Elliot Service and Company, 10 Barb Mews, London W6 (on behalf of John West PLC); Mr Marcel Forman, H. Forman and Son (Salmon Curers), 6 Queen's Yard, White Post Lane, London E9; Mr Stuart McKenzie, Fishmonger, Smithfield Market, London W1; Mrs Shirin Thobani, Frozen Fish Food Ltd., 10 Lansdowne Close, London SW20 8AS; Mr Richard West, Distributors of Frozen Fish, for Clouston Europe, 924 Oxford Road, Tilehurst, Reading; The French Government Tourist Office, 192 Piccadilly, London, W1; Fin Hawkes Ltd., Vegetable Merchants; Courtier Company, 267 Merton Road, London SW18, for the generous supply of china and glassware; Mr Costa, La Porcellana Ltd., 3 Somers Place, London SW2; Ms Jane Miller, Home Economist, for her valuable contribution to the photographic sessions.

To the following chefs, for their contributions and advice: Edward Mennie, Chairman of the Society of Master Chefs; Marc Legros, Chef de Cuisine, Brasserie de St Quentin; Anthony Baker, Executive Chef, Royal Westminster Hotel; Michel Hamiot, Proprietor, Atlantic Hotel, Wimereux, France; David Pippard, formerly of the Royal Overseas League Club; David Evans, The Bear Hotel, Hungerford.

To the Chairman of the Arts Club, Mr Stuart Rose; and to the staff, in particular Julio Alvarez, Sous Chef; Neal Findlay, Sous Chef; Michael Luck, Secretary; Sharon McAngus, designer. Our thanks for all your assistance.

To Mme Annie Wable of the Tourism Office of Boulogne-sur-mer, and to the Presidents of the Associations and Syndicates of *Armateurs* and *Mareyeurs* of Boulogne-sur-mer. To all friends from the fishing industry in both Boulogne and Billingsgate, who have given their wholehearted support to this project. And lastly to our families, and friends in the culinary world, especially the members of the Society of Master Chefs.

Preface

'I don't like fish,' say people who remember the horrors of school meals. How frustrating it is for anyone preparing a dinner party to hear a guest dismiss in that one phrase all the tastes and textures of fish, from the luxurious turbot and salmon to the humble whiting, and shellfish from lobsters to shrimps.

Fish is immensely adaptable: it can be found plain, smoked, breaded or battered; it can be served with all manner of sauces, and it can be made into pâtés or mousses which may be prepared well in advance of your special meal. The prawn cocktail is one of the most popular appetizers in hotels and restaurants of the world, but there are plenty of shellfish alternatives available to the creative cook, such as scampi, scallops and clams. And fish gives you something appropriate to go with the white wine that guests nearly always bring to dinner parties!

Meat fans might claim that fish is not satisfying, but the truth is that it makes a perfectly substantial and healthy main course. Fish is a very convenient food, too. The frozen varieties are often fully prepared, and your fishmonger can gut and fillet the fresh variety for you. And cooking times are minimal. What is more, fish is good for you: in days of increased awareness of healthy eating, here is a food which is high in protein and low in cholesterol.

My journal, *Fish Trader*, serves an industry which wholeheartedly welcomes the contemporary attitudes to diet. It also welcomes the efforts of a flamboyant culinary personality like Jean Conil to promote fish. This book is set to be even more successful than his recent *Cuisine Végétarienne Française*.

The son of one of Boulogne's finest fish restaurateurs, Jean grew up appreciating the joys of seafood, and he trained as a chef in some of the top Paris restaurants, where his mentors were all famous chefs. He went on to become executive chef in such establishments as Fortnum and Mason and, currently, the Arts Club in London.

Not only is Jean Conil a writer, broadcaster and lecturer on cookery, and founder of his own Academy of Gastronomy, but also president of the Society of Master Chefs. The Society has twice arranged spectacular presentations of fish at Billingsgate Market open days.

In this latest book, Jean Conil offers imaginative ideas for starters and main courses, with an emphasis on using small fillets for *nouvelle cuisine* dishes. So if your view of fish is limited to the local chip shop or those dreadful school meals of the past, turn these pages and see what colourful and appetizing dishes are possible.

JAMES PRINGLE
Editor, *Fish Trader*

Menu

Diner au Muscadet et Sancerre

☆

Truite Arc-en-Ciel Marinée
Noilly-Prat

☆☆☆☆☆

La Soupe des Pêcheurs de Boulogne

☆☆☆

Coquilles Saint-Jacques aux Corallines
Garni de Couscous à la Conil

☆☆☆☆☆

Le Gâteau D'Anniversaire Imbibé
au Rhum et Garni de Sorbet aux Fraises

Foreword

The true potential of fish has not yet perhaps been fully realized in the new movement towards a healthy gastronomic tradition, so it is highly meritorious of Jean Conil — son of a Boulogne fish restaurateur — to draw these two concepts together in a single book.

Fish as a 'health food' has much to recommend it, as the millions of people who are turning to natural foods and cutting back their meat consumption have fast been realizing. Its nutritional qualities are excellent, it is easily digested, and it provides a light yet satisfying alternative to the richness of our modern diet — perhaps our forefathers were wiser than we had appreciated in observing the 'fish on Fridays' rule.

Yet the simple fact that something is good for us is not necessarily enough to convince us that it is good to eat. We should not forget the variety and versatility of this wholesome, natural food. We in France have, perhaps more than most, explored the culinary challenge of fish cuisine. We have been known to speak of the 'noble species', but even we are inclined to snub the common varieties which are so abundant in our oceans. It is part of the alchemy of this book that the authors have used all sorts of fish, from the most familiar to the rare and unusual, transforming each and every one into a delectable and appetizing treat that can be prepared by amateur and professional cook alike. Surely here is the best argument of all in the debate — fish is as delicious to eat as it is good for you!

In my role as Mayor of Boulogne and Minister of Fisheries for France, I am a frequent guest at official functions. So, just as I welcome the idea that a book such as this will inspire the consumer to ask for and purchase more varieties of fish, I delight in the thought that chefs will take up Jean Conil's ideas and the dishes on the menus of restaurants and caterers will become more diverse. I think that many people, when dining out, will welcome as I do the opportunity of choosing a fish main course so that they can eat well without ending the meal feeling over-indulged and even unwell. Of course, I may be thought of as biased when I choose fish in preference to meat, but I see many of my fellow officials doing likewise so I know that I am not alone in this preference.

As a gourmet, too, I rejoice in Jean Conil's approach to fish cuisine. None of the pleasures of the palate are lost in this approach to healthy eating. Richness is balanced by lightness, the finest of classic cuisine is reappraised in light of the concepts of the new. The knowledge and experience distilled into these pages makes each and every recipe a gastronomic treat — for this especially the authors must be particularly and warmly congratulated.

As Mayor of France's first sea port, and as Minister of Fisheries, I welcome this book

as something of a trump card in putting fish into its rightful place at the forefront of good food. Jean Conil and Fay Franklin deserve great success with their happy collaboration. I cannot help but remember, too, that a book such as this will be welcomed by the many thousands of fishermen and their families whose livelihood is in the hands of the consumer just as much as on the perilous seas. It is to their labours and endeavours that this book pays a special tribute in the unequalled style of French cuisine, and for that, too, I wish it every success.

GUY LENGAGNE
Secrétaire d'État chargé de la Mer
Maire de Boulogne-sur-mer

Introduction

I was brought up in Boulogne, the fish capital of France, where my father owned two restaurants famed for their seafood specialities. At the Buffet de la Halle, which was the main fish restaurant, we featured over fifty seafood dishes and the splendid, many-coursed dinners featuring all aspects of fish cuisine were renowned throughout Northern France. Our family lived above the modern fish market so, as you can imagine, our lives were interwoven with the bustling trade carried out below. As a child I would stand at the window, looking down on the boats unloading their catch straight onto the quay at the edge of the market, and everything from sprat to shark would come up in its turn for auction to buyers from both France and England. My youth was spent learning the business of cooking, under the guidance of my father Octave, and the sea influenced my every waking hour in some way. Not so surprising, then, that even when I left Boulogne, I was soon even more closely involved with the sea as the War drew me aboard ship in first the French, and then the British, Navy.

I have always loved fish as a food, from earliest days when my childish palate appreciated — as does that of every French child — all sorts of tasty fish delicacies. Later, as I learned my trade, I came to realize the versatility of this special food. All chefs appreciate the opportunity of creating new dishes, of trying new styles of cooking, and of using ingredients which respond to careful handling in interesting and appetizing ways, and fish has always appeared to me far and away more challenging and exciting to cook than meat.

It has always seemed especially sad to me, in light of this, that my chosen home of England had, until recently, apparently lost its taste for fish. With the exception of that classic dish of fish and chips (which, when well prepared can be food fit for a king, yet is more often to be found with little more flavour and texture than the newspaper in which it is served) little else in the way of fish was likely to be part of the typical British diet. But times are changing, I am pleased to say.

Over the past few years there has been a resurgence of interest in fish in many parts of the world. I feel it is very much in response to the growing interest in health and vitality that has been so evident of late. As my training as a chef led me into the field of food technology I was at the forefront of this movement towards a healthier diet. I realized many years ago that fish has even more going for it than fine flavour and versatility — it is also one of the most nutritious and healthy foods you can eat.

Fish is an excellent source of protein, and contains many essential vitamins and minerals. White fish, especially, contains very little fat, making it an ideal food for those on a low-fat diet, and even the traditionally 'oily' varieties such as herring or mackerel are high in unsaturated fats, unlike the high-cholesterol fats in meats and dairy produce, so anyone worried about heart disease can enjoy a rich meal of fish without affecting their health. Many types of fish are low in calories and carbohydrate,

and so can be enjoyed as part of a slimming diet.

Fish finds favour, too, with a large number of semi-vegetarians. This is for several reasons, as well as the obvious health advantages. I think many people are now aware of the use of hormones in meat products, to produce bigger, leaner cattle more quickly. Despite the way our seas sometimes appear to be growing more polluted over the years, this does not affect the fish that live in it, for the most part, and the mercury scandal that rocked the Japanese tuna industry some years ago was a rare incident — the fuss and outcry it caused proving amply how rare it is to meet serious problems of polluted fish. There is also the question of meat production in terms of quality of life. Fish is at least 'free range', unlike so many of the other 'healthy' foods being promoted as part of a 'natural' diet — like veal calves in their pens and battery chickens on their cramped perches.

So you see, my whole background had led me to an understanding of the values of fish, from my earliest days as a boy in Boulogne, to my recent researches into vegetarianism for my last book, *Cuisine Végétarienne Française*.

We should now spend a moment looking at the different types of fish, and the ways they can be cooked. After all, there are over 100 species of fish on the market! Fish are generally divided into three main types: demersal, which live on or near the sea-bed (and include round as well as flat fish); pelagic, which live near the surface, usually in shoals; and shellfish, which in turn divide into molluscs (scallops, oysters etc.) and crustaceans (such as lobsters and shrimps). Fish can also be divided into white and oily varieties, or into sea or freshwater — some would add farmed fish to the latter division, too.

You will find ample examples of all these types of fish in this book. In a field such as French fish cuisine one can only hope to skim the surface of the art — an encyclopaedia would be needed to come close to taking in all the thousands of recipes and variations my countrymen and women have devised over the centuries to use the harvest of their lakes, streams and shores. But we have tried to give you a taste of as many fish and styles of cooking as possible without becoming too overwhelming. Some fish will be familiar and, of course, where a fish is specified — a flat white fish, for example — you can use whichever is local or most appealing to you. The dish may taste different to the way it did when it was tested in my kitchens, but the principle by which it is prepared and cooked should hold sound, and it will certainly taste as good. As always, variety is the keyword — a recipe should inspire and enlighten, it should never be held as a law graven on stone. Good cooks will always take what they think is best from the printed page and make it their own. If they understand what they are doing they are assured of my blessing on their meal.

The observant reader will note that I have avoided too much emphasis on the earliest stages of preparing fish and shellfish in my recipes. This is by no means as a result of a lack of desire to pass on my tips and skills in these techniques. Rather it is because my researches have shown me that it is a natural squeamishness which exists in many countries (not in France, I hasten to add) that has led to the decline in popularity of fish. I have taken great care in this book to omit the use of all meat and poultry, such was the response to my book of vegetarian cuisine by people who asked for a fish book to follow it, and I feel that they above all will not want to be faced with a page of description on boiling a live lobster! So for the sake of my readers I will ask you to find a good supplier who will do the initial preparation for you — and take great care with it — and suggest that you concentrate on the all-important job of cooking and serving your fish with equal care and attention. Since a decent approach to the written and photographic description of correct fish preparation would take a book in itself anyway, I prefer to concentrate here on the culinary aspects, and would refer those readers who wish to tackle the procedure themselves to a good, plain, catering text book from which they can really learn.

So let us move to a brief look at the ways of preparing fish. I use the word preparing advisedly, since it is worth first mentioning the delights of properly prepared raw fish. Some people find the idea of raw fish very off-putting, but they are usually those who have never tried it, or who have not thought about the fact that traditional dishes such as rollmops, for example, are raw. Of primary importance when serving raw fish is that it should be absolutely fresh. So long as this is the case, your food will be palatable and with far more subtlety of flavour than cooked fish. In most cases, the fish is 'cooked' by being marinated in an acid or saline mixture, such as vinegar, citrus fruit juice or herbs and sea salt. This changes the appearance of the fish from a translucent, uncooked look to the opaque appearance we associate with fish cooked by heat. Fish to be eaten raw is usually sliced very finely to allow the marinade to permeate right through. The marinade fulfils the same function as cooking, in making it sterile and safe to eat. Since fish is naturally tender, heat is not applied for this purpose — in fact, as most people realize, overcooking will make fish drier and less tender, and must be finely gauged to get the balance just right. A marinade allows far more flexibility in this respect, making for a dish which is moist and appetizing as well as safe to eat.

Steaming is the best method of cooking fish, but still needs careful timing and a close eye on the proceedings to ensure perfection. Remember, your fish is cooked as soon as a skewer, gently inserted, enables the fish to flake. You will soon come to be able to judge this by eye, without making a mark on the fish itself. This method of cooking came to us from the Orient, and I think an inexpensive bamboo steamer from that region is the best type to use. Delicate *julienne* strips of vegetables can be cooked at the same time to preserve all their flavour and texture, and to enhance the colour of the finished dish. The steam in which the fish cooks can be flavoured with the addition of sea vegetables such as kelp to the water, or a delicate fish can be wrapped in leaves such as spinach before cooking. Whatever you choose to do, your fish will be delicious in flavour and texture — steamed fish has come a long way from its old associations with 'hospital food'.

Baking is a good cooking process for fish. The fish is cooked in a parcel which retains all the juices and prevents dehydration. This parcel can be the traditional paper or more modern and simple foil, in which the seasoned fish is placed with a little liquid — wine or melted butter are good — before being sealed and baked. Of course, the parcel might even be pastry, when the fish is boned and prepared before being sealed in its edible parcel.

Grilling (broiling) can be excellent for some fish, especially oilier varieties that retain their moisture well. But grilled fish passes very quickly from perfection to disaster, due to the fierceness of the heat. Basting will help prevent this, and will ensure you stay with the fish to keep an eye on it. Charcoal grilling (broiling) is one of the pleasures of the summer for fish-lovers, and adds a wonderful flavour to small oily fish, delicate steaks and chunky kebabs alike. Since food eaten outdoors always tastes extra-good, you may be excused for being more relaxed about the cooking, but it should never be an excuse for sloppy or careless cooking.

Frying is a technique open to terrible abuse. Deep frying should be carried out only by the most confident cook, not simply because it can be dangerous but because if the oil is too cool your fish will become soggy, greasy and unpalatable, too hot and it will be dry and singed. The heat must be just right to instantly seal the exterior of the fish, keeping the juices in and the oil out, and this will depend on the size and type of fish involved. A modern deep-fat fryer can help with this, but it cannot decide for you when your fish is cooked! Shallow frying is easier to manage, but care must still be exercised to get the heat just right, for the reasons already discussed. The Oriental technique of stir-frying is my favourite, with thin strips of fish being tossed in just a tiny amount of hot oil, along with vegetables. Cooking is almost instantaneous, and the flavour is exquisite.

A process which should never be used for fish is boiling, with the exception of

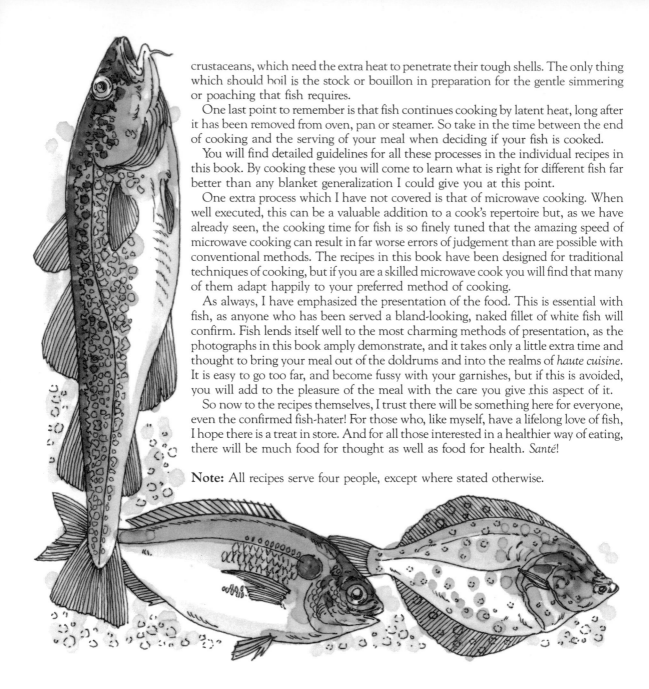

crustaceans, which need the extra heat to penetrate their tough shells. The only thing which should boil is the stock or bouillon in preparation for the gentle simmering or poaching that fish requires.

One last point to remember is that fish continues cooking by latent heat, long after it has been removed from oven, pan or steamer. So take in the time between the end of cooking and the serving of your meal when deciding if your fish is cooked.

You will find detailed guidelines for all these processes in the individual recipes in this book. By cooking these you will come to learn what is right for different fish far better than any blanket generalization I could give you at this point.

One extra process which I have not covered is that of microwave cooking. When well executed, this can be a valuable addition to a cook's repertoire but, as we have already seen, the cooking time for fish is so finely tuned that the amazing speed of microwave cooking can result in far worse errors of judgement than are possible with conventional methods. The recipes in this book have been designed for traditional techniques of cooking, but if you are a skilled microwave cook you will find that many of them adapt happily to your preferred method of cooking.

As always, I have emphasized the presentation of the food. This is essential with fish, as anyone who has been served a bland-looking, naked fillet of white fish will confirm. Fish lends itself well to the most charming methods of presentation, as the photographs in this book amply demonstrate, and it takes only a little extra time and thought to bring your meal out of the doldrums and into the realms of *haute cuisine*. It is easy to go too far, and become fussy with your garnishes, but if this is avoided, you will add to the pleasure of the meal with the care you give this aspect of it.

So now to the recipes themselves, I trust there will be something here for everyone, even the confirmed fish-hater! For those who, like myself, have a lifelong love of fish, I hope there is a treat in store. And for all those interested in a healthier way of eating, there will be much food for thought as well as food for health. *Santé*!

Note: All recipes serve four people, except where stated otherwise.

1 Les Chef-d'Oeuvres

Appetizers

If you look at the sea and the sky from the heights of Boulogne — be it from the clifftops or from Napoleon's memorial to his army — you will be amazed at the sight which confronts you. I loved to gaze out across the Channel when I was young, catching glimpses of Dover's famous white cliffs on clear days and little realizing that I would one day make the island beyond them my home. You will see, as I did, the breathtaking kaleidoscope of changing light. From the dawn mists, pierced by the first few rays of sunlight, promising the fisherman a fine, safe day's work; to the first wisps of fog, rolling off the Channel and obscuring the sky — nicknamed by mariners 'the shroud of the sun' — bringing with it the melancholy call of the foghorns which all seafaring folk know spells danger; to the dazzling greens and golds and reds of a fine sunset, which in turn lead to a spectacular vision of harbour lights reflected on the water, with a luminescent line of thin surf breaking gently on the beaches beyond the brightly lit casino, and above, the sparkle of the constant stars and changing moon.

All these different patterns of light have their meaning to the sailors of Boulogne, and each is noted with care by the folk whose very lives may depend on the changing moods of the weather seen through the rigging of their vessels as they set out to sea.

Yet go to sea they do, almost whatever the weather, for Boulogne is France's most important fishing port, teeming with boats of every size, from great trawlers, bound for the deep waters of the North Sea, to little boats whose catch will be sold by the fishwives on the stalls that line the Quai Gambetta. You can select as fine a meal from these stalls as in the days of my father's acclaimed seafood restaurant, the Buffet de la Halle, which was one of the finest of Boulogne's many great restaurants in the 1920s and 30s. We could seat as many as 300 people at our splendid eight-course banquets, and people came from miles around to sample the pick of the day's catch, transformed into a meal of style, flair and imagination.

These days, the cook in Boulogne requires only these same qualities to prepare just as fine a meal, whether for the family table or the *table d'hôte*. Flair and imagination to select the best from the fabulous displays of silvery fish and mysterious seafood, style to match them with the best country produce on sale in the market of the Place Dalton and the breathtaking choices of cheeses, wines and coffees which perfume the bustling streets of the Lower Town, shadowed as it is by the monumental walls of the Old Town, its quieter streets steeped in the history and traditions of a seafaring people in both war and peace.

And despite a volume of tourist traffic undreamed of in my father's day, it is the people of Boulogne themselves who are most frequently to be found at the stalls of quay and market, for Boulogne is all too often viewed only from the car or train window

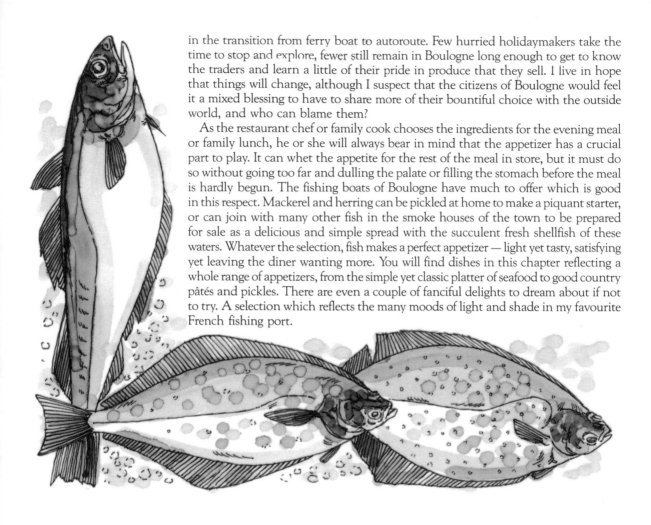

in the transition from ferry boat to autoroute. Few hurried holidaymakers take the time to stop and explore, fewer still remain in Boulogne long enough to get to know the traders and learn a little of their pride in produce that they sell. I live in hope that things will change, although I suspect that the citizens of Boulogne would feel it a mixed blessing to have to share more of their bountiful choice with the outside world, and who can blame them?

As the restaurant chef or family cook chooses the ingredients for the evening meal or family lunch, he or she will always bear in mind that the appetizer has a crucial part to play. It can whet the appetite for the rest of the meal in store, but it must do so without going too far and dulling the palate or filling the stomach before the meal is hardly begun. The fishing boats of Boulogne have much to offer which is good in this respect. Mackerel and herring can be pickled at home to make a piquant starter, or can join with many other fish in the smoke houses of the town to be prepared for sale as a delicious and simple spread with the succulent fresh shellfish of these waters. Whatever the selection, fish makes a perfect appetizer — light yet tasty, satisfying yet leaving the diner wanting more. You will find dishes in this chapter reflecting a whole range of appetizers, from the simple yet classic platter of seafood to good country pâtés and pickles. There are even a couple of fanciful delights to dream about if not to try. A selection which reflects the many moods of light and shade in my favourite French fishing port.

Opposite: Panir de Crevettes Mediterranée Surprise (page 164); *Cassolette de Rouget Cannoise* (page 30).

Plat de la Flotte Boulonnaise
Smoked Fish Medley

Illustrated opposite.

A platter of fish, based upon whatever is freshest and best in the market on that particular day, is hard to beat as an appetizer, and well-prepared smoked fish is perhaps best of all. If you are far from the sea it has the advantage, too, of remaining at its peak far longer than fresh seafood. At our restaurant the Buffet de la Halle in Boulogne we could pick and choose from the finest *mareyeurs* in all France, and our displays of fresh, pickled and smoked fish was enough to whet the appetite of even the most discerning customer. Use your imagination to create combinations of fish which will appeal to your guests — if you are unsure of their tastes, arrange your display on a single large platter and let them choose for themselves, but if you are confident of your choice then arrange your selection charmingly on individual plates, as shown opposite.

Imperial (Metric)	American
4 thin slices smoked salmon	4 thin slices smoked salmon
12 thin slices smoked halibut	12 thin slices smoked halibut
12 thin slices smoked tuna	12 thin slices smoked tuna
4 small fillets smoked eel	4 small fillets smoked eel
4 oz (100g) cream cheese	½ cup cream cheese
2 oz (50g) cooked asparagus tips	½ cup cooked asparagus tips
4 cooked asparagus spears	4 cooked asparagus spears
Sea salt and freshly ground black pepper	Sea salt and freshly ground black pepper
2 oz (50g) celeriac, cut into *julienne*	⅓ cup celeriac, cut into *julienne*
1 small carrot, cut into *julienne*	1 small carrot, cut into *julienne*
Sprigs corn salad or other garnish of choice (see below)	Sprigs corn salad or other garnish of choice (see below)
Mango Sauce (page 189)	Mango Sauce (page 189)
Sauce Raifort (page 178)	Sauce Raifort (page 178)

1 Place the slices of smoked salmon on a flat work surface. Arrange the smoked halibut and tuna attractively on the plate or plates of your choice. Reserve the smoked eel.

2 In a bowl, beat together the cream cheese and the asparagus tips, or blend to a smooth cream. Season with salt and pepper.

3 Spread a little of this mixture onto each slice of salmon, then place a spear of asparagus across the width of the slice and roll the fish up around it. Place alongside the smoked halibut and tuna.

4 Skin the smoked eel and check for any remaining bones. Using a very sharp knife, cut the fish into *julienne* of a similar size to the vegetables. Arrange these in heaps on the serving plate, or make an attractive lattice pattern, as shown opposite. Garnish and serve with a choice of sauces.

Variations:
These are, of course, almost endless but, in particular, certain garnishes suit the fish we have used here. Sprigs of dill, as shown, add an attractive flavour and look to the dish. Batons of cucumber and slices of kiwi fruit are delicious with the salmon, as is a tiny heap or sprinkling of black lumpfish caviar. Slices of mango and a few leaves of fresh mint add tang to the mellow-flavoured halibut, while slices of lime and ripe avocado harmonize well with the richer smoked tuna. Black olives look good with the dish, too. Leaves of radicchio provide a pleasant contrast of colour, as does a pool of jelly made by boiling ½ tablespoon agar-agar with 2 fl oz (60ml/¼ cup) Martini Rosso and ¼ pint (150ml/⅔ cup) fish stock which is then left to cool before being spooned onto the plate to set before the fish is arranged on top or alongside it. Oak leaf lettuce is another unusual and pretty salad leaf to try as a garnish.

Other combinations of seafood were particular favourites at the Buffet de la Halle, but two are worth special mention:

Le Plateau des Pêcheurs

Per portion:

Imperial (Metric)	American
2 poached oysters, served on the half-shell	2 poached oysters, served on the half-shell
2 boiled king prawns	2 boiled jumbo shrimps
1 small piece grilled red mullet	1 small piece grilled snapper
1 small marinated kipper fillet	1 small marinated kipper fillet
4 oz (100g) mixed *julienne* of blanched carrot, celery, leek, preserved ginger and samphire fronds	⅔ cup mixed *julienne* of blanched carrot, celery, leek, preserved ginger and samphire fronds
8 tablespoons raspberry vinegar (page 189)	8 tablespoons raspberry vinegar (page 189)
2 tablespoons sour cream	2 tablespoons sour cream

The fish was served on a bed of fresh seaweed such as kelp, and the *julienne* would be marinated in the vinegar and cream dressing before being served set in a small bowl in the centre of the platter. The fish could be served on a bed of lettuce if preferred, or simply on a platter.

Le Plateau Côte d'Opale

Per portion:

Imperial (Metric)	American
1 fresh, raw, deep-shelled oyster, served on the half-shell	1 fresh, raw, deep-shelled oyster, served on the half-shell
1 fresh, raw clam, served on the half-shell	1 fresh, raw clam, served on the half-shell
1 sea urchin, poached briefly and with top removed like a boiled egg	1 sea urchin, poached briefly and with top removed like a boiled egg
1 small cooked crab	1 small cooked crab
1 large crab claw, cracked	1 large crab claw, cracked
1 poached crayfish	1 poached crawfish
1 poached king prawn	1 poached jumbo shrimp
Lemon wedges	Lemon wedges
¼ quantity Sauce Conil (page 181)	¼ quantity Sauce Conil (page 181)

In fact, the portions we served were more often than not three of each of these ingredients, and the dish was served in stages — first, the oysters, clams and sea urchins, on a bed of crushed ice; then the dish of crabs and other crustaceans with a bowl of Sauce Conil in which to dip the shelled fish. Much good French bread was served as an accompaniment, since the fishermen of Boulogne were hearty eaters, especially when it came to the fruits of their own labours, and they would mop up the last juices rather than let any go to waste.

Les Oeufs du Poulailler aux deux Caviars

Fresh Eggs Stuffed with Caviar

In my younger days I worked in places where caviar was dished out by the ton — just as if it were the 'black jam' of its Russian nickname. Nowadays only the very rich can affort to be so liberal, but surely it is worthy trying even just a teaspoonful once in a lifetime if you have aspirations towards gastronomy or the finer things of life. Serve this dish to your very favourite friends, or those you wish to impress — you will create a memory that will last for ever. Or why not halve the ingredients to make the most perfect starter for a *diner à deux* . . . or even a romantic honeymoon breakfast!

Imperial (Metric)	American
8 fresh free-range eggs	8 fresh free-range eggs
1 oz (25g) unsalted French butter	2 tablespoons unsalted French butter
1 tablespoon sour cream	1 tablespoon sour cream
Sea salt and freshly ground black pepper	Sea salt and freshly ground black pepper
1 shallot, chopped	1 shallot, chopped
1 clove garlic, chopped	1 clove garlic, chopped
1 teaspoon tomatoe purée	1 teaspoon tomatoe paste
Juice of ½ lemon	Juice of ½ lemon
1 tablespoon sunflower oil	1 tablespoon sunflower oil
3 oz (75g) smoked cod's roe	½ cup smoked cod's roe
3 oz (75g) Sevruga caviar (use less, or substitute black lumpfish roe if necessary)	8 teaspoons Sevruga caviar (use less, or substitute black lumpfish roe if necessary)

1. With a saw-toothed knife, very carefully slice off the top of each egg, taking great care to avoid cracking the shells badly. Tip the contents of six eggs into a small bowl (use the others for another dish).

2. Wash the shells of all eight eggs very well. Pat dry with kitchen paper towels and leave in a warm place to dry completely.

3. Beat the eggs very lightly, just to mix white and yolk. In a pan, heat the butter and stir in the eggs. Whisk gently so that the eggs cook to a creamy consistency. Stir in the cream and season to taste. Remove the pan from the heat to stop the eggs cooking further.

4. Place in a blender the shallot, garlic, tomato purée (paste), lemon juice, oil and smoked cod's roe. Reduce to a smooth purée. If the mixture is very thick, thin with a little boiling water (about ½ tablespoon).

5. Beat the cod's roe mixture into the scrambled eggs.

6. Place the eggshells in egg cups and carefully fill with the mixture, which should still be pleasantly warm. Top with a little caviar and cover with eggshell 'lids' for your guests to remove. Serve with fingers of wholemeal toast or steamed asparagus spears to dip into the delicious filling.

Crudités de Saumon et Turbot, Sauce aux Pistaches

Marinated Salmon and Turbot with a Pistachio Sauce

Serves 4 to 6

The technique of pickling raw fish in an acid liquid such as fruit juice or vinegar and salt is not new. The Japanese and Pacific islanders have done it for centuries. But it is the Scandinavian and Russian regions who until recently had had the most influence in making such concepts fashionable, simply because in cold countries the fish was likely to stay fresh and appealing for longer. Remember that, correctly done, acid marination will render the food sterile and safe — but the fish must always be at its peak of freshness when it is prepared.

Imperial (Metric)	American
For the marinade:	For the marinade:
Juice of 3 limes	Juice of 3 limes
Juice of 2 lemons	Juice of 2 lemons
4 fl oz (120ml) Marc de Bourgogne or Grappa	½ cup Marc de Bourgogne or Grappa
1 teaspoon sea salt	1 teaspoon sea salt
12 tinned green peppercorns	12 canned green peppercorns
Pinch cayenne	Pinch cayenne
Grated rind of 2 limes and 2 lemons	Grated rind of 2 limes and 2 lemons
1 piece preserved ginger, cut into *julienne*, plus 2 fl oz (60ml) of the syrup	1 piece preserved ginger, cut into *julienne*, plus ¼ cup of the syrup
For the fish roulade:	For the fish roulade:
10 oz (300g) salmon fillets, thinly sliced	2 cups salmon fillets, thinly sliced
10 oz (300g) turbot fillets, thinly sliced	2 cups turbot fillets, thinly sliced
4 large cabbage leaves, core removed, blanched and refreshed	4 large cabbage leaves, core removed, blanched and refreshed
For the sauce:	For the sauce:
2 oz (50g) skinned pistachio nuts	¼ cup skinned pistachio nuts
4 oz (100g) silken tofu *or* ¼ pint (150ml) natural yogurt	⅔ cup silken tofu *or* plain yogurt
2 cloves garlic, crushed	2 cloves garlic, crushed
1 small shallot, chopped	1 small shallot, chopped
Sea salt and freshly ground black pepper	Sea salt and freshly ground black pepper

1 In a small bowl, mix together the marinade ingredients.

2 Lay the slices of fish in a large, shallow earthenware dish. Pour over the marinade, cover the dish with foil and refrigerate for about 6 hours, turning the fish once during this time if it is not immersed in the marinade.

3 Place the turbot fillets on a piece of oiled greaseproof (parchment) paper, to form a complete layer. Cover the fish with the cabbage leaves. Over the cabbage lay the salmon slices in a complete layer.

4 Carefully roll up the layers, Swiss-roll fashion, pressing tightly with the paper but taking care not to roll the paper up inside the sausage. Trim the ends neatly and wrap tightly in foil. Freeze for 10 to 15 minutes to firm the roll.

5 Place all the sauce ingredients in a blender or food processor and reduce to a smooth, thick sauce.

6 Remove the roll from the freezer and slice into 10 or 12 pieces — removing the foil *after* slicing.

7 On individual serving plates, spoon an attractive swirl of sauce. Lay two or three slices of the fish roulade over this and garnish as wished. Tiny diamonds of tomato flesh and cubed cucumber look especially pretty. A sprinkling of fresh chopped mint or basil could also be used.

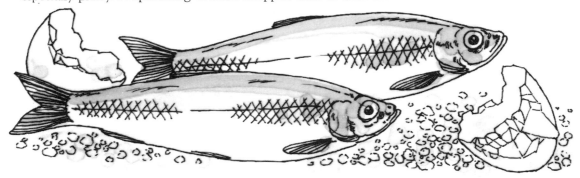

Cartouches de Sardines Saint Jean de Luz
Stuffed Sardines, Baked in Puff Pastry

Serves 6

Enormous quantities of sardines are landed all along the Basque coastline, and the inventive recipes of that region using this versatile little fish are sheer delight to any fish-lover. This baked roll makes a perfect starter to an informal dinner party, but is equally good as part of a buffet spread, as a snack, or as picnic fare. Ask your fishmonger to remove the heads and central bones to make the preparation easier for you.

Imperial (Metric)	American
6 medium sardines, boned, scaled and gutted, heads removed	6 medium sardines, boned, scaled and gutted, heads removed
2 oz (50g) *fromage blanc* or Boursin	¼ cup *fromage blanc* or Boursin
2 oz (50g) crushed walnuts	⅓ cup crushed English walnuts
1 hard-boiled egg, sieved to a paste	1 hard-cooked egg, strained to a paste
1 small shallot, finely chopped	1 small shallot, finely chopped
1 tablespoon fresh chopped tarragon	1 tablespoon fresh chopped tarragon
Juice of 1 lemon	Juice of 1 lemon
Sea salt and freshly ground black pepper	Sea salt and freshly ground black pepper
8 oz (225g) puff pastry (page 58)	8 ounces puff pastry (page 58)
1 egg yolk plus 1 tablespoon water, for eggwash	1 egg yolk plus 1 tablespoon water, for eggwash

1 Wash the fish, drain well and pat dry.
2 In a bowl, beat together the cheese, nuts, egg, shallot, tarragon and lemon juice. Season to taste.
3 Spoon or pipe a little of this paste into the cavities of the sardines and shape them neatly around it.
4 Roll the pastry out to a thickness of about ⅛ inch (3mm). Cut it into 6 oblongs, each of which should be about 3 times the width of a sardine and 1½ times the length. Brush the edges with water.
5 Place a sardine on each piece of pastry. Pinch the edges together, folding the ends over the seam side of the tube and then laying each roll seam-side down on a greased baking tray.
6 Brush the roll with eggwash and mark the tops with a criss-cross pattern using the back of a knife. Bake in a preheated oven at 400°F/200°C (Gas Mark 6) for 15 minutes until puffed up and golden-brown. Serve hot or cold.

Mousse de Saumon au Fromage Blanc

Fresh Salmon Mousse with Soft White Cheese

This is a luxury dish when made with fresh salmon, and it is worth investing in an attractive copper fish-shaped mould in which to prepare it — it will look delightful when turned out as the centrepiece of your dining table at the start of a meal, and the empty mould will add a special, old-fashioned glow to your kitchen *batterie de cuisine*. For a less extravagant occasion, a good brand of canned salmon will provide an equally delicious, and more economical, appetizer, and can be used as a dip for crudités or Melba toast if the occasion merits a less formal presentation.

Imperial (Metric)	American
1 lb (450g) piece fresh salmon	1 pound piece fresh salmon
1 oz (25g) butter for greasing dish	2 tablespoons butter for greasing dish
1 pint (600ml) hot court bouillon (page 170)	2½ cups hot court bouillon (page 170)
¼ pint (150ml) natural yogurt	⅔ cup plain yogurt
5 oz (150g) *fromage blanc*	⅔ cup soft white cheese
2 oz (50g) softened butter	¼ cup softened butter
4 fl oz (130ml) dry white wine	½ cup dry white wine
2 tablespoons lemon juice	2 tablespoons lemon juice
Sea salt and paprika	Sea salt and paprika
¼ oz (7g) agar-agar	½ tablespoon agar-agar
½ cucumber, finely sliced	½ cucumber, finely sliced
Twists of lemon, to garnish	Twists of lemon, to garnish
Mayonnaise Paloise (page 180)	Mayonnaise Paloise (page 180)

1 Place the salmon — first wiped with a damp cloth — in a lightly buttered ovenproof dish.

2 Cover the salmon with hot court bouillon, then cover the dish with foil and bake at 350°F/180°C (Gas Mark 4) for 20 minutes. Leave the salmon in the dish when it is removed from the oven. It will continue to cook gently as the liquid cools, and will end up perfectly cooked and moist.

3 Remove the skin and bones from the cold salmon. Place the flesh in a food processor with the yogurt, cheese and butter. Process to a thick cream. Alternatively, pound the salmon in a bowl and beat in the yogurt, cheese and butter with a wooden spoon.

4 Stir in the wine, lemon juice and seasoning.

5 Measure 6 tablespoons of the hot court bouillon into a bowl and sprinkle the agar-agar on top. Set the bowl over a pan of hot water and allow the court bouillon to just simmer for a few minutes, until the agar-agar is completely dissolved and cooked. Allow this mixture to cool slightly, then beat into the salmon mousse mixture.

6 If using a mould, rinse the insides with cold water, then spoon in the mousse. Alternatively, pile the mousse into an attractive serving bowl. Place in the refrigerator and leave to chill and set for several hours or overnight.

7 To serve from a mould, invert the mould over a serving platter which has been lined with slices of cucumber, overlapped like fish scales, and shake the mould very gently so that the salmon mousse settles intact onto the cucumber. Decorate with twists of lemon and serve with mayonnaise Paloise. Offer Melba toast and crudités with a bowl of salmon mousse.

Rillettes de Maquereau Fumé au Beurre de Normandie
Mackerel Pâté with Normandy Butter

Serves 6

The traditional characteristic of *rillettes* is that the main ingredients are blended with equal their amount in fat. In these more enlightened days of healthy, low-fat diets, it is rare for recipes to suggest this balance, though the *rillettes* you would buy in France, made from fatty pork or poultry, could still match this quantity. In the old days, *rillettes* were intended to make a palatable, easy-to-preserve dish from the cheaper or less versatile cuts of meat. But the judicious use of an oily fish, balanced with other ingredients including a more sensible amount of butter, will provide a tasty dish which is both healthier and rather different from the classic country pâté.

Imperial (Metric)	American
1 lb (450g) smoked mackerel, skinned, boned and minced	1 pound smoked mackerel, skinned, boned and minced
2 oz (50g) butter, preferably unsalted from Normandy	¼ cup butter, preferably unsalted French
1 tablespoon olive oil	1 tablespoon olive oil
1 red onion, finely chopped	1 red onion, finely chopped
1 clove garlic, crushed	1 clove garlic, crushed
Sea salt and freshly ground black pepper	Sea salt and freshly ground black pepper
Freshly grated nutmeg	Freshly grated nutmeg
1 teaspoon chopped fresh tarragon	1 teaspoon chopped fresh tarragon
1 rounded tablespoon tomato purée	1 heaping tablespoon tomato paste
2 tablespoons cognac	2 tablespoons cognac
2 oz (50g) low-fat soft white cheese	¼ cup low-fat soft white cheese
1 tablespoon horseradish cream	1 tablespoon horseradish cream
2 tablespoons clarified butter, for topping	2 tablespoons clarified butter, for topping

1 Make sure the mackerel is completely free of bones, and is reduced to a smooth, fibrous purée. Place in a large bowl.
2 Heat the butter and oil in a pan and sauté the onion and garlic very gently until tender and translucent — do not allow to brown.
3 Beat the onion mixture into the fish. Season with salt, pepper and nutmeg to taste, then stir in the tarragon, tomato purée (paste) and cognac. Beat in the cheese thoroughly, and blend in the horseradish cream.
4 Spoon the *rillettes* into an earthenware terrine and chill well.
5 Melt the clarified butter and drizzle over the *rillettes* to seal the top completely. Refrigerate until needed.

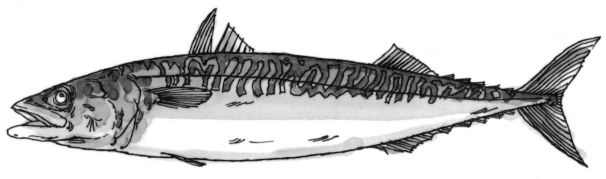

Petits Pains en Mosaïque

Soft Wholemeal (Whole Wheat) Rolls with a Mosaic Mousseline

Here is a perfect dish for a wide range of party situations. Picnics, barbecues, parties for young people at Hallowe'en or other informal gatherings — even a formal event such as a wedding or anniversary buffet will suit a pretty display of these little rolls, neatly sliced. And they have the extra advantage in all these situations of actually benefiting from advance preparation!

Imperial (Metric)	American
8 oz (225g) skinned rainbow trout fillets, minced	1⅓ cups skinned, filleted and minced rainbow trout
1 egg white	1 egg white
4 oz (100g) low-fat curd cheese	½ cup low-fat soft white cheese
Juice of ½ lemon	Juice of ½ lemon
Sea salt and freshly ground black pepper	Sea salt and freshly ground black pepper
1 good pinch dried dill	1 good pinch dried dill
1 hard-boiled egg, finely chopped	1 hard-boiled egg, finely chopped
1 spring onion, finely chopped	1 scallion, finely chopped
1 oz (25g) cooked green peas	2 tablespoons cooked green peas
1 oz (25g) cooked sweetcorn kernels	2 tablespoons cooked corn kernels
1 oz (25g) finely diced red pepper	2 tablespoons finely diced red pepper
4 wholemeal baton rolls	4 whole wheat hoagies

1 Place the minced trout in a bowl and beat in the egg white, cheese, and lemon juice. Season to taste with salt, pepper and dill.
2 Stir in the chopped egg, spring onion (scallion), peas, corn and red pepper. Mix well.
3 Slice the rolls one-third of the way along. Carefully scoop out the soft bread from the centres — this can be used to make breadcrumbs for use in other dishes. It freezes well if stored in polythene bags in the freezer.
4 Fill each section of hollowed-out roll with the trout mixture, then set the sections of roll back together.
5 Wrap each roll individually in foil, sealing tightly together. Chill for at least 2 hours.
6 To serve, cut each roll into thick slices and arrange in a decorative, flower-like pattern, on a serving dish.

Chartreuse de Truite Saumonée aux Crevettes Roses

Salmon Trout and Prawn (Shrimp) Mould

The mild, sweet flavour of both trout and prawn (shrimp) lends itself well to a delicate appetizer which can both interest the palate and leave it fresh and whetted for the next course. The busy host will see instantly that this is a dish which is easy to prepare and that can be chilled ahead of time to allow extra effort to be devoted to a main course, or to free him or her for the all-important aspect of any dinner party — mingling with charming guests, creating a relaxed and friendly atmosphere in which food can be savoured, wine enjoyed, and conversation stimulated and appreciated.

Imperial (Metric)	American
5 oz (150g) salmon trout fillets, skinned	1 cup skinned and filleted salmon trout
3 oz (75g) king prawns, shelled and diced	½ cup shelled and diced jumbo shrimp
1 egg, beaten	1 egg, beaten
4 fl oz (120ml) natural yogurt	½ cup plain yogurt
1 teaspoon dried dill	1 teaspoon dried dill
1 oz (25g) crushed matzos	¼ cup crushed matzos
Sea salt and freshly ground black pepper	Sea salt and freshly ground black pepper
1 teaspoon tomato purée	1 teaspoon tomato paste
4 fl oz (120ml) double cream, whipped	½ cup heavy cream, whipped
2 oz (50g) softened butter	¼ cup softened butter
4 small fillets salmon trout (approx. 3 oz/75g each)	4 small fillets salmon trout (approx. 3 ounces each)
Chive and yogurt sauce (see below)	Chive and yogurt sauce (see below)

1 Place the skinned salmon trout fillets in a food processor and mince finely.
2 Mix the salmon trout in a bowl with the diced prawns (shrimp), beaten egg, yogurt, dill, crushed matzos, seasoning and tomato purée (paste). Chill this mixture for 20 minutes.
3 Gently fold the whipped cream into the fish mixture.
4 Line four buttered dariole moulds or ramekins with the lightly beaten trout fillets. Into these spoon the fish mousse, folding over any loose edges of trout fillet.
5 Place the ramekins in a baking tin and add hot water to come half way up their sides. Bake at 400°F/200°C (Gas Mark 6) for 15 minutes. Remove from the oven and allow to cool.
6 When the mousses are cold, turn out onto individual serving plates and decorate as you choose — twists of lemon and peeled prawns (shrimp) with their heads left on are good. Serve with chive and yogurt sauce, made by beating ¼ pint (150ml/⅔ cup) plain yogurt with 1 tablespoon chopped chives and 1 tablespoon mayonnaise and seasoning to taste.

Hareng au Cidre

Herrings with Cider, Normandy-style

Cider has been a speciality of Normandy since the Middle Ages, and its production is treated with as much care and devotion as that of the finest wine — indeed, *cidre bouché* is made by the *méthode champenoise*. You need not use such fine quality cider for this dish — save it to drink with your meal. But choose a good country cider, preferably strong and dry (hard) for best results.

Imperial (Metric)	American
4 herrings, boned, cleaned and laid flat	4 herrings, boned, cleaned and laid flat
Sea salt and freshly ground black pepper	Sea salt and freshly ground black pepper
1 small onion, finely chopped	1 small onion, finely chopped
1 small apple, finely chopped	1 small apple, finely chopped
1 tablespoon fresh chopped parsley	1 tablespoon fresh chopped parsley
2 oz (50g) butter	¼ cup butter
½ pint (300ml) Normandy or other cider	1⅓ cups Normandy or other cider
Fresh single cream (optional)	Fresh single cream (optional)
Extra chopped parsley to garnish	Extra chopped parsley to garnish

1 Lay the herrings out on a clean flat surface. Season them inside with salt and pepper.
2 Spoon over the flesh equal amounts of the mixed onion, apple and parsley. Carefully roll up the fish, securing with a cocktail stick if necessary.
3 Place the fish in a buttered ovenproof dish. Pour on the cider and dot with extra butter.
4 Bake at 350°F/180°C (Gas Mark 4) for 25 to 30 minutes. Place a herring on each of four warmed serving plates, removing the cocktail stick if used.
5 If you wish to serve a richer dish, beat a little cream into the cider and fish juices before spooning over the mackerel — otherwise just drizzle the fish with the tasty liquid as a sauce. Sprinkle with parsley and serve at once.

Variation:
The herrings could be covered and left to cool in the cooking liquid, then served cold as part of a buffet, or simply as a chilled appetizer. Do not use cream if serving the fish this way.

Aiguillettes de Truite Marinée au Vinaigre de Framboise
Rainbow Trout Fillets, Marinated in Raspberry Vinegar

Illustrated opposite page 177.

Vinegar can absorb the essential oils from herbs and spices. It can also take on the flavour of other ingredients left to soak in it — garlic and onions, or soft fruits such as raspberries or black currants. Raspberry vinegar has become very fashionable of recent times, and is inclined to be over-used in dishes which it does not suit, but this aromatic, heady marinated appetizer is quite exquisite because of the elusive aroma of fruit which accompanies every delicious morsel.

Imperial (Metric)	American
2 lb (900g) rainbow trout, skinned, filleted and washed	2 pounds rainbow trout, skinned, filleted and washed
Juice of 2 lemons	Juice of 2 lemons
Juice of 1 lime	Juice of 1 lime
6 fl oz (180ml) raspberry vinegar (page 189)	¾ cup raspberry vinegar (page 189)
2 fl oz (60ml) French dry vermouth	¼ cup French dry vermouth
2 fl oz (60ml) cognac Lagrange	¼ cup cognac Lagrange
2 tablespoons olive oil	2 tablespoons olive oil
Sea salt and freshly ground black pepper	Sea salt and freshly ground black pepper
1 oz (25g) chopped red onion	2 tablespoons chopped red onion
1 crushed clove garlic	1 crushed clove garlic
2 tablespoons honey	2 tablespoons honey
8 coriander seeds	8 coriander seeds
1 tablespoon pink or green peppercorns	1 tablespoon pink or green peppercorns
Dried chillies (optional)	Dried chilies (optional)
Sprigs fresh dill, to garnish	Sprigs fresh dill, to garnish
½ honeydew melon, sliced, to garnish	½ honeydew melon, sliced, to garnish
Slices of fresh lime, to garnish	Slices of fresh lime, to garnish

1 Using a very sharp knife, slice the raw, filleted trout as thinly as possible. Lay the slices in a shallow, flat dish. Coat them in a mixture of the lemon and lime juice, the vinegar, vermouth, cognac, olive oil and seasoning. Cover the dish, place in the refrigerator and leave to marinate for up to 2 days, turning the fish occasionally.

2 Before serving, drain off the marinade, reserving about 4 fl oz (120ml/½ cup).

3 Place the reserved marinade in a blender with the onion, garlic and honey. Blend to a thin cream.

4 Drizzle this mixture over the fish on a serving platter, then sprinkle with the coriander seeds, peppercorns, chillies if used, and garnish with sprigs of dill, slices of melon and slices of lime.

Escabèche de Raie au Cidre de Picardie
Skate Poached in Cider with Apples

The wonderful aromas which will emanate from your kitchen during the cooking of this dish, and the richness of flavour which results from the ingredients used, will belie the fact that it is lower on calories and cholesterol than many more frugal-looking appetizers. Nonetheless, it is more substantial than most dishes in this chapter, so be careful to balance it with a lighter main course than usual.

Imperial (Metric)	American
4 small wings of skate, skinned	4 small wings of skate, skinned
1 pint (600ml) fish stock (page 170), made with 2 fl oz (60ml) cider vinegar	2½ cups fish stock (page 170), made with ¼ cup cider vinegar
1 tablespoon tomato purée	1 tablespoon tomato paste
4 tablespoons Calvados	4 tablespoons Calvados
4 tablespoons dry cider	4 tablespoons hard cider
1 tablespoon cider vinegar	1 tablespoon cider vinegar
Sea salt and freshly ground black pepper	Sea salt and freshly ground black pepper
4 tablespoons natural low-fat yogurt	4 tablespoons plain low-fat yogurt
1 teaspoon cornflour	1 teaspoon cornstarch
2 French Golden Delicious apples, finely diced and tossed in a little lemon juice	2 Golden Delicious apples, finely diced and tossed in a little lemon juice
2 tomatoes, skinned, seeded and finely diced	2 tomatoes, skinned, seeded and finely diced
¼ teaspoon chopped parsley	¼ teaspoon chopped parsley
¼ teaspoon chopped mint	¼ teaspoon chopped mint

1 Rinse the skate in a bowl with cold running water for 5 minutes. Then place in a pan, cover with stock and poach gently for 10 minutes. Keep the fish warm while preparing the sauce.

2 Drain ¼ pint (150ml/⅔ cup) stock into a pan and bring to the boil. Stir in tomato purée (paste), Calvados, cider, cider vinegar and seasoning. Boil for 5 minutes.

3 Meanwhile, in a bowl beat together the yogurt and cornflour (cornstarch). Add 2 teaspoons water to this mixture, then beat it gradually into the sauce. Simmer a further 5 minutes until the sauce is smooth and creamy. Check the seasoning and strain.

4 Pour a little sauce onto 4 warmed plates, lay a skate wing over each, then cover with a little more sauce. Decorate the edges of the plate with tiny mounds of chopped apple and tomato and sprinkle the fish with the chopped herbs. Serve at once.

Saumon Saumuré à la Moutarde

Marinated Salmon with a Mustard Sauce

Serves 8

This dish from Northern France bears a close similarity to the acclaimed *gravlax* of Scandinavia. It makes an unusual alternative to the traditional smoked salmon as part of a formal buffet, especially if served on thin slices of country bread, instead of the more strongly-flavoured 'black' bread or rye bread. It is also quite delicious as an appetizer served with thin slices of cantaloup melon or chopped cucumber bound with a garlic-flavoured yogurt.

Imperial (Metric)	American
2 lb (1 kilo) tail piece of salmon	2 pounds tail piece salmon
4 tablespoons coarse sea salt	4 tablespoons coarse sea salt
4 tablespoons raw cane sugar	4 tablespoons raw cane sugar
2 teaspoons black peppercorns, crushed	2 teaspoons black peppercorns, crushed
2 teaspoons mustard seeds	2 teaspoons mustard seeds
2 teaspoons vegetable oil	2 teaspoons vegetable oil
Large bunch fresh dill, chopped	Large bunch fresh dill, chopped

For the mustard sauce:	For the mustard sauce:
½ tablespoon moutarde des graines	½ tablespoon moutarde des graines
¼ pint (150ml) natural yogurt	⅔ cup plain yogurt
1 tablespoon honey	1 tablespoon honey
1 tablespoon port	1 tablespoon port
Juice of ½ lemon	Juice of ½ lemon
Sea salt and freshly ground black pepper	Sea salt and freshly ground black pepper

1 Carefully scrape off the fish scales, leaving the skin intact. Rinse under running water and pat dry. Cut the piece of fish lengthways and remove the backbone as well as any smaller bones.

2 Rub the flesh with a mixture of the salt, sugar, peppercorns, mustard seeds and oil. Reassemble the fish into its original form.

3 Place a layer of dill at the bottom of a smallish, shallow dish which is big enough to hold the piece of salmon. Lay the salmon on top of the layer of dill, then cover with the remaining dill.

4 Cover the salmon with a plate, place a small weight onto this. Refrigerate the salmon for a minimum of 2 days, or as long as 5 days, turning the salmon halfway through marinating time.

5 Before serving, scrape off most of the dill. Slice the salmon very thinly.

6 Prepare the mustard sauce by placing all the ingredients in a bowl and beating well. One teaspoon chopped basil may be added if wished.

7 Serve with the garnish of your choice — cornichons or small pickled onions are good, as are hot new potatoes, boiled in their skins.

Note:
A beautiful way to serve the marinaded salmon is as follows: place a 3 inch (7cm) pastry ring on a plate and fill it almost to the top with diced salmon, blended with the mustard sauce. Cover with a spoonful of whipped cream and level up with a palette knife. Decorate top with lemon wedges, rosemary and salmon caviar and surround with a circle of cucumber slices. Remove the pastry cutter and repeat the operation for each guest.

Cassolette de Rouget Cannoise
Provencale Red Mullet (Snapper) Pâté with Fennel

Illustrated opposite page 16.

The basis for this recipe was developed when I was working at the Hotel des Pins and the Beau Site Palace Hotel at Cannes. Along the Riviera at Monte Carlo a man who was later to become a colleague and a great friend had worked under Prosper Montagné at the luxurious Hotel de Paris — Adolphe Cadier. Adolphe and I sat on many committees together in the post-war years and he became the first and most respected President of the International Academy of Chefs. I was later honoured to follow in his footsteps as the fourth President of this famed institution. I consider him to have been one of the greatest exponents of fish cookery and dedicate this recipe to his memory.

Imperial (Metric)	American
4 small red mullet (approx. 8 oz/225g each)	4 small red snapper (approx. 8 ounces each)
½ pint (300ml) reduced fish stock (page 170)	2½ cups reduced fish stock (page 170)
1 tablespoon agar-agar	1 tablespoon agar-agar
3 fl oz (90ml) olive oil	⅓ cup olive oil
1 small onion, chopped	1 small onion, chopped
2 cloves garlic, chopped	2 cloves garlic, chopped
4 tomatoes, skinned, seeded and chopped	4 tomatoes, skinned, seeded and chopped
1 tablespoon tomato purée	1 tablespoon tomato paste
1 green chilli, seeded and chopped	1 green chili, seeded and chopped
3 oz (75g) pine nuts	⅓ cup pignoli
1 teaspoon fresh chopped basil	1 teaspoon fresh chopped basil
1 oz (25g) wholemeal breadcrumbs	⅓ cup whole wheat breadcrumbs
Sea salt and freshly ground black pepper	Sea salt and freshly ground black pepper
2 eggs, beaten	2 eggs, beaten
2 tablespoons Pernod	2 tablespoons Pernod
1 head fennel, trimmed and segmented to give 8 good-sized pieces	1 head fennel, trimmed and segmented to give 8 good-sized pieces
8 stoned black olives	8 stoned black olives
½ pint (300ml) tomato coulis (page 187)	2½ cups tomato coulis (page 187)

1 Gently scale the fish and fillet them. Use the heads and bones for stock. You will be using half the fillets for the pâté and half for grilling, so choose the four best fillets for the latter and set aside.

2 Boil the agar-agar in the stock until dissolved and cooked, then set the mixture aside to cool.

3 Heat half the oil in a pan and sauté the fillets for use in the pâté for 4 minutes only. Flake into a bowl.

4 In the same oil sauté the onion and garlic until softened but not browned. Add the fresh tomatoes and the tomato purée (paste), the chilli, pine nuts (pignoli), basil, breadcrumbs and seasoning. Stir the mixture together for a minute.

5 Add the beaten egg to the pan and stir well. Cook for 2 minutes, then remove the pan from the heat.

6 Beat this mixture into the flaked fish, and stir in the Pernod. Allow to cool, then add half the jellied stock. (The rest can be chopped like aspic to use as a garnish for this or another dish.)

7 This mixture can then be processed in a blender or food processor for a smooth pâté, or beaten well for a coarser type.

8 Fill the fennel cavities with the fish pâté and decorate with black olives. Arrange to one side on serving plates and spoon some tomato coulis on the other side of the plate.

9   Just before serving, brush the reserved fillets with oil and grill (broil) for 2 minutes on each side. Sear the skin, as shown, with a hot skewer for a decorative appearance. Lay the sizzling fillets onto the chilled coulis and serve at once, garnished with chopped fish aspic if wished.

Variations:
Fronds of leaves from the fennel make a pretty garnish, as do basil leaves, and this dish is even more delicious served with segments of orange and slices of lemon — these enhance the Mediterranean flavour.

Brandade de Cabillaud Fumé Elizabeth
Smoked Cod and Cod's Roe Purée with Whisky

I had the great honour of cooking a special buffet at Windsor for Her Majesty Queen Elizabeth II, at which a variation on this delicious pâté was served. I have chosen to include it here because a brandade is a typical dish of the Languedoc region of France, although here it is given a flavour of *entente cordiale* with the addition of good Scotch whisky, reflecting one branch of Royal ancestry.

Imperial (Metric)	American
8 oz (225g) smoked cod fillet, skinned	1⅓ cups smoked cod fillet, skinned
1 shallot, finely chopped	1 shallot, finely chopped
2 cloves garlic, chopped	2 cloves garlic, chopped
3 fl oz (90ml) milk	⅓ cup milk
8 oz (225g) smoked cod's roe, skinned	1 cup smoked cod's roe, skinned
Juice of 2 lemons	Juice of 2 lemons
2 tablespoons Johnny Walker Red Label whisky	2 tablespoons Johnny Walker Red Label whisky
1 tablespoon tomato purée	1 tablespoon tomato paste
8 oz (225g) smoothly mashed, cooked potato	1 cup smoothly mashed, cooked potato
2 egg yolks	2 egg yolks
4 fl oz (120ml) natural yogurt	½ cup plain yogurt
2 fl oz (60ml) walnut oil	¼ cup walnut oil
Sea salt and freshly ground black pepper	Sea salt and freshly ground black pepper
Pinch mace	Pinch mace

1   Place the smoked cod in a pan with the shallot, garlic and milk. Poach for 4 minutes, then place the contents of the pan in a bowl and flake the fish with two forks.
2   Crumble in the smoked cod's roe, lemon juice, whisky and tomato purée (paste). Using an electric whisk, beat the ingredients together until fairly smooth.
3   Add the potato and egg yolks and beat again.
4   Gradually whisk in alternate small amounts of yogurt and oil. The mixture should thicken up into a smooth, rich cream. Season to taste with salt (do not over-salt — taste the mixture first), pepper and mace. Beat the mixture again and chill for 1 hour before serving.
5   Serve the brandade in small, chilled glass bowls with crudités or Melba toast.

Les Blinis au Caviar de Saumon

Russian-style Pancakes (Crêpes) with Salmon Caviar

Serves 4 to 6

Caviar is a food which provokes one of two reactions in those who try it — either delight at this exotic and extravagant food, or a grimace of displeasure at what is, after all, an acquired taste. True caviar comes from the roe of the sturgeon, and is far beyond the pocket of most of us. Lumpfish roe is what most people who claim to have eaten caviar were really given, and it is a tasty and colourful treat which should not be underrated. Other roes are commonly used, too — smoked cod's roe for taramasalata, and herring roes which are a delicious savoury when spread on hot wholemeal toast. But this dish uses salmon roe, which I consider to be the most subtle and superior caviar after the 'real thing'. Matched with light, spongy, muffin-like blinis, the recipe for which was brought back from Russia by the French chefs to the Tsar, this is a gourmet experience not to be missed.

Imperial (Metric)	American
For the blinis:	For the blinis:
½ oz (15g) brewer's yeast	1 tablespoon brewer's yeast
¼ pint (150ml) tepid water	⅔ cup tepid water
¼ pint (150ml) tepid milk *or* cream	⅔ cup tepid milk *or* cream
2 eggs, beaten	2 eggs, beaten
5 oz (150g) wholemeal flour	1¼ cups whole wheat flour
2 fl oz (60ml) vegetable oil	¼ cup vegetable oil
For the topping:	For the topping:
8 oz (225g) salmon caviar, or other type	1 cup salmon caviar, or other type
¼ pint natural yogurt, whipped	⅔ cup plain yogurt, whipped
4 spring onions, chopped	4 scallions, chopped
4 sprigs dill	4 sprigs dill

1 Crumble the yeast into a bowl containing the water and milk or cream. Leave it for 10 minutes to ferment — it should become foamy or frothy in this time.

2 Gradually beat in the eggs and flour to form a smooth batter. Leave for 1 hour at room temperature to ferment again, then beat the mixture.

3 Heat the oil in a large frying pan and pour in small quantities of batter (about 3 tablespoons each) to make 4 to 6 pancakes (crêpes). Cook for 1 minute, then turn and cook for another minute, so they are golden on each side and are risen and fluffy.

4 Allow the blinis to cool slightly, then top with a generous spoonful each of caviar and whipped yogurt, sprinkle with chopped spring onion (scallion) and fronds of dill, and serve.

Opposite: *Zephir de Truite Princesse Diana* (page 50).
Overleaf: *Côtriade Brestoise au Rameaux de Salicorne* (page 44).

2   *Les Soupes de nos Pêcheurs*

Fishermen's Soups and Chowders

'*Zuppa di pesce* . . . this is the stuff for which Neapolitans sell their female relatives . . . how unfavourably this hotch-potch compares with Marseillaise Bouillabaisse! . . . The fact is, there is hardly a fish in the Mediterranean worth eating, and therefore *ex nihilo ninil fit*. Bouillabaisse is only good because cooked by the French.'

Norman Douglas, *Siren Land*

Well! While I would not go quite so far as *that*, I am inclined to agree that bouillabaisse, so often regarded as the best — if not the only — fish soup, is inclined to overshadow others which I personally think are better. The rich coastline of Brittany, for example, cannot be beaten for its wealth of different fish all admirably suited to use in soups from chunky chowders to elegant consommés. My old friend Louis Garault and I once collaborated on a book about the region, and the recipes for soups which we gathered then have stood me in good stead for many years, always receiving high praise when I have served them. Of course, over the years I have modified them in one way or another, and the ones featured here are designed to satisfy modern trends — light, aromatic, avoiding bones and shells — without losing any of the flavour and character which have always been their appeal.

I am afraid it is those bits of bone and shell which many people recall from sampling a soup such as bouillabaisse, and which puts them off trying any other fish soup, for fear of a repeat performance. Only the most dedicated 'foodie' can possibly enjoy struggling with shellfish in a bowl of rich and spicy soup, splashing clothes and tablecloth in the process more often than not — or, worse still, extricating an unnoticed fish bone from their throat before asphyxia sets in! It seems so unnecessary to me. All the rich flavour of the bones can be distilled into the stock before the soup itself is prepared. Then just the tasty and succulent fish itself may be enjoyed to the full without fear of embarrassment or choking. I do not deny that, say, a mussel in the half-shell makes a pretty and satisfying garnish to a bowl of soup, but it can be served in such a way that diners can cope easily with it, or leave it to one side as they choose.

You will find all sorts of fish soup in this chapter, from good and filling country soups, which make a meal in themselves when served with crusty bread and good French butter, to extravagant and unusual dinner party dishes which will make your guests feel pampered and honoured to be served.

Few accompaniments better suit a fish soup than the traditional Breton drinks of

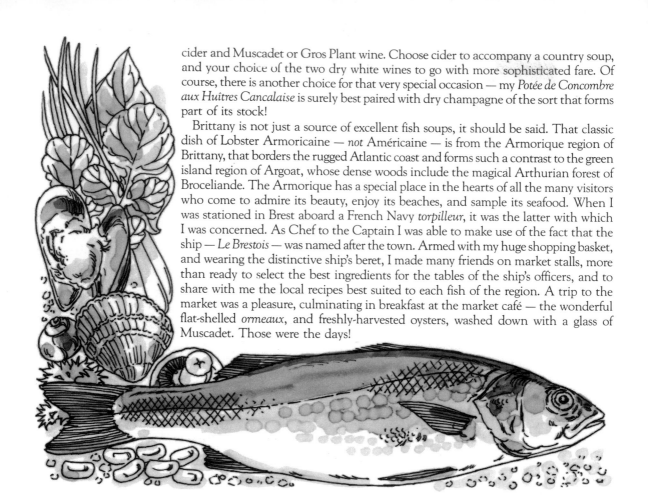

cider and Muscadet or Gros Plant wine. Choose cider to accompany a country soup, and your choice of the two dry white wines to go with more sophisticated fare. Of course, there is another choice for that very special occasion — my *Potée de Concombre aux Huîtres Cancalaise* is surely best paired with dry champagne of the sort that forms part of its stock!

Brittany is not just a source of excellent fish soups, it should be said. That classic dish of Lobster Armoricaine — *not* Américaine — is from the Armorique region of Brittany, that borders the rugged Atlantic coast and forms such a contrast to the green island region of Argoat, whose dense woods include the magical Arthurian forest of Broceliande. The Armorique has a special place in the hearts of all the many visitors who come to admire its beauty, enjoy its beaches, and sample its seafood. When I was stationed in Brest aboard a French Navy *torpilleur*, it was the latter with which I was concerned. As Chef to the Captain I was able to make use of the fact that the ship — *Le Brestois* — was named after the town. Armed with my huge shopping basket, and wearing the distinctive ship's beret, I made many friends on market stalls, more than ready to select the best ingredients for the tables of the ship's officers, and to share with me the local recipes best suited to each fish of the region. A trip to the market was a pleasure, culminating in breakfast at the market café — the wonderful flat-shelled *ormeaux*, and freshly-harvested oysters, washed down with a glass of Muscadet. Those were the days!

Bouillure de Maquereau à la Boulonnaise

Mackerel and Spinach Soup

Serves 8-10

Mackerel has a high fat content, reaching as much as 20 per cent in Summer and Autumn, so is usually best served grilled, or marinated in vinegar or a dry wine. Because of this, it cannot be used to make stock for ordinary sauces but for this soup a stock made from the bones and heads produces a rich and strongly-flavoured stock which is perfectly balanced by the distinctive character of the spinach.

Imperial (Metric)	American
1 lb (450g) fresh spinach	1 pound fresh spinach
1 lb (450g) fresh mackerel fillets*	1 pound fresh mackerel fillets*
1½ oz (40g) butter	3 tablespoons butter
1½ fl oz (50ml) olive oil	3 tablespoons olive oil
8 oz (225g) chopped onions	1⅓ cups chopped onions
8 oz (225g) sliced leeks	1⅓ cups sliced leeks
3½ pints (2 litres) water	8¾ cups water
¼ cup (140ml) dry white wine	⅔ cup dry white wine
2 oz (50g) tomato purée	¼ cup tomato paste
1 tablespoon crushed black peppercorns	1 tablespoon crushed black peppercorns
1 tablespoon *Crème de Cassis* or blackcurrant juice	1 tablespoon *Crème de Cassis* or blackcurrant juice
A few strands saffron	A few strands saffron
2 oz (50g) wholemeal vermicelli	1 cup whole wheat vermicelli
Sea salt	Sea salt
Slices French bread, toasted	Slices French bread, toasted

1 Wash and drain the spinach leaves and shred finely.
2 Skin the mackerel fillets and cut into chunks. Wash in cold water and drain.
3 Heat the butter and oil and sauté the onions and leeks for 5 minutes, then add the fish heads and bones and brown them for 4 minutes.
4 Stir in the water, wine, tomato purée (paste), peppercorns, *Cassis* or blackcurrant juice, and the saffron. Simmer gently for 25 minutes.
5 Strain the broth into a fresh saucepan. Add the shredded spinach and simmer for 3 minutes, then add the vermicelli and cook for a further 4 minutes. Season to taste.
6 Place the fish in a shallow baking tin, cover just level with the soup and poach gently for 5 minutes.
7 Transfer the fish to individual serving bowls and cover with spinach soup. Serve with toasted French bread.

*Ask the fishmonger to give you the bones and heads when he fillets your fish.

Marmite de Poisson Berquoise aux Betteraves
Beetroot (Beet) Soup with Fish Dumplings

Serves 8

This soup is delicious eaten hot or cold, and has a sweet-sour taste which will appeal to anyone who likes beetroot (beet). Readers of my last book, *Cuisine Végétarienne Française*, may be familiar with the beetroot (beet) soup in that book — '*Le Dragon Rouge*'. But it is worth noting that this soup, too, can be just as enjoyable in its vegetarian form, made with a well-flavoured vegetable stock and, of course, without the fish dumplings. I have made a point, throughout this book, to create wholesome and balanced recipes which make good use of vegetables, grains, seeds and pulses, so that many can be adapted to omit the fish yet remain as appetizing and attractive as before.

Imperial (Metric)	American
8 oz (225g) cooked beetroot	2 cooked beet
½ pint (300ml) red wine	1⅓ cups red wine
1 teaspoon raw cane sugar	1 teaspoon raw cane sugar
1 teaspoon aniseeds	1 teaspoon aniseeds
1 oz (85g) tomato purée	2 tablespoons tomato paste
2 pints (1.15 litres) fish stock (page 170)	5 cups fish stock (page 170)
1 small carrot	1 small carrot
½ turnip	½ turnip
1 small leek	1 small leek
1 stick celery	1 stalk celery
1 oz (25g) cabbage	½ cup cabbage
1 small potato	1 small potato
1 oz (25g) cooked brown rice	¼ cup cooked brown rice
1 lb (450g) raw white fish of choice, minced	1 pound raw white fish of choice, minced
1 egg	1 egg
2 oz (50g) fresh wholemeal breadcrumbs	1 cup fresh whole wheat breadcrumbs
Sea salt and freshly ground black pepper	Sea salt and freshly ground black pepper
4 fl oz (120ml) soured cream	½ cup sour cream

1 Cut the beetroot (beet) into small cubes and marinate in a mixture of the wine, sugar, aniseeds and tomato purée (paste).

2 Bring the fish stock to the boil and add all the vegetables, cut into small pieces. Simmer for 10 minutes, or until the vegetables are just tender.

3 Add the beetroot (beet) in its marinade, and the rice. Cook for a further 10 minutes, without allowing the vegetables to overcook and break up.

4 In a bowl, mix the minced fish with beaten egg and breadcrumbs. Season with salt and pepper. Roll into 8 large or 16 small dumplings (roll in a little whole wheat flour if this makes handling easier for you).

5 Place the dumplings in a sauté pan, with just enough soup to cover them. Simmer for 10 minutes. Remove the dumplings with a slotted spoon and place in individual soup bowls.

6 Check the seasoning of the soup, then ladle into the bowls over the dumplings.

7 Serve with the sour cream in a separate bowl, to be added by your guests if liked.

Potée de Concombre Cancalaise aux Huitres
Cucumber and Oyster Soup with Champagne

Serves 8

The quality and season of oysters vary considerably from place to place. French oysters, for example, can be light brown or — most highly prized — green. This green colour is achieved by breeding the oysters in special lakes called *claires*, which are full of a special green algae on which the oysters feed. The Common European oyster, as eaten in Britain, is the subject of the classic 'R-in-the-month' rule, because during their breeding season (the summer months, when there is no letter R in the name of the month!) they are extremely unpalatable to eat. The American, Australian and Portuguese oysters do not suffer from this restriction, though each region may still have a season when oysters are at their best. It takes three or four years to produce an oyster of an acceptable size for consumption, which is why they are so expensive; although many years ago, when oyster beds were far more widespread, they were the food of the poor, being used to supplement meat in many dishes. Now their cost makes them a luxury item, and so I have spared no expense in this special-occasion soup, by pairing them with some champagne — the rest of the bottle can be served with the soup or saved, suitably capped, to accompany dessert.

Imperial (Metric)	American
2 oz (50g) butter	¼ cup butter
2 shallots, chopped	2 shallots, chopped
1 small cucumber, peeled and diced	1 small cucumber, peeled and diced
3½ pints (2 litres) fish stock (page 170)	8¾ cups fish stock (page 170)
Juice and grated rind of 1 lemon	Juice and grated rind of 1 lemon
3 egg yolks	3 egg yolks
2 teaspoons cornflour	2 teaspoons cornstarch
8 shallow oysters	8 shallow oysters
Sea salt and freshly ground black pepper	Sea salt and freshly ground black pepper
¼ pint (150ml) champagne	⅔ cup champagne
¼ pint (150ml) soured cream	⅔ cup sour cream
1 small branch dill	1 small branch dill

1 Heat the butter in a large soup pan and sauté the shallots and cucumber for 5 minutes without allowing to brown. Stir in the stock, simmer for 10 minutes, then blend in a food processor or blender.

2 Return the soup to the pan and stir in the lemon juice and rind.

3 In a small bowl, mix the egg yolks and cornflour (cornstarch). Gradually add this to the hot soup, bring the mixture to the boil and simmer for 5 minutes. Season to taste.

4 Remove the oysters from their shells and clean them well. Place in a small pan with the champagne, bring slowly to the boil and simmer for 2 minutes.

5 Remove the oysters with a slotted spoon and place in individual serving bowls.

6 Stir the champagne which has been used to poach the oysters into the soup, then ladle soup over the oysters. Garnish each bowl with a swirl of cream and a sprig of dill and serve.

La Crème de la Crème au Limande

Lemon Sole Soup with a Citrus Flavour

Dover sole is far too expensive to use in a soup, so I have developed this recipe using lemon sole. I have accentuated its natural flavour with the lemon-scented herb known as citronelle. If this is unobtainable, then use lemon mint along with ordinary mint, to achieve a lemon flavour. If lemon sole is unobtainable, then any flat white fish will do just as well — few people would spot the very subtle difference in flavour and the soup tastes just as good.

Imperial (Metric)	American
1 oz (25g) butter	2 tablespoons butter
1 fl oz (30ml) vegetable oil	2 tablespoons vegetable oil
2 oz (50g) chopped celery	⅓ cup chopped celery
2 oz (50g) chopped fennel	⅓ cup chopped fennel
2 oz (50g) chopped celeriac	⅓ cup chopped celeriac
2 oz (50g) chopped leek	⅓ cup chopped leek
1 *bouquet garni*	1 *bouquet garni*
3 leaves citronelle	3 leaves citronelle
3 leaves mint	3 leaves mint
1¾ pints (1 litre) water	4½ cups water
4 fl oz (120ml) dry white wine	½ cup dry white wine
1 lb (450g) white fish bones	1 pound white fish bones
1 vegetable stock cube (optional)	1 vegetable stock cube (optional)
Sea salt and freshly ground black pepper	Sea salt and freshly ground black pepper
4 fl oz (120ml) soured cream	½ cup sour cream
2 egg yolks	2 egg yolks
Juice and grated rind of 1 lemon	Juice and grated rind of 1 lemon
2 teaspoons cornflour	2 teaspoons cornstarch
4 lemon sole fillets *or* other flat fish	4 lemon sole fillets *or* other flat fish
1 oz (25g) melted butter	2 tablespoons melted butter
1 lemon, skin grooved, then thinly sliced	1 lemon, skin grooved, then thinly sliced

1 Heat the butter and oil in a saucepan and sauté the vegetables for 5 minutes without browning. Add the herbs, half the water, and the wine. Simmer for 15 minutes, discard the herbs and liquidize the soup.

2 In the remaining water, boil the fish bones with the stock cube for 15 minutes. Strain and add the stock to the soup. Check seasoning and adjust if necessary.

3 In a bowl, blend together the cream, eggs, lemon juice and rind and cornflour (cornstarch) to a smooth paste. Stir into the soup and reheat to boiling, stirring constantly.

4 Cut the fish into thin slivers. Brush with melted butter and grill for 4 minutes to develop their flavour.

5 Place the fillets in individual soup bowls and pour soup over them, so that the flavours are brought together only at the last minute. Decorate each bowl with slices of lemon and serve.

L'Oignonnade Charentaise

Seafood and Onion Soup with Cognac

Serves 8

The region of Poitou-Charentes is situated between the Loire Valley and the vineyards of Bordeaux. Two of its finest features are represented in this recipe — the lovely Atlantic coastline of Charente-Maritime provides the seafood and the inland region of Charente adds its most famous export, fine brandy from the town of Cognac. Brandy is often used in cooking, but the idea of using it in a soup is quite a surprise to most people. Combined with a full, onion flavour — and sweet red onions are very much the best type for this dish — and the luscious flavour and texture of the mussels and prawns (shrimp), the rich taste and aroma of the cognac makes this a dish you will want to serve again and again.

Imperial (Metric)	American
3½ pints (2 litres) fish stock (page 170) made with red Bordeaux	8⅓ cups fish stock (page 170) made with red Bordeaux
3 oz (75g) butter	⅓ cup butter
8 oz (225g) red onions, sliced	2 cups sliced red onions
3 cloves garlic, chopped	3 cloves garlic, chopped
5 oz (10g) potatoes, thinly sliced	1 medium potato, thinly sliced
Sea salt and freshly ground black pepper	Sea salt and freshly ground black pepper
8 raw mussels, cleaned and shelled	8 raw mussels, cleaned and shelled
8 king prawns, cooked and peeled	8 jumbo shrimp, cooked and peeled
16 small pieces toasted French bread	16 small pieces toasted French bread
6 oz (175g) grated Gruyère cheese	1½ cups grated Gruyère cheese
2 fl oz (60ml) cognac	¼ cup cognac

1 Bring the stock to a boil and leave to simmer, uncovered, for 10 minutes, to reduce and increase in flavour.

2 In a saucepan, heat the butter and gently sauté the onions until soft and lightly browned. Add the chopped garlic and the potato and stir to coat evenly in the butter.

3 Gradually add the stock, bring back to the boil and simmer gently for 15 minutes or until the potatoes are soft.

4 Remove the soup from the heat and stir to mash the potatoes roughly. This will thicken the soup and give it a good, coarse and satisfying consistency. Season to taste.

5 Place a mussel and a prawn (shrimp) in each individual ovenproof bowl, top up with soup, then place 2 slices of toast on top and sprinkle with grated cheese.

6 Place the ovenproof bowls in the oven at 400°F/200°C (Gas Mark 6) and bake for 10 minutes. Remove from the oven, sprinkle each bowl with a little cognac and serve immediately.

Bisque de Crabe Boulonnaise
Crab Soup

Serves 8

Bisque is a term used to describe any thick seafood soup made with fish from the crustacean family. Originally, bisques were thickened with stale crusts or biscuits — hence their name. More often these days they are thickened with flour, usually rice flour. However, a good bisque really needs no artificial thickening, relying on the ingredients themselves to provide a creamy, unctious soup with a well-harmonized and mellow flavour.

Imperial (Metric)	American
2 oz (50g) butter	¼ cup butter
1 large onion, finely chopped	1 large onion, finely chopped
2 cloves garlic, crushed	2 cloves garlic, crushed
1 lb (450g) tomatoes, skinned, seeded and chopped	1 pound tomatoes, skinned, seeded and chopped
1½ pints (850ml) fish velouté (page 176)	3¾ cups fish velouté (page 176)
10 oz (275g) sweetcorn kernels	1⅔ cups corn kernels
1 lb (450g) crab meat (white and brown)	1 pound crab meat (white and brown)
¼ pint (150ml) sherry	⅔ cup sherry
2½ fl oz (75ml) soured cream	5 tablespoons sour cream
3 tablespoons cognac Lagrange	3 tablespoons cognac Lagrange
2 tablespoons chopped fresh parsley	2 tablespoons chopped fresh parsley
Sea salt and freshly ground black pepper	Sea salt and freshly ground black pepper
Pinch curry powder or saffron	Pinch curry powder or saffron

1 Melt the butter in a large pan and sauté the onion until soft but not browned. Add the garlic and cook for a few seconds.

2 Stir in the tomatoes, cover and simmer for 5 minutes.

3 Stir in the velouté, corn kernels and crab meat. Cover and simmer gently for a further 10 minutes. Blend briefly, then return to the pan.

4 Stir in the sherry, cream and cognac. Add the chopped parsley and season to taste with salt, pepper and curry powder or saffron. Reheat the bisque gently to simmering point.

5 Serve with crusty whole wheat bread.

L'Assiette de Thon au Maïs Rochefort

Tuna and Sweetcorn Chowder

I have found that, while tuna canned in oil is perfectly suited to salads — such as the classic *Salade Niçoise* in which its rich flavour is complemented by the tang of black olives, capers and tomatoes, and the fresh crispness of lettuce and lightly cooked French beans — tuna canned in brine is a better choice for soups and light mousses or dips. Of course, fresh tuna is well worth trying if you are in a region where it is available, but the standard of the canned varieties is such that, for a dish such as this rich soup, only a very well-trained palate would notice the difference. Tuna's firm, close-grained texture is ideal for a satisfying country soup, combining to good effect with the kernels of sweetcorn.

Imperial (Metric)	American
1 oz (25g) butter	2 tablespoons butter
8 oz (225g) onions, chopped	1⅓ cups chopped onions
8 oz (225g) potatoes, diced	1½ cups diced potatoes
½ pints (300ml) fish stock (page 170)	1⅓ cups fish stock (page 170)
11 oz (325g) tinned *or* frozen sweetcorn	2 cups canned *or* frozen corn kernels
Approx. 1 pint (600ml) milk	Approx. 2½ cups milk
7 oz (200g) tin tuna in brine	1 medium can tuna in brine
1 tablespoon lemon juice	1 tablespoon lemon juice
5 tablespoons Madeira	5 tablespoons Madeira
Sea salt and freshly ground black pepper	Sea salt and freshly ground black pepper
1 tablespoon chopped fresh parsley	1 tablespoon chopped fresh parsley
2 oz (50g) grated Gruyère cheese	½ cup grated Gruyère cheese

1 Melt the butter in a large pan and sauté the onions for 5 minutes, without browning.

2 Add the potatoes and stir to coat in butter. Add the fish stock, bring to the boil and simmer, covered, for 10 to 15 minutes or until the potatoes are just tender.

3 If using frozen corn, allow it to defrost then drain the liquid from either canned or defrosted corn into a measuring jug and make up to 1 pint (600ml/2½ cups) with milk.

4 Add the milk to the pan, along with the corn.

5 Drain the tuna well, roughly flake and add to the pan, along with the lemon juice and Madeira. Stir everything together well and season to taste.

6 Heat the soup gently to serving temperature, remove from the heat and stir in the parsley and cheese. Serve at once.

Note: The soup can also be liquidized to a smooth creamy texture.

La Bourride Narbonnaise

Provençale Mixed Fish Soup with Saffron

Serves 8-10

This recipe may at first look rather complex, but once you have made your special fish stock it is, in fact, very simple. The result is a sort of bone- and shell-free bouillabaisse which, because of the stock, has all the full flavour of that traditional soup, but involves none of the complications people often find in eating a fish soup complete with its non-edible items!

Imperial (Metric)	American
3½ pints (2 litres) water	8¾ cups water
1 small lobster (approx. 14 oz/400g)	1 small lobster (approx. 14 ounces)
6 Dublin Bay prawns	6 Dublin Bay prawns
1 gurnard (approx. 8 oz/225g)	1 gurnard (approx. 8 ounces)
1 small red mullet (approx. 8oz/225g)	1 small red mullet (approx. 8 ounces)
1 small John Dory (approx. 2 lb/900g)	1 small John Dory (approx. 2 pounds)
2 whitings *or* other white fish (approx. 1 lb/450g total, including bones)	2 whitings *or* other white fish (approx. 1 pound total, including bones)
3 fl oz (90ml) brandy	⅓ cup brandy
10 strands saffron	10 strands saffron
4 cloves garlic, crushed	4 cloves garlic, crushed
1 medium onion, sliced	1 medium onion, sliced
1 stick celery, chopped	1 stalk celery, chopped
1 stick fennel, sliced	1 stick fennel, sliced
2 carrots, chopped	2 carrots, chopped
4 basil leaves	4 basil leaves
1 large sprig thyme	1 large sprig thyme
4 oz (100g) tomato purée	⅔ cup tomato paste
Sea salt and freshly ground black pepper	Sea salt and freshly ground black pepper
Extra basil for garnish	Extra basil for garnish

1 Bring the water to a boil in a large pan and simmer the lobster for 10 minutes. Remove.

2 Simmer the prawns in the same liquid for 5 minutes, then remove.

3 Shell both the lobster and the prawn, slicing the lobster flesh finely and leaving the prawns whole. Retain the coral from the lobster, and any eggs, to blend with 2 oz (50g/¼ cup butter) as a paste to spread on bread.

4 Fillet and skin all the fish. (If you are leaving this task to your fishmonger, make sure to ask for all the trimmings and bones, which you will need for your stock.) Cut the flesh into small pieces, about 1 inch (2.5cm) square. Place in a bowl with the brandy, saffron and garlic to marinate.

5 Wash the fish bones and heads and lobster shells and place them in the lobster broth, along with all the vegetables and herbs. Simmer for 20 minutes, then strain the liquid into another pan.

6 Reheat this broth, add the tomato purée (paste) and season to taste.

7 Place the raw fish, along with the brandy in which it was marinated, in a large, shallow pan. Cover with stock and poach for 5 minutes, then add the lobster and prawns and poach for a further 2 minutes to reheat.

8 Divide the fish between 8 soup plates, cover with hot stock and garnish with 1 basil leaf each. Serve with toasted French bread and garlic butter.

Note: As with traditional bouillabaisse, this soup is especially delicious served with the Provençale sauce called *Rouille*. You can find a recipe for this sauce on page 181.

Consommé d'Homardeau Roscoff
Lobster Broth with Asparagus and Truffles

Serves 6-8

The delicate flavour of this luxurious soup is enhanced by the use of a hen lobster with eggs. You must make an especially fine-flavoured stock for this soup, and I would suggest using halibut, brill or turbot bones and trimmings along with a fortified wine such as red or white port, or vermouth which will also lend the flavours of its herbs to the broth. This makes a beautiful soup for a special dinner party, and the dish can be served hot or cold — in which case it would look especially attractive served in a glass bowl over a container of crushed ice.

Imperial (Metric)	American
3½ pints (2 litres) fish stock (page 170)	8¾ cups fish stock (page 170)
1 hen lobster (approx. 1 lb/450g)	1 hen lobster (approx. 1 pound)
¼ pint (150ml) equal parts dry white wine and brandy	⅔ cup equal parts dry white wine and brandy
2 egg whites	2 egg whites
5 oz (150g) minced white fish	1 cup minced white fish
2 oz (50g) each of the following, finely chopped: celery, fennel, beetroot, carrot and celeriac	⅓ cup each of the following, finely chopped: celery, fennel, beet, carrot and celeriac
Sprig thyme *or* tarragon, chopped	Sprig thyme *or* tarragon, chopped
Sea salt and freshly ground black pepper	Sea salt and freshly ground black pepper
4 asparagus tips, blanched for 7 minutes	4 asparagus tips, blanched for 7 minutes
1 truffle, fresh *or* tinned, thinly sliced	1 truffle, fresh *or* tinned, thinly sliced
4 white mushrooms, sliced	4 white mushrooms, sliced

1 Boil the stock for 1 hour, or until reduced by half. Allow to cool.
2 Place the lobster in a pan with the stock, bring to a boil and cook for 10 minutes. Cool the lobster, remove the tail meat and slice thinly. Place in a bowl with the wine and brandy mixture.
3 Blend the lobster's coral and eggs with the egg whites and minced fish.
4 In a large bowl, combine the chopped vegetables and herbs with the egg and fish mixture, then stir in the cold stock.
5 Return this mixture to the saucepan and reheat slowly, so that the solids coagulate and rise to the surface. Strain the cleared broth into another saucepan and reheat. Season to taste.
6 Serve hot or cold, decorated with asparagus, truffle, mushrooms and lobster tail meat slices.

Côtriade Brestoise aux Rameaux de Salicorne
A Clear Fish Soup with Samphire

Serves 8

Illustrated opposite page 33.

The ship on which I served in the French Navy was named by the town of Brest in Brittany, and was called the *Brestois*. You can imagine how popular we sailors were whenever we landed there, since our berets, with their famous red pom-pom, bore a ribbon with the ship's name on it. The cafés would serve us with their best food, and I especially remember, one bitter Winter's day, enjoying a fantastic *cotriade*, the flavour of which has stayed in my memory ever since. The closest I have come to recreating it is in this variation of a recipe by my old friend Louis Garault, which he used to serve in his restaurant *La Brétagne* in Paris.

Imperial (Metric)	American
3 pints (1.7 litres) fish stock (page 170)	7½ cups fish stock (page 170)
2 oz (50g) butter	¼ cup butter
8 oz (225g) sliced onions	2 cups sliced onions
1 leek, sliced	1 leek, sliced
2 cloves garlic, crushed	2 cloves garlic, crushed
8 oz (225g) potatoes, diced	2 cups diced potatoes
Sprig thyme	Sprig thyme
Sprig celery leaves	Sprig celery leaves
8 oz (225g) cod fillets, skinned and minced	2 cups cod fillets, skinned and minced
2 oz (50g) wholemeal breadcrumbs	1 cup whole wheat breacrumbs
1 egg, beaten	1 egg, beaten
Sea salt and freshly ground black pepper	Sea salt and freshly ground black pepper
Seasoned wholemeal flour	Seasoned whole wheat flour
¼ pint (150ml) Muscadet	⅔ cup Muscadet
8 oz (225g) mackerel fillets	2 cups mackerel fillets
8 oz (225g) Dublin Bay prawns, shelled	4 cups Dublin Bay prawns, shelled
4 oysters, shelled	4 oysters, shelled
4 oz (100g) samphire	1 cup samphire
4 slices wholemeal bread	4 slices whole wheat bread
1 tablespoon chopped fresh parsley	1 tablespoon chopped fresh parsley
1 tablespoon chopped fresh chervil	1 tablespoon chopped fresh chervil
8 mussels, half-shelled	8 mussels, half-shelled

1 Prepare a fish stock as directed on page 170, using the bones, heads and trimmings from the fish in this recipe. Strain the prepared stock.

2 In a large soup pan — a *marmite* as it is known in France — melt the butter and gently sauté the onion, leek and garlic for 3 minutes. Add the potatoes and cover with two-thirds of the fish stock. Add the thyme and celery leaves. Simmer for 20 minutes.

3 Place the minced cod in a bowl with the breadcrumbs and beaten egg. Season. Beat the mixture until it forms a smooth paste, then shape into quenelles. Roll in seasoned flour for easier handling.

4 Place the remaining stock and the wine in a large shallow pan and poach the quenelles, mackerel fillets cut into thin strips, and prawns for 3½ minutes, then add the oysters for ½ minute. Remove with a slotted spoon.

5 Blanch the samphire for 30 seconds only, then place on ice to refresh.

6 Place the slices of bread in soup bowls and spoon equal amounts of the fish over them.

7 Cover with soup and decorate with samphire, chopped herbs and the mussels on their half-shells. Serve at once as a main-course soup.

La Chaudrée de la Côte d'Opale

Scallop, Clam and Cockle Chowder

Serves 6-8

Cockles and clams are to be found along almost every sandy beach in France, and children are often sent out to gather them for the family's supper. They can, too, be found in any fish market, along with the more expensive scallop. Any shellfish can be used to make this delicious chowder, so if you cannot find one at a particular time, substitute something else or increase the quantity of the sort you have got.

Imperial (Metric)	American
3½ pints (2 litres) fish stock (page 170)	8¾ cups fish stock (page 170)
1¾ pints (1 litre) cockles	1 quart cockles
3 tablespoons white wine vinegar	3 tablespoons white wine vinegar
8 fresh scallops	8 fresh scallops
8 fresh clams	8 fresh clams
2 oz (50g) butter	¼ cup butter
2 oz (50g) chopped onion	½ cup chopped onion
1 sliced leek	1 sliced leek
4 egg yolks	4 egg yolks
3 fl oz (100ml) soured cream	⅓ cup sour cream
Sea salt and freshly ground black pepper	Sea salt and freshly ground black pepper
4 oz (100g) wholemeal croûtons	2 cups whole wheat croûtons
2 tablespoons chopped chives	2 tablespoons chopped chives

1 Bring the stock to the boil and simmer for 45 minutes to reduce to about half.

2 While the stock is simmering, prepare the seafood. Soak the cockles in salted water with the vinegar, so that they disgorge any sand. Rinse well then boil for 5 minutes and discard the shells.

3 Open the scallops and clams, remove the flesh and slice thinly, literally. Add the scallop 'beards' to the stock.

4 Heat the butter in a saucepan and sauté the onion and the white part of the leek. Add the green part to the stock. Sauté the onion and leek for 5 minutes without browning, then add the clams and scallops. Sauté for a further 2 minutes.

5 Add the cockles and the strained stock, check the seasoning and then simmer for 6 minutes.

6 In a bowl, blend together the egg yolks and cream. Remove the soup from the heat and gradually beat in the egg and cream mixture. Season to taste.

7 Return the soup to the heat, simmer for a further 6 minutes, then serve with a sprinkling of croûtons and chives.

Pot-au-Feu de Poisson à la Mode de Quimper
Rich Fish and Vegetable Soup from Brittany

Serves 8

Like the *côtriade* on page 44, this is very much a main course soup, and makes a delicious and filling supper dish. During my years as a chef in Britain, it has always seemed to me that cod and other fish of the same type have been so 'typecast' into Fish and Chips that they have not been properly exploited for all their other many uses. Here, I have used cod to make tasty little dumplings to float in your soup — they help to make a meal which is just as flavoursome as fried fish and fried potatoes, but which is *far* more healthy for you!

Imperial (Metric)	American
2 lb 4 oz (1 kilo) whole cod — this will yield 1 lb (450g) skinned fillets	2¼ pounds whole cod — this will yield 1 pound skinned fillets
1 egg white	1 egg white
2 oz (50g) wholemeal breadcrumbs	1 cup whole wheat breadcrumbs
Sea salt and freshly ground black pepper	Sea salt and freshly ground black pepper
3 pints (1.7 litres) water	7½ cups water
½ pint (300ml) Muscadet	1⅓ cups Muscadet
1 *bouquet garni*	1 *bouquet garni*
3 leaves basil	3 leaves basil
1 stick fennel, chopped	1 stalk fennel, chopped
1 stick celery, including leaves, chopped	1 stalk celery, including leaves, chopped
3 carrots, sliced	3 carrots, sliced
1 small beetroot, sliced	1 small beet, sliced
2 leeks, green part only washed, white part washed and sliced	2 leeks, green part only washed, white part washed and sliced
2 turnips, sliced	2 turnips, sliced
½ small green cabbage, cored and sliced	½ head small green cabbage, cored and sliced
1 small onion, studded with 3 cloves	1 small onion, studded with 3 cloves
2 chopped cloves garlic	2 chopped cloves garlic
2 oz (50g) butter	¼ cup butter
Sea salt and freshly ground black pepper	Sea salt and freshly ground black pepper
1 pint (½ litre) fresh mussels	2½ cups fresh mussels
8 slices buckwheat *or* wholemeal bread	8 slices buckwheat *or* whole wheat bread
4 oz (100g) grated Gruyère cheese	1 cup grated Gruyère cheese
1 tablespoon chopped fresh parsley and chervil	1 tablespoon chopped fresh parsley and chervil

1 Fillet the cod and mince the skinned fillets.
2 Place the minced fish in a bowl with the egg white and breadcrumbs. Season and beat the mixture into a paste. Cover the bowl and refrigerate while you prepare the stock.
3 Place the cod bones and head in a large pan with the water and Muscadet. Add the herbs, fennel, celery, one-third of the carrots, beetroot (beet) and the green part of the leeks. Bring to the boil and simmer for 30 minutes. Strain into a clean pan.
4 Into this pan put the sliced white of leeks, turnips, cabbage, onion and garlic. Simmer for 20 minutes.
5 Shape the minced fish mixture into 16 quenelles, rolling in seasoned flour for easier handling if necessary.

6 Coat a large shallow pan with butter, place the quenelles gently in this and cover with just enough broth to cover them. Poach gently for 4 to 6 minutes only.

7 Clean the mussels and add them to the main pan of soup 5 minutes before the end of cooking. Season the soup to taste.

8 Place 4 quenelles and a few mussels in each serving bowl and cover with soup.

9 Toast the bread, top with cheese and brown under the grill (broiler) to serve with the soup. Sprinkle the soup with herbs and serve.

Potage Paysanne Vallée de la Loire aux Truites Fumées
Country Vegetable Soup with Smoked Trout

Serves 8

The Loire valley is rich in freshwater fish, not just from the great river which gives it its name, but also from the smaller — and often prettier — rivers of the region, such as the Loiret, Cher, Vienne, Creuse and *Le* Loir, the 'little brother' of its larger namesake. The wines of the region understandably complement its wealth of fish, from Muscadet at the seaward end of the river, to Sancerre and Pouilly-Fumé from the upper reaches of the river, and with the light and appealing rosés of Touraine and Anjou, and the sparkling delights of Vouvray and Saumur in-between. For this dish I have chosen Pouilly-Fumé, so called for its supposedly 'smoky' taste, to enhance the subtle smoked flavour of the trout.

Imperial (Metric)	American
4 smoked trout, filleted	4 smoked trout, filleted
¼ pint (150ml) Pouilly-Fumé	⅔ cup Pouilly-Fumé
1 tablespoon cream of horseradish	1 tablespoon cream of horseradish
3½ pints (2 litres) fish stock (page 170)	8¾ cups fish stock (page 170)
2 oz (50g) butter	¼ cup butter
2 oz (50g) sliced white of leek	⅓ cup of sliced white of leek
2 oz (50g) carrot, cut into *julienne*	⅓ cup *julienne* sticks carrot
2 oz (50g) celery, cut into *julienne*	⅓ cup *julienne* sticks celery
1 teaspoon turmeric powder	1 teaspoon turmeric powder
1 oz (25g) tomato purée	2 tablespoons tomato paste
2 oz (50g) cucumber, cut into *julienne*	⅓ cup *julienne* sticks cucumber
2 oz (50g) watercress, leaves only	½ cup watercress leaves
Sea salt and freshly ground black pepper	Sea salt and freshly ground black pepper
1 teaspoon chopped chives	1 teaspoon chopped chives

1 Skin the trout and cut into small pieces. Marinate in a mixture of the wine and horseradish for 30 minutes.

2 Boil the fish stock until it is reduced to 3 pints (1.7 litres/7½ cups).

3 Heat the butter in a large pan and sauté the leek, carrot and celery for 5 minutes, without browning. Add the turmeric towards the end of the time.

4 Add the fish stock and simmer for 10 minutes, then add the tomato purée (paste) and simmer for 2 minutes more.

5 Season to taste, then add the fish, with its marinade, the cucumber and the watercress leaves.

6 Bring back to the boil and simmer for 5 minutes. Serve sprinkled with chives.

3

Les Petites Entrées Froides et Chaudes Maritimes

Cold and Hot Entrées

Fish makes the perfect base for a light meal of any kind. You might choose to serve a feathery salmon mousse for lunch with a salad, or choose a tasty and satisfying fish pâté to serve with crusty bread for a cosy supper. A supper of a more sophisticated kind would be the perfect occasion for elegant fish *quenelles*, accompanied by a chilled bottle of Entre-Deux-Mers, and golden vol-au-vents or spicy fritters will suit any light meal or serve as cocktail party fare — just vary the size to suit finger or fork! A true fish fanatic will also point out that fish is the ideal choice for that most important of light meals — breakfast. Many of my clientèle over the years, especially the British, would agree with this, and enjoy with great relish the classic fish-based breakfasts of grilled kippers or kedgeree. However, in this chapter you will find a selection of recipes with a little more *je ne sais quoi*, gathered from the many regions of France which border on the sea and all its wealth, or make full use of the many fast-flowing, clear and bountiful rivers which irrigate the countryside.

I seem to have spent a great many years of my career in places where I could learn to take full advantage of seafood of all kinds, from my time in the French Navy to my idyllic stay in Port Antonio, Jamaica, as Chef-Manager of the celebrated Frenchman's Cove Hotel. I was even born near one of France's most agreeable beaches — Les Sables d'Olonne — and spent much of my youth in Boulogne, that important sea port. So my use of fish spreads across half the globe, and you will find recipes to cool you in the heat of summer, or sustain you when you come home from a chilly day to eat in front of the fire.

Of course, as always, these recipes are very flexible. Just as you will find dishes in other chapters which fit your requirements for a light meal, so you can adapt the recipes here to suit your needs. As I have already mentioned, many will make very appetizing snacks for a drinks party, or appetizers in themselves for a formal meal. Any occasion is complemented by a judiciously selected recipe centred on the special qualities of fish — light, mouth-watering and nutritious, and always imbued with that special air of elegance and luxury.

The Aquitaine region of France has a long, straight coastline that stretches for hundreds of miles from the Gironde estuary in the north to fashionable holiday resorts such as Biarritz in the south. A wide variety of fish is caught off its sandy Atlantic beaches, including tuna in the south and salmon, eels, and even sturgeon to the north. But whatever fish is served to you in this part of France, an important part of the culinary treat will be the wine or spirit in which it is cooked. For this is the region of Bordeaux, Graves, Sauternes, Saint-Emilion, Entre-Deux-Mers and Monbazillac to the north, Armagnac to the south. In the past it was considered a *faux pas* to match

red wine with fish, but now such rules are seen as being made to be broken — so long as you are careful with your choice of fish and wine. In Bordeaux, for example, eels and red wine are a classic combination. But if you are uncertain, the dry white wines of this region are delicious with fish of all sorts.

You may live near the sea, or simply spend your holidays by a river or on the coast. Whichever it may be, if you have the chance, sample the local produce of fish just as you might the fruit and vegetables. Because both give you an opportunity to try truly *fresh* produce — an ever-increasing luxury in these days of refrigeration and preservation. There is nothing to beat freshly picked asparagus *or* the trout fresh from the stream!

Champignons Farcis au Loup de Mer Ciotat
Mushrooms Stuffed with Sea Bass

The Sea Bass, known in France as *Loup de Mer* or *Bar* is a favourite fish of the South of France. A tail piece of this fish makes a delicious meal grilled with fennel stalks, or poached in wine. The flesh can be flaked for all sorts of dishes, and is particularly well suited to this type of *bonne-bouche* or light entrée.

Imperial (Metric)	American
8 large, cupped mushrooms	8 large, cupped mushrooms
6 oz (150g) filleted sea bass, minced	1½ cups filleted sea bass, minced
1 egg, beaten	1 egg, beaten
1 oz (25g) wholemeal breadcrumbs *or* matzo meal	½ cup whole wheat breadcrumbs *or* matzo meal
1 small shallot, chopped	1 small shallot, chopped
½ oz (15g) fennel, chopped	3 tablespoons chopped fennel
Sea salt and freshly ground black pepper	Sea salt and freshly ground black pepper
1 tablespoon cognac	1 tablespoon cognac
2 tablespoons double cream	2 tablespoons heavy cream
Vegetable oil, for basting	Vegetable oil, for basting
Wholemeal toast	Whole wheat toast

1   Clean the mushrooms thoroughly. Remove the stalks, trim their ends, chop the stalks finely and reserve.

2   In a bowl, combine the minced fish, beaten egg, breadcrumbs or matzo meal, shallot, fennel, chopped mushroom stalks and seasoning. Add the cognac and cream and keep beating the mixture until it reaches a light texture but is well bound together.

3   Place the mushroom caps in a shallow baking dish which has been brushed with oil.

4   Divide the mixture into 8 balls, and place one on each inverted mushroom cap. Brush the tops with oil.

5   Bake at 400°F/200°C (Gas Mark 6) for 10 to 12 minutes until the stuffing is golden and sizzling but before the mushrooms have had time to soften and flatten too much.

6   Serve two mushrooms per portion on slices of toast.

Note: If sea bass is unavailable, the flesh of any firm white fish may be used.

Zéphir de Truite Princesse Diana
A Light Trout Mousse with a Hint of Vermouth

Serves 8

Illustrated opposite page 32.

A carefully balanced combination of fish, fruit and green vegetables is ideal for keeping a beautiful figure, shining hair and sparkling eyes, as well as good health and a boundless reserve of energy. It seems to me — and I am sure everyone would agree — that these qualities are epitomized by the lovely Princess of Wales, and if we are to believe what we read in the papers her diet is just such a light and carefully chosen one as I have mentioned. For that reason, I would like to dedicate this dish in her honour.

Imperial (Metric)	American
For the mousse:	For the mousse:
1 lb (450g) trout fillets, skinned	1 pound trout fillets, skinned
3 egg whites	3 egg whites
Sea salt and freshly ground black pepper	Sea salt and freshly ground black pepper
⅔ pint (350ml) double cream	1½ cups heavy cream
1 oz (25g) dry spinach purée	¼ cup dry spinach paste
5 fresh mint leaves	5 fresh mint leaves
1 kiwi fruit, peeled and chopped	1 kiwi fruit, peeled and chopped
2 oz (50g) softened butter	¼ cup softened butter
For the sauce:	For the sauce:
½ oz (15g) butter	1 tablespoon butter
½ oz (15g) vegetable oil	1 tablespoon vegetable oil
1 shallot, chopped	1 shallot, chopped
2 tablespoons Noilly Prat vermouth	2 tablespoons Noilly Prat vermouth
¼ pint fish velouté (page 176)	⅔ cup fish velouté (page 176)
3 fl oz (90ml) single cream	⅓ cup light cream
Sea salt and freshly ground black pepper	Sea salt and freshly ground black pepper
2 oz (50g) skinned, seeded and chopped tomato	¼ cup skinned, seeded and chopped tomato
For decoration:	For decoration:
24 peeled prawns	24 peeled large shrimp
8 whole king prawns	8 whole jumbo shrimp
8 sprigs mint	8 sprigs mint
8 thin slices truffle (tinned)	8 thin slices truffle (canned)
16 slices kiwi fruit	16 slices kiwi fruit

1 Mince the fish finely, then blend in the egg whites and seasoning. Place the mixture in the freezer for 15 minutes, then remove and gradually beat in the cream.
2 Blend the spinach purée, mint and kiwi fruit with a quarter of the fish mixture, then add this to the rest of the fish mixture and stir until an evenly-mixed, pale green paste is achieved. (These two stages can be done in a food processor if you have one.)
3 Grease 8 ramekins (1 inch/2.5cm deep by 3 inches/7.5cm diameter) with the butter, and spoon the mixture into them.

4 Place the moulds in a baking tray, add water to come half-way up their sides, and bake for 25 to 30 minutes in an oven preheated to 350°F/180°C (Gas Mark 4). Allow to rest for a few moments.

5 While the mousses are cooking, prepare the sauce. Heat the butter and oil and sauté the shallot for 2 minutes, then add the vermouth and boil for 5 minutes to reduce by half. Stir in the fish velouté and simmer for 5 minutes, then add the cream and seasoning. Simmer for 5 minutes more, then strain. Return to the pan and stir in the chopped tomato just before serving.

6 To serve the dish, turn out the mousse onto individual serving plates. Spoon a ribbon of sauce on one side of the plate, and on this arrange the peeled prawns (shrimp), truffle and kiwi fruit. Over the fish mousse or 'zéphir', place a sprig of mint and a whole prawn (shrimp). Alternatively, the mousses could be served in their ramekins, with the sauce served separately, in which case, decorate just with a whole prawn (shrimp) and a slice of kiwi fruit. Remember, the key to the presentation of this dish should be that it reflects the elegant beauty of the charming lady for whom it is named!

Cantaloupe aux Fruits de Mer

Cantaloupe Melon Filled with Fish and Fruits

Melon is a beautiful fruit — delicate of flavour, easily digested, light and refreshing to eat, and it combines well with all manner of savoury foods to make a piquant dish suited to a summer buffet, a light lunch or an appetizing first course. The cantaloupe melon has a wonderful aroma which would whet the dullest of appetites, and a sweetness of flavour which is perfectly complemented by the tang of citrus fruits and the subtle flavour of the seafood.

Imperial (Metric)	American
4 small, ripe cantaloupe melons	4 small, ripe cantaloupe melons
2 oz (50g) seedless grapes	⅓ cup seedless grapes
2 oz (50g) sliced peach	⅓ cup sliced peach
8 cooked scampi, chopped	8 cooked scampi, chopped
2 fl oz (60ml) Saint-Raphaël vermouth	¼ cup Saint-Raphaël vermouth
4 fl oz (120ml) natural yogurt	½ cup plain yogurt
4 sprigs mint	4 sprigs mint
4 slices orange	4 slices orange
4 stoned cherries	4 pitted cherries

1 Cut the top off the melon in a zig-zag line. Scoop the seeds from the melon, and discard. Remove a little melon flesh if wished and place in a bowl. (You may need to trim the base of the melon to make it stand upright on a plate.)

2 Put the grapes, peach, scampi and Saint-Raphaël in the bowl with the melon flesh and leave to marinate for a little while.

3 Spoon the fruit mixture into the melon, top with a swirl of yogurt, a sprig of mint, a slice of lemon and a fresh cherry. Serve on a bed of crushed ice.

Variations:
Nuts make a pleasant addition to this dish — cashews and walnuts are especially good. Almost any other type of fruit or fish can take the place of the ones given — and you can change the liqueur to suit the fruits selected. Look upon this as a fish cocktail which you can adapt to suit your mood, and your situation.

Mousseline de Mangetouts aux Crevettes Roses Royale
Mangetout (Snow) Pea Mousse with Prawns (Shrimp)

Serves 8

The French have always preferred tiny peas — *petits pois* or *mangetouts* — to the larger, mushier types preferred by some nations, but at present we seem to be experiencing a surfeit of mangetout (snow) peas. Since they are so readily available, and their flavour is so good, it is worth thinking of more exciting things to do with them than simply blanching them to serve as a garnish. In my last book, *Cuisine Végétarienne Française*, I gave you a recipe for making a most delicious and elegant soup with them. This recipe, too, is based originally on a soup — one which my grandmother used to make, combining mangetout (snow) peas with goat's cheese. Experimenting with this recipe I have found that the flavours are better when it is cooled and set, and from that idea I have created this moussseline, the flavour of which complements king prawns (shrimp) perfectly to make a most elegant and luxurious dish.

Imperial (Metric)	American
1 lb (450g) mangetout peas	1 pound snow peas
2 oz (50g) butter	¼ cup butter
1 shallot, chopped	1 shallot, chopped
4 hard-boiled eggs, sieved	4 hard-cooked eggs, finely minced
4 oz (100g) goat's cheese	½ cup goat's cheese
Sea salt and freshly ground black pepper	Sea salt and freshly ground black pepper
4 fl oz (120ml) natural yogurt	½ cup plain yogurt
1 sprig fresh mint	1 sprig fresh mint

For decoration:	For decoration:
16 perfect mangetout peas	16 perfect snow peas
16 large king prawns, shelled but with heads left on	16 large jumbo shrimp, shelled but with heads left on
4 spring onions	4 scallions
4 strips tomato peel	4 strips tomato peel

1 Trim the mangetout (snow) peas.
2 Melt the butter in a pan and sauté the shallot and peas for 5 minutes. Add just enough water to cover the peas and simmer for a further 5 minutes.
3 Drain, leaving just a little liquid with the peas, sufficient to allow them to be puréed in a blender or processor.
4 Mix the purée thoroughly with the eggs and goat's cheese. Season to taste and chill, covered.
5 Blend the yogurt with the mint, season to taste and set aside for flavours to develop.
6 On individual plates arrange two spoonsful of the mousseline, moulded attractively, and around this place four prawns (shrimp) and four uncooked pea pods per plate.
7 Slice the spring onions (scallions) lengthwise at each end and place in iced water so that they curl attractively. Place a little pile of drained strips on each plate.
8 Curl the tomato peels into rose shapes, and place one on each plate. Serve, with the yogurt and mint sauce offered separately in a sauce boat.

Variations:
The mousselines could be served on a bed of shredded escarole leaves, or on a pool of the sauce. The prawns (shrimp) could be decorated with twisted slices of lemon or lime.

If you feel unsure about whether your mousseline will set, you could thicken it with a setting agent. Gelatine is made of animal bones and hooves, so it is appropriate, in this meat-free context, to use agar-agar, which is made from seaweed (though it does not taste of it!). Use ½ oz (15g) agar-agar to each pint (600ml) liquid and boil until the agar-agar is completely dissolved. Still, I think it is best if one can learn to achieve the right consistency with just the dish's ingredients alone.

Gougeonnade de Plie et Langoustines au Poivre Vert
Plaice (Flounder) and Scampi with Green Peppercorns

Serves 8

Canned green peppercorns are becoming more and more readily available, and are worth hunting out for the beautiful flavour they give to a sauce. The best come from Madagascar, an old French colony whose Creole food, featuring a wealth of fish, exotic fruits and spices, is highly praised. I have adapted an island recipe, using pineapple, garlic and fresh ginger, to make a light and sophisticated dish with flavours which contrast yet harmonize beautifully.

Imperial (Metric)	American
1 slice fresh pineapple	1 slice fresh pineapple
1 small slice (10g) fresh ginger	1 small slice fresh ginger
2 cloves garlic, peeled	2 cloves garlic, peeled
Juice and rind of 1 lemon (rind cut into thin *julienne* strips)	Juice and rind of 1 lemon (rind cut into thin *julienne* strips)
Juice and rind of 1 orange (rind cut into thin *julienne* strips)	Juice and rind of 1 orange (rind cut into thin *julienne* strips)
8 oz (225g) plaice fillets	2 cups flounder fillets
8 oz (225g) shelled scampi	2 cups shelled scampi
Sea salt and freshly ground black pepper	Sea salt and freshly ground black pepper
2 oz (50g) seasoned wholemeal flour	½ cup seasoned whole wheat flour
3 oz (75g) mixed butter and olive oil	⅓ cup mixed butter and olive oil
1 teaspoon canned green peppercorns	1 teaspoon canned green peppercorns
Salad of choice, to serve	Salad of choice, to serve

1 Place the pineapple, ginger, garlic and juice of the orange and lemon in a blender or food processor and blend until smooth.

2 Slice the fish fillets into strips and marinate these and the scampi in the pineapple mixture, sprinkled with salt and pepper, for 30 minutes.

3 While the fish is marinating, blanch the *julienne* strips of orange and lemon rind in boiling water for 6 minutes. Refresh under cold running water, drain and reserve.

4 Remove the fish from the marinade, reserving the liquid.

5 Toss the fish in seasoned flour. Heat the oil and butter mixture in a pan and sauté the fish, tossing and stirring all the time, for 4 minutes.

6 Add the marinade, peppercorns and lemon and orange strips and cook for 2 minutes, stirring so that all the flavours mingle.

7 Serve on a bed of salad — watercress or bean sprouts are good, but any type of salad leaves will do.

Maquereau Fumé à la Rhubarbe Porteloise
Marinated Mackerel with Rhubarb Purée

All smoked fish benefit from being partnered with an acid ingredient, which adds piquancy to the mellow, smoky flavour of the fish. Mackerel is often served with a gooseberry purée, a sour cream and horseradish sauce, or even a sauce of sharp apples. In this recipe I have chosen to use rhubarb for a change, but have not left out the classic ingredients as I use a little cream of horseradish to add smoothness, and a sharp green apple for extra tang. Some people find smoked mackerel slightly indigestible, but rhubarb aids the digestion — yet another way in which these two ingredients complement each other.

Imperial (Metric)	American
For the mackerel:	For the mackerel:
4 smoked mackerel, skinned and filleted	4 smoked mackerel, skinned and filleted
¼ pint (140ml) cider vinegar	⅔ cup cider vinegar
1 tablespoon pickling spices (coriander seeds, chilli, peppercorns and aniseeds)	1 tablespoon pickling spices (coriander seeds, chili, peppercorns and aniseeds)
For the rhubarb purée:	For the rhubarb purée:
1 lb (450g) rhubarb stems, trimmed and chopped small	1 pound rhubarb stems, trimmed and chopped small
4 oz (100g) sour green apple, chopped	1 sour green apple, chopped
1 small piece preserved stem ginger	1 small piece preserved stem ginger
2 tablespoons honey	2 tablespoons honey
1 tablespoon cream of horseradish	1 tablespoon cream of horseradish
Pinch of cinnamon	Pinch of cinnamon
Watercress to garnish	Watercress to garnish

1 Place the mackerel fillets in a shallow dish. Cover with cider vinegar and spices. Cover with foil and leave for at least 8 hours, turning occasionally.

2 Boil all the ingredients for the purée together for 5 to 10 minutes, until the rhubarb is soft. Push through a sieve (strainer) or purée in a blender or food processor. Leave to cool.

3 Arrange the mackerel fillets on individual plates, with a spoonful or two of the purée by their sides. Garnish with watercress leaves.

Variation:
Baked fillets of fresh mackerel are also delicious served with this sauce.

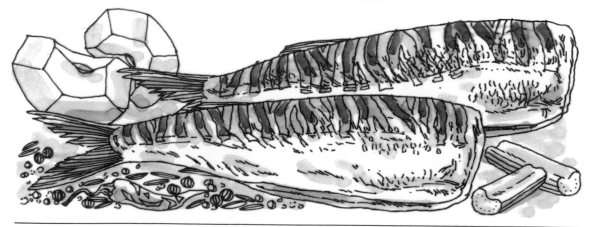

Mousseline de Saint-Jacques Valéscure

Scallop Mousseline with Grand Marnier Mayonnaise

I am often struck by the way that certain new dishes presented by young chefs evoke memories of those I created many years ago . . . *plus ça change!* I recall having cooked a mousseline of scallops during my time in the French Navy, to honour the visit of a high-ranking officer, Admiral Darlan. He took great pains to compliment me on the dish — a very unusual occurrence in those days. Of course, in Brittany, where we were stationed, scallops of such quality that they almost melted in the mouth were in great abundance. In other parts of the world they are usually something of a luxury so I have created this dish to team just three scallops per person with other delicious ingredients to please the palate in such a way that a small quantity is totally satisfying.

Imperial (Metric)	American
Rind of 1 orange, cut into fine strips	Rind of 1 orange, cut into fine strips
2 tablespoons Grand Marnier	2 tablespoons Grand Marnier
12 fresh scallops	12 fresh scallops
3 fl oz (90ml) dry white wine	⅓ cup dry white wine
8 oz (225g) red mullet *or* trout fillets	1⅓ cups red snapper *or* trout fillets
2 egg whites	2 egg whites
6 fl oz (170ml) double cream	¾ cup heavy cream
2 oz (50g) butter	¼ cup butter
¼ pint (150ml) Mayonnaise Sauce (page 179)	⅔ cup Mayonnaise Sauce (page 179)
1 piece preserved ginger, to garnish	1 piece preserved ginger, to garnish
1 tablespoon green peppercorns, to garnish	1 tablespoon green peppercorns, to garnish

1 Blanch the orange strips in boiling water for 7 minutes. Drain, refresh in cold water, and drain again. Leave to soak in the Grand Marnier.

2 Poach 4 scallops in the wine for 3 minutes, drain and reserve as a garnish. The wine could be used as part of the court bouillon for another dish.

3 Mince the remaining scallops to a paste with the fish fillets. Gradually add the egg whites and cream, working the mixture into a smooth, creamy consistency. Chill the mixture for 20 minutes.

4 Grease 4 dariole moulds with butter and fill them with fish paste. Place them in a baking tin and add hot water to come half-way up their sides. Bake at 350°F/180°C (Gas Mark 4) for 15 to 20 minutes, or until set.

5 Remove from the oven and leave to rest for 10 minutes before unmoulding.

6 Remove the orange strips from the liqueur, reserving the Grand Marnier.

7 Place a spoonful of Mayonnaise onto each individual serving plate, then unmould the mousseline on top of the sauce. Place a scallop at the side or on top of each mousseline, and sprinkle the dish with orange strips. Cut the ginger into thin strips and sprinkle these on, too, and scatter a few canned green peppercorns if wished.

8 Serve, with the remaining Mayonnaise beaten together with the reserved Grand Marnier as a separate sauce.

Rouget et Truite au Bleu à la Vapeur Sous Cloche

Red Mullet (Snapper) and Blue Trout, Steamed and Served in a Bell Dish

The Oriental style of steaming fish has become very popular in five-star hotels, in Paris as in other parts of the world. Personally, I prefer a fish to be cooked in its own juices in the oven, rather than in a steam of water or stock — but you may take your choice, since I have created this recipe as a simple example of this new fashion. The bell dish is a lovely thing to use for an elegant meal, since as the lid is lifted at the table all the beautiful aromas of the dish are wafted straight to the diners rather than being lost on the way from kitchen to dining room.

Imperial (Metric)	American
2 rainbow trout, filleted	2 rainbow trout, filleted
2 red mullet, filleted	2 red snapper, filleted
Sea salt and freshly ground black pepper	Sea salt and freshly ground black pepper
4 large leaves of spring cabbage	4 large leaves of spring cabbage
4 courgettes	4 zucchini
4 small carrots	4 small carrots
4 spring onions	4 scallions
2 sprigs fresh basil	2 sprigs fresh basil
2 sprigs fresh mint	2 sprigs fresh mint

For the sauce:	For the sauce:
2 tablespoons raspbery *or* sherry vinegar	2 tablespoons raspberry *or* sherry vinegar
2 tablespoons natural yogurt	2 tablespoons plain yogurt
4 tablespoons fish stock (page 170)	4 tablespoons fish stock (page 170)
2 tablespoons chopped shallots	2 tablespoons chopped shallots
1 teaspoon honey	1 teaspoon honey
Sea salt and freshly ground black pepper	Sea salt and freshly ground black pepper

1 Sprinkle the fillets with salt and pepper and lay them on top of the cabbage leaves in the top of a steamer. Cover and steam for 5 minutes.

2 Meanwhile, thinly slice the courgettes (zucchini) and carrots, lengthways. Blanch in boiling water for 30 seconds and drain well. Slice the spring onions (scallions) diagonally.

3 On the dish of the serving bell, place the cabbage leaves with one red and one blue fillet on each, skin side up. Decorate with the vegetables and sprigs of fresh herbs. Cover the dish with the bell.

4 Place the covered dish in the oven at 400°F/200°C (Gas Mark 6) for 4 minutes.

5 Place all the sauce ingredients in a blender and blend to a smooth emulsion.

6 Take the covered dish to the table, and serve the sauce separately.

Note: A handful of sea vegetables, placed in the water of the steamer, gives an even better flavour to this dish.

Accra de Morue Féroce Perpignannaise
Smoked Cod Fritters with a Chilli Sauce

This is a dish typical of Mediterranean cuisine, with its Moorish influences clearly shown in the spicy and rich tomato sauce and the use of preserved fish. Now that fresh fish is so readily available, and modern refrigeration techniques enable fish to be kept quite safely, free of harmful bacteria, the use of smoked or salted cod has lessened somewhat. But there is still much potential in these ingredients and this dish combines the subtle smoky taste of the fish with the other clasic Mediterranean ingredients, tomatoes, peppers and — of course — garlic. It is a very versatile dish which can be served as here as a light lunch or supper dish, or as picnic or party nibbles if you decrease the size of the fritters, or as an elegant appetizer for a dinner party.

Imperial (Metric)	American
For the fritters:	For the fritters:
1 lb (450g) smoked cod	1 pound smoked cod
¼ pint (150ml) fish stock (page 170) *or* dry white wine	⅔ cup fish stock (page 170) *or* dry white wine
8 oz (225g) potatoes, peeled and sliced	1 large *or* 2 small potatoes, peeled and sliced
4 cloves garlic, crushed	4 cloves garlic, crushed
Freshly ground black pepper	Freshly ground black pepper
Vegetable oil for frying	Vegetable oil for frying
For the sauce:	For the sauce:
2 tablespoons olive oil	2 tablespoons olive oil
1 onion, chopped	1 onion, chopped
1 clove garlic, crushed	1 clove garlic, crushed
12 oz (350g) tomatoes, skinned, seeded and chopped (to make ½ pint/300ml)	12 ounces tomatoes, skinned, seeded and chopped (to make ⅔ cup)
2 red chillies, seeded and chopped	2 red chilies, seeded and chopped
1 red pepper, chopped	1 red pepper, chopped
For the garnish:	For the garnish:
2 avocados	2 avocados
4 crisp lettuce leaves	4 crisp lettuce leaves
4 slices lemon *or* lime	4 slices lemon *or* lime

1 Soak the smoked cod in cold water for 1 hour. Drain and place in a pan with the stock or wine, adding just enough water to cover the fish. Poach the fish for 15 minutes, then drain. (The fish stock can be kept for use in another dish, if it is not too salty.)

2 Boil the potatoes until tender, drain and mash. While they are still hot, add them to the fish, pounding the mixture to a smooth paste. Beat in the garlic and season with black pepper.

3 Chill the mixture and then shape into balls about the size of a small egg.

4 Roll the fritters in a little seasoned flour and then shallow-fry them, for 3 to 4 minutes or until golden, and drain on kitchen paper towels and keep hot.

5 To make the sauce, heat the olive oil and sauté the onion and garlic for 4 minutes, then add the tomatoes, chillies and red pepper. Cook for a few minutes, then blend the sauce in a blender or food processor. Keep the sauce warm.

6 Arrange the fritters on a serving plate decorated with slices of peeled avocado, lettuce leaves and slices of acid fruit to sprinkle over the fritters, and serve the sauce separately. Alternatively, place one lettuce leaf on each individual plate and pile a few fritters onto each, then decorate with avocado and citrus fruit. Guests can help themselves to sauce to drizzle over the fritters or to act as a dip for them.

Boîtes de Feuilletage Garnies de Truite Fumées
Puff Pastry Cases Filled with Smoked Trout

I think that square vol-au-vent cases are far more attractive than the usual round ones, and they are more straightforward to prepare (alternatively, you can purchase a special cutter to make them from any good kitchen supplies store). They make perfect containers for all sorts of fillings, and you can vary the size of the 'boîte' according to the occasion, from tiny ones to serve as appetizers or cocktail snacks, to the size I suggest here with 3-inch (7cm) sides which make a perfect light entrée or luncheon dish with a salad.

Imperial (Metric)	American
For the puff pastry:	For the puff pastry:
½ lb /225g) wholemeal bread flour	2 cups wholewheat bread flour
Pinch sea salt	Pinch sea salt
½ lb (225g) butter	1 cup butter
4 fl oz (120ml) water	½ cup water
1 tablespoon lemon juice	1 tablespoon lemon juice
Extra wholemeal flour for dusting	Extra whole wheat flour for dusting
1 egg, beaten, for glazing	1 egg, beaten, for glazing

1 Sift the flour and salt into a large bowl. Reserve the bran for some other dish.
2 Rub a quarter of the butter into the flour.
3 Make a well in the mixture and add the water and lemon juice. Knead the mixture to a dough and roll into a ball.
4 Slash the top of the dough in a cross shape, cover with a damp cloth and leave to rest for 30 minutes.
5 While the dough is resting, knead the butter until it is the same consistency as the pastry dough, and then roll it out on a floured board to a neat oblong ⅛ inch (3mm) thick. You will need to flour the butter and the rolling pin, as well as the board, very carefully so that the butter does not stick.
6 Roll out the dough to the same thickness as the butter. Place the butter piece on top of the dough and fold the two layers three times. Roll again into an oblong, fold into three again and rest the dough for 20 minutes.
7 Repeat this procedure twice more, then wrap in clingfilm and chill until needed.

Imperial (Metric)	American
For the sauce:	For the sauce:
2 oz (50g) butter	¼ cup butter
2 shallots, chopped	2 shallots, chopped
1 clove garlic, crushed	1 clove garlic, crushed
1 tablespoon tomato purée	1 tablespoon tomato paste
3 fl oz (90ml) dry white wine	⅓ cup dry white wine
3 fl oz (90ml) natural yogurt	⅓ cup plain yogurt
1 teaspoon cornflour	1 teaspoon cornstarch
Sea salt and freshly ground black pepper	Sea salt and freshly ground black pepper
4 smoked trout, skinned, boned and flaked	4 smoked trout, skinned, boned and flaked
Pinch cayenne pepper	Pinch cayenne pepper
1 tablespoon chopped fresh dill, chervil *or* basil	1 tablespoon chopped fresh dill, chervil *or* basil

1 Roll out the pastry to a depth of ⅛ inch (3mm) and cut four or six 3-inch (7cm) squares. Then, ¼-inch (5mm) in from the edges mark another square, ⅛-inch (3mm) deep. Allow the pastry squares to rest on a greased baking sheet at room temperature for at least 2 hours to prevent them shrinking when they are baked.

2 Bake the vol-au-vents for 20 minutes at 400°F/200°C (Gas Mark 6). Then lift off the central 'lid', scoop out the soft pastry inside and your 'boîtes' are ready for filling.

3 While the pastry is baking, prepare the sauce. Melt the butter in a pan and sauté the shallots for 3 minutes. Add the garlic and cook for a further 30 seconds, then stir in the tomato purée (paste) and the wine. Cook this mixture for 10 minutes.

4 In a bowl, mix together the yogurt and cornflour (cornstarch) to a smooth paste. (The cornflour/cornstarch will prevent the yogurt from curdling when heated — you could use sour cream and leave out the cornflour/cornstarch if preferred.)

5 Stir about half the sauce mixture into this bowl, stirring constantly, then transfer all this to the pan. Simmer for 5 minutes, stirring. Season to taste.

6 Stir in the flaked fish and add a pinch of cayenne pepper. Allow the fish to heat through but do not let the sauce boil at this stage.

7 Spoon the mixture into the pastry cases when they are removed from the oven. Sprinkle the tops with herbs, and replace the pastry lids if wished. Serve at once with curly lettuce leaves or radicchio as garnish.

Ratatouille de Sole à la Conil

Goujons of Sole in Ratatouille

This is a ratatouille with a difference. For one thing, the cooking time is considerably shorter than that usually suggested for this dish, so that rather than a rich stew in which all the flavours have had time to amalgamate the result is a very satisfying dish which allows each ingredient to retain its individual character and texture. But the main difference between this and other ratatouilles is that, for the last few minutes of cooking, lightly floured strips of sole are stirred into the vegetables — not for too long, because the fish would break down resulting in an unpalatable mess, but for just long enough to allow the dish to taken on a special and very pleasing quality which I feel sure you will enjoy.

Imperial (Metric)	American
4 fillets of sole (3 oz/90g each)	4 fillets of sole (3 ounces each)
2 oz (50g) seasoned flour	½ cup seasoned flour
1 courgette	1 zucchini
1 aubergine	1 eggplant
1 large onion	1 large onion
2 cloves garlic	2 cloves garlic
4 tomatoes	4 tomatoes
3 fl oz (75ml) olive oil	⅓ cup olive oil
1 tablespoon chopped fresh parsley	1 tablespoon chopped fresh parsley
1 tablespoon chopped fresh basil	1 tablespoon chopped fresh basil

1 Cut the fish into thin strips and toss in seasoned flour, shaking off any surplus.
2 Trim the ends of the courgette (zucchini) and cut in slanting slices.
3 Trim the end of the aubergine (eggplant), halve down the length of it if large, and then cut into slices.
4 Chop the onion and crush the garlic.
5 Skin, seed and chop the tomatoes roughly.
6 Heat the oil in a large, shallow pan and sauté the onion and garlic for 3 minutes. Add all the other vegetables and cover with a tight lid. Cook for 20 minutes over a low heat, stirring occasionally. Add a little fish stock if the mixture gets too dry.
7 Grill the sole fillets for 5 minutes, then add with the herbs to the stew.
8 Check the seasoning and serve on a bed of crisp lettuce or cress as a *salade tiède*.

Flamique d'Aiglefin aux Haricots Verts à la Boulonnaise
Haddock and Green Bean Quiche

This is a far cry from the ordinary cheese custard based quiche. Its filling tastes so luxurious that it could be served at even a quite sophisticated party. Yet it is basically a country dish, known as a *flamique* in Northern France — using good, nourishing ingredients from the countryside and the harbour.

Imperial (Metric)	American
For the pastry:	For the pastry:
1 oz (25g) cornflour	2 tablespoons cornstarch
½ lb (225g) wholemeal flour	2 cups whole wheat flour
5 oz (125g) butter	⅔ cup butter
1 egg	1 egg
4 tablespoons water *or* milk	4 tablespoons water *or* milk
Good pinch sea salt	Good pinch sea salt

1 To make the pastry: in a bowl, sift the cornflour (cornstarch) and wholemeal (whole wheat) flour together. Rub the butter into the flour.
2 Beat the egg and add it, with the water or milk and salt, to the flour and mix to form a soft dough. Roll into a ball and leave to rest for 20 minutes.

Imperial (Metric)	American
For the filling:	For the filling:
4 oz (100g) fresh, skinned haddock fillets	1⅓ cups fresh, skinned haddock fillets
4 oz (100g) smoked haddock fillets	1⅓ cups smoked haddock fillets
Grated rind and juice of 1 lemon	Grated rind and juice of 1 lemon
2 fl oz (60ml) light beer	¼ cup light beer
5 oz (170g) chopped onion	1 cup chopped onion
2 oz (50g) French beans	½ cup snap beans
2 eggs	2 eggs
¼ pint (150ml) double cream	⅔ cup heavy cream
Sea salt and freshly ground black pepper	Sea salt and freshly ground black pepper

1 Cut the fish into small pieces.
2 In a bowl, mix the lemon rind and juice, the light beer and the chopped onion. Stir the fish into this mixture and leave to marinate for a while.
3 Top and tail the beans, slice them if long, and blanch in boiling water for 3 minutes. Drain, refresh under cold running water and drain again. Cut into chunks.
4 Roll or press out the pastry to line an 8-inch (20cm) quiche ring. Arrange the beans in the bottom of this.
5 Drain off the beer and lemon juice from the marinating ingredients (save the marinade for *court bouillon*) and arrange the fish mixture over the beans.
6 In a bowl, beat together the eggs and cream, season to taste, then pour this mixture over the fish.
7 Bake in a preheated oven for 35 minutes, at 400°F/200°C (Gas Mark 6).
8 Serve hot or cold with salad.

Terrine des Deux Poissons Atlantique

Terrine of Sea and River Fish

Serves 8-10

I demonstrated this dish on British TV-am in May 1985, and was inundated with letters asking for the recipe. As with any recipe I have made one or two changes since it was broadcast, but this is in essence the dish which was so popular. I trust you will enjoy it — certainly the guests at various Arts Club functions at which it has been served have done. Those of you for whom it is a new dish will, I hope, like it as much as those hundreds of people whom I thank for their interest — especially at that time of the morning — in being spurred to put pen to paper asking for the recipe. If you have that recipe, I do hope you will enjoy trying it afresh with these variations as much as I have enjoyed making them.

Imperial (Metric)	American
8 green cabbage *or* spinach leaves	8 green cabbage *or* spinach leaves
4 oz (100g) butter, softened	½ cup butter, softened
8 oz (225g) skinned haddock fillets, minced	2 cups skinned haddock fillets, minced
2 shallots, finely chopped	2 shallots, finely chopped
1 egg white	1 egg white
4 fl oz (120ml) double cream	½ cup heavy cream
Sea salt and freshly ground black pepper	Sea salt and freshly ground black pepper
8 oz (225g) rainbow *or* salmon trout fillets, skinned and minced	2 cups rainbow *or* salmon trout fillets, skinned and minced
2 eggs, beaten	2 eggs, beaten
2 tablespoons tomato purée	2 tablespoons tomato paste
4 fl oz (120ml) double cream *or* yogurt	½ cup heavy cream *or* yogurt
1 teaspoon paprika	1 teaspoon paprika
3 oz (75g) cooked peas	½ cup cooked peas
2 oz (50g) cooked sweetcorn kernels	⅓ cup cooked corn kernels
½ red pepper, seeded, blanched and diced	½ red pepper, seeded, blanched and diced

1 Blanch the cabbage or spinach leaves for 30 seconds in boiling salted water, then refresh in iced water. Drain and pat dry.

2 Cut the thick core from each leaf, then line a buttered 2 lb (500g/4 cup) earthenware terrine with 4 leaves.

3 In a bowl, blend together the minced haddock with half the shallots, the egg white, cream and seasoning.

4 In another bowl, mix the minced trout with the beaten egg, tomato purée (paste), yogurt or cream and paprika. Season to taste. Place both bowls in the freezer for 6 minutes to firm.

5 Stir the peas, corn and diced pepper into the haddock mixture so that the colours are evenly distributed.

6 Pack half the haddock mixture firmly into the terrine.

7 Spread the trout mixture onto two cabbage or spinach leaves and roll them up, Swiss-roll (jelly-roll) fashion. Place these lengthways in the dish.

8 Cover with the remaining haddock mixture and level the top. Cover with the remaining leaves and trim neatly.

9 Cover the dish with a lid or foil, and bake at 350°F/180°C (Gas Mark 4) for 45 minutes. Cool and then chill.

10 Prepare a sauce of your choice. Spoon onto individual plates, then cut thin slices of the terrine and

lay them on the sauce. Serve garnished with the item of your choice — lightly steamed asparagus tips are most attractive, as are tiny flowers made of radishes. But even unadorned, the terrine is a visual delight which is matched by its exquisite flavour.

Le Pâté d'Aiglefin au Cognac
Brandied Haddock Pâté

Makes 12 portions

Haddock which has been correctly smoked has a most delicate flavour, and to use artificially coloured and dyed fish in this — or any other — dish would be a disgrace. This pâté combines it with a dash of cognac to give a richness of taste, and the tang of lemon for piquancy. The pâté is very versatile — it can be served in individual ramekins, shaped into quenelles and served with salad, used to fill pancakes or blanched lettuce leaves. At the Arts Club we often feature it on our menus, and use it as a filling for the famous Omelette Arnold Bennett, a dish created at the Savoy in honour of the author.

Imperial (Metric)	American
For the court bouillon:	For the court bouillon:
¾ pint (425ml) water	2 cups water
¼ pint (140ml) dry white wine	⅔ cup dry white wine
2 tablespoons white wine vinegar	2 tablespoons white wine vinegar
1 onion, sliced	1 onion, sliced
2 carrots, sliced	2 carrots, sliced
1 sprig thyme	1 sprig thyme
6 crushed black peppercorns	6 crushed black peppercorns
For the pâté:	For the pâté:
2 lb (900g) boned, smoked haddock	2 pounds boned, smoked haddock
3 oz (75g) wholemeal flour	¾ cup whole wheat flour
3 oz (75g) butter	⅓ cup butter
3 fl oz (75ml) cognac	⅓ cup cognac
2 hard-boiled eggs, sieved	2 hard-cooked eggs, finely minced
Juice of 1 lemon	Juice of 1 lemon
Sea salt and freshly ground black pepper	Sea salt and freshly ground black pepper

1 Boil all the court bouillon ingredients together for 20 minutes. Discard the thyme.
2 Poach the fish in the liquid for 15 minutes and allow to cool in the liquor.
3 Remove the fish, the carrots and the onion, and blend or process together.
4 Reserve ½ pint (250ml/1⅓ cups) of the liquid.
5 In a clean pan, make a *roux* with the flour and butter. Add the brandy to the reserved stock and add slowly to the *roux*, stirring constantly, to make a thick sauce.
6 Stir the haddock mixture, and the eggs, into this sauce. Add the lemon juice and check the seasoning. Cool the pâté quickly and serve in whatever manner you choose. This pâté can also be frozen, so it is well worth making this amount at one time especially since it is so versatile.

Les Quenelles et Timbales Sauce aux Huitres
Different-coloured Fish Mousses on an Oyster Sauce

Illustrated opposite.

This charming and elegant dish is perfect for a special supper party. It uses the principle of a fish mousse to achieve four different flavoured morsels which are then presented in two contrasting ways — as quenelles and as the filling for a timbale. Chilled Entre-Deux-Mers is the ideal accompaniment to this dish, perhaps along with a basket of warm Melba toast. Your guests will be enchanted by the prettiness and the subtle flavours of this dish, as well as with the care you have taken in preparing it.

Imperial (Metric)	American
For the quenelles:	For the quenelles:
4 oz (100g) rainbow trout fillet	1 cup rainbow trout fillet
4 oz (100g) smoked cod	1 cup smoked cod
4 oz (100g) whiting *or* other white fish	1 cup whiting *or* other white fish
2 oz (50g) smoked haddock	½ cup smoked haddock
2 oz (50g) shelled prawns	½ cup shelled shrimp
4 egg whites	4 egg whites
12 fl oz (340ml) double cream	1⅓ cups heavy cream
4 large blanched chard leaves	4 large blanched chard leaves
Sea salt and freshly ground black pepper	Sea salt and freshly ground black pepper
Sauce aux Huitres (page 175)	Sauce aux Huitres (page 175)
½ oz (15g) each red and black lumpfish roe, to garnish	2 teaspoons each red and black lumpfish roe, to garnish

1 Mince each type of fish separately. Place the first three fish in individual bowls, and the haddock and prawn (shrimp) in a fourth.

2 Add to each bowl 1 egg white and 3 fl oz (85ml/⅓ cup) cream. Season and blend the mixtures well. Place all the bowls in the freezer or on ice to chill for 10 minutes.

3 Line four greased dariole moulds with the blanched chard leaves.

4 Prepare the Sauce aux Huitres as instructed on page 175. Reserve the sauce while the quenelles are prepared.

5 Remove the quenelle pastes from the freezer. Using two dessertspoons, shape oval portions of the pink (trout), yellow (smoked fish) and white (whiting) pastes. You should have four of each. (Dipping the spoons in hot water will make the shaping process easier.)

6 Use the fourth paste (the haddock and shrimp) to fill the four dariole moulds. Place these in a baking tray and fill with hot water to come half-way up the sides of the moulds. Place in a preheated oven at 350°F/180°C (Gas Mark 4) and cook for 15 to 20 minutes, or until set.

7 Poach the 12 quenelles in hot stock — *not* boiling — for 8 minutes. When they are cooked they will float to the surface. Remove with a slotted spoon and keep warm (you may find it easiest to cook a few at a time).

8 Arrange the quenelles decoratively on individual plates, along with the timbales, turned out of their dariole moulds. Decorate with the lumpfish roe. You could arrange the quenelles on a pool of sauce, or drizzle a little over each, so that their colours still show through, and serve the rest of the sauce separately. You can see how we chose to present this dish in the illustration opposite.

Overleaf: *Paupiettes de Sole Vigneronne* (page 76).

4 *Les Plats Poissonniers Chauds*

Hot Main Courses

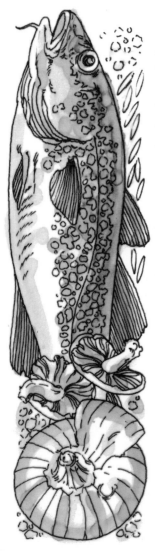

Every year, statistics tell us, the numbers of people turning towards a healthier diet grow and grow. There are probably as many reasons for this as there are individuals on the face of our planet, from compassion for fellow creatures to a greater awareness of one's own physical and mental health. Whether you feel unhappy at the conditions in factory farms and abbatoirs, or are simply worried about the saturated fats and growth hormones you might be consuming with your meat, if you are reading this book it is, I think, safe to assume that you are a person who cares about the quality of their food and the quality of life. If so, you have come to the right place. For a judicious balance of fish and other good, natural foods like vegetables, beans and grains, will provide you with an almost unbeatable diet — high in protein, unsaturated fats, vitamins and minerals, easy to digest and good to eat. You can eat as simply as your needs and purse dictate, or as luxuriously as any carnivorous gourmet could manage. I might even add that you could dine as well as a future King!

In this chapter you will find a wealth of dishes from simple to exotic; to suit a quiet supper or an extravagant dinner party; lightly cooked in the simplicity of a foil parcel or poached in wine and cream for a special occasion; paired with pasta, pulses or grains for a substantial, nourishing meal or accompanied by green vegetables to tempt event the most jaded palate.

Several of the dishes in this chapter have a flavour of Southern France — notably the region of Languedoc-Roussillon. My aunt Thérèse married the brother of the Bishop of Albi, so many a holiday was spent with relatives in this region. From what I recall, the Bishop's table was the best in the diocese, since he had a taste and a talent for gastronomy traditional with the high dignitaries of the Church of Rome. Of course, Friday was the customary day for fish, but the seafood of the region is so plentiful and of such fine quality that almost every day could have been a Friday. The Cassoulet de Cabillaud Carcassonnaise is a dish which has remained especially fresh in my memory, and which I include here for you to try. The region has a wealth of these richly-flavoured dishes, bordering as it does on the Catalan region of Spain and being almost ringed with wine regions, notably that of the Côtes-du-Rhône. The produce of the ports and vineyards is matched by that of the fields and orchards — citrus fruits, olives, aubergines (eggplants), garlic, tomatoes, truffles and *cèpes* all lend their special properties to the cuisine of the region, making it a paradise for vegetarians as well as their fish-eating friends.

As usual, you will find a balance of classic dishes, country fare, and my own creations both old and new. The variety is as boundless as the sea itself, and your imagination is your passport to culinary adventure!

Loup de Mer Catalane au Riz Basquaise

Sea Bass with a Spicy Rice Pilaff

Serves 6

This dish is as rich in colour as it is in flavour, and both are evocative of the scents and sights of Southern France — pungent aromas of garlic, peppers and olives are complemented by rich reds, browns and golds. You could choose brown rice for this dish, or make it special by using wild rice. Both can be cooked easily without the loss of fibre or flavour, and add to the character of this rustic country food.

Imperial (Metric)	American
For the pilaf:	For the pilaf:
8 oz (225g) *Uncle Ben's* wholegrain *or* wild rice	1⅓ cups *Uncle Ben's* wholegrain *or* wild rice
1 oz (25g) butter	2 tablespoons butter
1 fl oz (30ml) olive oil	2 tablespoons olive oil
1 oz (25g) chopped onion	2 tablespoons chopped onion
2 cloves garlic, crushed	2 cloves garlic, crushed
Sea salt and freshly ground black pepper	Sea salt and freshly ground black pepper
5 strands saffron, crushed	5 strands saffron, crushed
1 teaspoon turmeric	1 teaspoon turmeric
2¼ pints (1.3 litres) fish stock (page 170)	5⅔ cups fish stock (page 170)
For the fish:	For the fish:
6 fillets sea bass (approx. 6 oz/150g each)	6 fillets sea bass (approx. 6 ounces each)
Seasoned wholemeal flour	Seasoned whole wheat flour
2 oz (50g) butter	¼ cup butter
2 fl oz (60ml) olive oil	¼ cup olive oil
1 red onion, sliced	1 red onion, sliced
4 cloves garlic, crushed	4 cloves garlic, crushed
1 lb (450g) tomatoes, skinned, seeded and diced	1 pound tomatoes, skinned, seeded and diced
1 oz (25g) tomato purée	2 tablespoons tomato paste
2 tablespoons Pernod *or* Ricard	2 tablespoons Pernod *or* Ricard
Sea salt and freshly ground black pepper	Sea salt and freshly ground black pepper
Fresh basil	Fresh basil
Fresh tarragon	Fresh tarragon
Black olives, stoned	Black olives, pitted

1 To cook the rice, heat the butter and oil in a flameproof casserole dish and sauté the onion and garlic briefly, then add the rice and toss in the mixture until every grain is impregnated with flavour.

2 Add seasoning and stir in the saffron and turmeric, then immediately pour on the stock. Bring to a boil, stirring, and simmer for 3 minutes. Cover and transfer the casserole to the oven. Cook at 400°F/200°C (Gas Mark 6) for 20 minutes.

3 Meanwhile, prepare the fish. Turn the fillets in seasoned flour. Heat half the butter and oil in a large pan and sauté the fish for 5 minutes on each side. Remove from the pan and keep warm while the sauce is prepared.

4 Add the remaining butter and oil to the pan and sauté the onion and garlic for a minute. Stir in

the tomatoes and the tomato purée (paste). Add the Pernod and 4 fl oz (120ml/½ cup) water. Bring to the boil and simmer for 5 minutes or until rich and thickened. Check the seasoning.

5 Turn the rice out onto a warmed serving dish, in a deep ring. (Alternatively, for a more special dish, the rice could be moulded into a savarin ring once cooked, and then turned out.)

6 Arrange the fish fillets decoratively either within or over the rice, and pour in the sauce. Sprinkle with plenty of chopped herbs, garnish with olives, and serve at once with a light, southern French white wine, such as Clairette du Clos de la Rouquette, Grenache or sparkling Gaillac.

Variation:
For a more elegant presentation, use individual savarin moulds and turn them out on individual warmed plates which have already been decorated with a pool of sauce. Arrange the fillet of bass prettily in the centre of the crown of rice.

Couronne Néptune aux Deux Poissons
A Crown of Fish on an Oyster Sauce

Serves 8
Illustrated opposite page 80.

This moulded crown of white fish fillets and pink fish mousse is baked in a savarin mould for a most charming effect. Served on a delicate oyster sauce, with a light garnish and perhaps a simple green vegetable accompaniment, it makes a perfect main course for a supper party. The oyster sauce which accompanies the *couronne* is basically like a Sauce Normande (page 177), enriched with extra oysters and then liquidized, and made more piquant by the use of sour cream and the addition of a splash of Tabasco.

Imperial (Metric)	American
1 oz (25g) butter	2 tablespoons butter
8 fillets of sole *or* whiting (approx. 2 oz/50g each)	8 fillets of sole *or* whiting (approx. 2 ounces each)
Sea salt and freshly ground black pepper	Sea salt and freshly ground black pepper
8 oz (225g) rainbow trout fillets, finely minced	1⅓ cups rainbow trout fillets, finely minced
1 egg white	1 egg white
½ pint (300ml) double cream	1⅓ cups heavy cream
Sea salt and freshly ground black pepper	Sea salt and freshly ground black pepper
For the sauce aux huitres:	For the sauce aux huitres:
½ pint (300ml) fish velouté (page 176)	1⅓ cups fish velouté (page 176)
8 small oysters, shelled	8 small oysters, shucked
3 fl oz (90ml) dry white wine	⅓ cup dry white wine
2 fl oz (60ml) sour cream	¼ cup sour cream
2 drops Tabasco	2 drops Tabasco
For the garnish:	For the garnish:
8 button mushrooms	8 button mushrooms
1 tomato	1 tomato
Small piece red pepper	Small piece red pepper
Coriander leaves *or* fresh parsley	Coriander leaves *or* fresh parsley

1 Grease an 8-inch (20cm) savarin mould with butter. Line with the white fish fillets seasoned with a little salt and pepper. Make sure there are no gaps in the lining, but do not worry if the fillets overhang the edge for now.

2 In a bowl, place the minced trout and beat in the egg white and cream. Season. Place this mixture in the freezer for 8 minutes to firm up.

3 Spoon the chilled trout mousse into the savarin mould, pressing down evenly. Fold the edges of the fish fillets over the top.

4 Cover the mould with greaseproof (parchment) paper, place in a bain marie and bake at 350°F/180°C (Gas Mark 4) for 45 minutes.

5 While the *couronne* is baking, prepare the sauce. Prepare a fish velouté as described on page 176.

6 Poach the oysters in the wine for 2 minutes, then blend to a smooth purée and add this mixture to the velouté sauce. Stir in the sour cream and Tabasco, bring the sauce to the boil and simmer for 4 minutes. Check the seasoning.

7 Trim the mushrooms and carve prettily if wished. Skin and seed the tomato and cut diamond-shaped lozenges from the flesh. Cut the red pepper into tiny cubes and trim the coriander or parsley leaves into sprigs.

8 When the crown is baked, remove from the oven and leave it in the mould for 10 minutes before turning out onto a warmed serving plate. (If liked, some of the sauce could be spooned onto the plate first.) Decorate with the mushrooms, tomato, pepper and leaves. Cut slices from the crown, revealing the attractive combination of colours, and serve individual portions on a spoonful of sauce.

La Tentation du Diable Boulonnaise

Herrings Baked with Potatoes and Sour Cream

Serves 8

One of the finest fish products of Boulogne, in my days there, was the *hareng saur* — herring, filleted and smoked and preserved in brine. We often ate them cold as a simple family meal, with new potatoes and a sour cream dressing. But in the winter my father would prepare this dish, which marries the tang of the fish with the luscious, creamy smoothness of potatoes cooked in the Savoyard style — all in all, a dish to tempt the devil!

Imperial (Metric)	American
4 oz (100g) butter	½ cup butter
8 oz (225g) onions, sliced	2 cups sliced onions
8 smoked herring fillets	8 smoked herring fillets
8 fl oz (250ml) sour cream	1 cup sour cream
8 fl oz (150ml) water	1 cup water
Freshly ground black pepper	Freshly ground black pepper
3 cloves garlic, finely chopped	3 cloves garlic, finely chopped
4 sprigs thyme, chopped	4 sprigs thyme, chopped
1 lb (450g) medium-sized potatoes	1 pound medium-sized potatoes

1 Heat the butter in a pan and sauté the onions gently until softened but not browned.

2 Place the herrings in a shallow dish and cover with a mixture of the cream, water, pepper, garlic and thyme. Leave to marinate for 10 minutes.

3 Slice the potatoes neatly into regular circles ⅛-inch (3mm) thick.

4 Divide half the potato slices between four ovenproof individual baking dishes (choose oven-to-table ware as the dish will be served in these).

5 Remove the fillets from the marinade and lay two in each baking dish.

6 Cover the fish with the remaining potato slices, taking care to overlap the slices attractively.

7 Pour an equal quantity of the cream mixture into each dish.

8 Bake for 45 minutes at 375°F/190°C (Gas Mark 5) until golden on top and the potatoes are tender when gently prodded with a knife or skewer.

9 Serve piping hot with a green salad on the side for a delightful supper.

Gigot de Lotte au Chou Bayonnaise

Roasted Monkfish (Anglerfish) with Cider and Cabbage

This fish has become increasingly popular over the past few years, as people have come to appreciate the many and varied uses of its firm flesh and good flavour. When cut into strips or chunks it hold together well, making it ideally suited to barbecue kebabs. Its texture is similar to that of scampi, too, and it can be breadcrumbed and substituted in a budget meal, such as a picnic. It makes a delicious *salade tiède*, tossed in a little hot olive oil with shallots and mushrooms and then served over a bed of lettuce, corn salad and radicchio. But in the fun of trying recipes which use monkfish in chunks, strips and slivers, do not forget that it is a delicious fish to serve in a piece, as in this recipe, where it is roasted on the bone and then served on a bed of aromatically scented cabbage, in a style traditional of the Mediterranean coastline from Perpignan to Marseilles.

Imperial (Metric)	American
1 whole monkfish, gutted, skinned and with head removed (about 2 lb/1 kilo)	1 whole anglerfish, gutted, skinned and with head removed (about 2 pounds)
Sea salt and freshly ground black pepper	Sea salt and freshly ground black pepper
8 cloves garlic, peeled and cut in slivers	8 cloves garlic, peeled and cut in slivers
4 tablespoons olive oil	4 tablespoons olive oil
2 lb (900g) cabbage	2 pounds cabbage
1 oz (25g) butter	2 tablespoons butter
3 apples, cored and sliced thinly	3 apples, cored and sliced thinly
3 fl oz (90ml) dry cider	⅓ cup hard cider
1 fl oz (30ml) Calvados *or* brandy	2 tablespoons Calvados *or* brandy
3 fl oz (90ml) sour cream *or* yogurt (optional)	⅓ cup sour cream *or* yogurt (optional)

1 Clean, wash and pat dry the fish. Season with salt and pepper, make small slits with a sharp knife and insert slivers of garlic into the flesh.

2 Brush the fish with oil and place in a lightly oiled earthenware oven dish. Bake for 20 to 30 minutes in a preheated oven at 400°F/200°C (Gas Mark 6), basting occasionally with a little cider and turning once or twice during cooking.

3 While the fish is cooking, prepare the cabbage. Slice the cabbage into thin shreds. Wash, drain and place in boiling salted water. Cook for 8-10 minutes, then drain thoroughly.

4 Heat the remaining oil with the butter in a sauté pan. Toss the cabbage and sliced apples in the pan until the apples are softened. Season to taste.

5 Stir the cider and Calvados into the cabbage mixture and transfer to a warm serving dish. Lay the roasted monkfish on top and serve at once. Sour cream or yogurt could be stirred into the cabbage before serving the fish, for a more tangy dish.

Saumon en Croûte

Salmon with a Mushroom Pâté in a Light Puff Pastry Parcel

Serves 8

This is an excellent dish for a buffet party. It can also be served cold as part of a picnic spread, although the delicate pastry will not withstand too much bumpy transporting. Yet it is probably best as the centrepiece of an elegant dinner party for guests who you wish either to spoil or impress. It is a classic which never fails in either of these respects. Served with a simple green salad dressed with a dill-flavoured yogurt mayonnaise, or with a selection of lightly-steamed green vegetables such as broccoli or courgettes (zucchini), your guests will feel replete but not bloated and your dinner will be a success, with conversation flowing as brightly as a sparkling Saumur.

Imperial (Metric)	American
1 onion, finely chopped	1 onion, finely chopped
1 large *or* 2 small bulbs fennel, finely chopped	1 large *or* 2 small bulbs fennel, finely chopped
2 oz (50g) butter	¼ cup butter
8 oz (225g) mushrooms, finely chopped	1 cup finely chopped mushrooms
2 oz (50g) wholemeal breadcrumbs	1 cup whole wheat breadcrumbs
2 tablespoons chopped parsley	2 tablespoons chopped parsley
Grated rind and juice of 1 lemon	Grated rind and juice of 1 lemon
Sea salt and freshly ground black pepper	Sea salt and freshly ground black pepper
1 lb (450g) prepared puff pastry (page 58)	1 pound prepared puff pastry (page 58)
1½ lb (675g) fresh salmon fillet	1½ pounds fresh salmon fillet
Beaten egg to glaze	Beaten egg to glaze

1 Gently sauté the onion and fennel in the butter until softened but not browned. Add the mushrooms and sauté until all the liquid has evaporated.

2 Remove the pan from the heat and stir in the breadcrumbs, parsley, lemon rind and juice and seasoning. Beat the mixture together well, then set aside to cool.

3 Roll out the pastry to a thickness of about ⅛ inch (3mm). Cut the pastry into rectangles or fish shapes, allowing two per portion.

4 Cut pieces of salmon fillet about ½ inch (1cm) thick to fit the pastry shapes, allowing a border of about ½ inch (1cm) around each edge. Grill for 5 minutes, then cool.

5 Spoon a layer of mushroom pâté on top of each fillet, brush the pastry edges with water and place the matching pastry lid over each fillet, sealing the edges together well. Decorate the tops with pastry off-cuts if wished.

6 Place the parcels on a lightly-oiled baking tray, brush the tops with beaten egg and bake at 400°F/200°C (Gas Mark 6) for 20 minutes, until the pastry is risen and golden-brown. Serve at once.

Loup de Mer aux Rameaux de Salicorne

Sea Bass with Vermouth, Saffron and Samphire

Sea Bass is an oily fish, so it is best cooked in a way which avoids the use of extra fat. It is very popular grilled, and I like it baked in foil, but a good way of bringing out its flavour is to steam it over a seaweed-flavoured stock. You will be amazed and delighted at the full flavour this gives the fish — a far cry from the use of steamed fish as 'invalid food'. The Oriental technique of steaming is emphasized by the use of ginger, and the addition of sea vegetables in the form of kelp and samphire give the dish a 'fresh from the ocean' flavour which is quite delicious.

Imperial (Metric)	American
4 sea bass (approx. 6 oz/175g each), filleted and scraped	4 sea bass (approx. 6 ounces each), filleted and scraped
½ oz (15g) fresh ginger, sliced into strips	1 tablespoon fresh ginger, sliced into strips
2 shallots, thinly sliced	2 shallots, thinly sliced
8 small sprigs fresh thyme	8 small sprigs fresh thyme
Sea salt and freshly ground black pepper	Sea salt and freshly ground black pepper
8 large chard leaves, blanched for 30 seconds	8 large chard leaves, blanched for 30 seconds
1 pint (600ml) fish stock (page 170)	2½ cups fish stock (page 170)
1 oz (25g) dried kelp, *or* a small handful fresh seaweed	½ cup dried kelp, *or* a small handful fresh seaweed

For the sauce:	For the sauce:
3 fl oz (75ml) Noilly Prat vermouth	½ cup Noilly Prat vermouth
8 threads saffron	8 threads saffron
1 clove garlic, crushed	1 clove garlic, crushed
1 teaspoon tomato purée	1 teaspoon tomato paste
Sea salt and freshly ground black pepper	Sea salt and freshly ground black pepper
3 oz (75g) butter	⅓ cup butter

For decoration:	For decoration:
4 wholemeal pastry boats	4 whole wheat pastry boats
2 oz (50g) red lumpfish caviar	2 tablespoons red lumpfish caviar
3 oz (75g) samphire, blanched for 30 seconds	½ cup samphire, blanched for 30 seconds
1 carrot, grooved, cut into thin slices and blanched for 30 seconds	1 carrot, grooved, cut into thin slices and blanched for 30 seconds

1 On each fillet of bass, place strips of ginger, slices of shallot, 2 sprigs of thyme and a sprinkling of seasoning. Lay the chard leaves out on a flat surface and carefully wrap one fish fillet in each leaf.

2 Bring the stock to a boil in the bottom part of a steamer, and add the dried kelp or well-washed fresh seaweed. Place the wrapped fish in the top part of the steamer and set this over the stock. Cover and steam for 10 minutes. When cooked, remove the fish from the steamer and keep warm.

3 Take ¼ pint (150ml/⅔ cup) stock from the steamer, strain and place in a pan with the vermouth, saffron and garlic. Boil for 5 minutes to reduce by one third, then strain into a clean pan. Stir in the tomato purée (paste). Season.

4 Whisk the butter into the sauce, then spoon 4 tablespoons sauce onto each serving plate.

5 Arrange two wrapped fillets on the sauce on each plate. Fill the pastry boats with caviar and place

them alongside, sprinkle samphire onto the sauce and arrange carrot slices along the top of each fillet. Serve at once.

Variation:
The adding of butter to the sauce at the end is known as *monter au beurre*. You can make a lighter sauce by adding a liaison of 1 egg yolk, ½ teaspoon cornflour (cornstarch) and 2 tablespoons water, mixed thoroughly in a cup and whisked into the sauce. Season to taste and cook for a few minutes for a good and less fatty sauce.

Truite Volante aux Cacahouettes
'Butterfly' Trout with Peanuts and a Spicy Ginger Sauce

Serves 2

The combination of fish and nuts is an attractive and unusual one. This dish uses that partnership in a light and novel way, using both ingredients and presentation which reflect a South-East Asian approach. The influence of this cuisine is strong in France at present, and its emphasis on a subtle blend of exotic flavours, along with a fresh and charming approach to the presentation of food, has brought a breath of fresh air to many a jaded palate.

Imperial (Metric)	American
For the fish:	For the fish:
1 lb (450g) rainbow trout	1 pound rainbow trout
1 oz (25g) seasoned wholemeal flour	¼ cup seasoned whole wheat flour
2 fl oz (60ml) vegetable oil	¼ cup vegetable oil
For the sauce:	For the sauce:
1 slice fresh pineapple	1 slice fresh pineapple
1 clove garlic, chopped	1 clove garlic, chopped
½ oz (15g) fresh ginger	½ tablespoon fresh ginger
1 tablespoon soya sauce	1 tablespoon soy sauce
2 oz (50g) peanuts	⅓ cup peanuts
4 tablespoons water	4 tablespoons water
For the garnish:	For the garnish:
Fresh grapefruit and orange segments	Fresh grapefruit and orange segments
1 oz (25g) butter	2 tablespoons butter
2 oz (50g) unsalted peanuts	⅓ cup unsalted peanuts
2 fl oz (60ml) grapefruit juice	¼ cup grapefruit juice
2 oz (50g) beansprouts, or more, to taste	1 cup beansprouts, or more, to taste
1 oz (25g) *julienne* of red pepper	½ cup *julienne* of red pepper

1 Prepare the trout in 'butterfly' fashion or have this done for you. Wash, dry and coat in seasoned flour. Heat the oil in a pan and place the fish, spread flat out, in the pan and sauté for 4 minutes. Do not turn but baste frequently.

2 Place the fish in a shallow baking dish and bake in a preheated oven at 400°F/200°C (Gas Mark 6) for 10 minutes.

3 Blend all the sauce ingredients together and place in a small pan. Bring to the boil and simmer for 2 minutes.

4 As soon as the fish is cooked, place, skin side down, on a warm serving dish and decorate the edges of the 'wings' with alternate segments of grapefruit and orange.

5 Heat the butter quickly in a pan, add the peanuts and toss briefly to toast them.

6 Add the grapefruit juice, bring to a boil and pour over the fish. Decorate the edge of the dish with the beansprouts and *julienne* of red pepper, drizzle the dish with the ginger sauce and serve at once.

Cabillaud au Cidre Normandie

Cod Baked in Cream and Cider

This is a traditional Normandy style of presentation, which makes a special treat out of any white fish. I have used cod since, in Britain where I live, it is a common yet very underexploited fish, usually to be found coated in heavy batter or blanketed in a dull and floury cheese sauce. Many regions and countries have an equivalent white fish which will lend itself just as well to this simple and delicious dish.

Imperial (Metric)	American
2 shallots	2 shallots
2 lb (900g) tail piece of cod, skinned and filleted	2 pound tail piece cod, skinned and filleted
1½ oz (40g) butter	3 tablespoons butter
2 tablespoons cider vinegar	2 tablespoons cider vinegar
8 oz (225g) button mushrooms	4 cups button mushrooms
Sea salt and freshly ground black pepper	Sea salt and freshly ground black pepper
4 fl oz (120ml) dry cider	½ cup hard cider
12 mussels	12 mussels
4 oz (100g) peeled, cooked prawns	¾ cup shelled, cooked shrimp
7 fl oz (200ml) double cream	Scant cup heavy cream
Freshly chopped parsley	Freshly chopped parsley

1 Peel and chop the shallots. Butter an ovenproof dish with a little of the butter and place the shallots in the bottom.

2 Wash and dry the filleted fish and lay this on top of the shallots. Sprinkle with half the cider vinegar.

3 Wash and trim the mushrooms. Slice them and place on top of the fish. Season with salt and pepper, then pour in the cider.

4 Cut the remaining butter into small pieces and dot the dish with it. Bake at 375°F/190°C (Gas Mark 5) for 30 minutes, basting occasionally.

5 While the fish is cooking, wash and scrape the mussels, discarding any that remain open (since you want to serve the dish with 12 mussels, you may wish to use extra, in case of rejects).

6 Place the mussels in a pan with a little water and the remaining cider vinegar. Cover and cook over a brisk heat for 5 minutes, shaking the pan occasionally. Discard any mussels which remain closed by the end of cooking. Drain and keep warm.

7 When the fish is cooked, drain the juices into a pan. Keep the fish warm.

8 Add the cooked prawns to the fish liquid and bring to the boil. Stir in the cream and boil for 5 minutes to reduce and thicken the sauce.

9 Place the fish in the centre of a serving dish, with the mussels around the edge. Pour over some of the sauce and sprinkle with parsley. Serve, with the remaining sauce offered separately.

Paupiettes de Sole Vigneronne

Stuffed Sole Fillets, Garnished with White Grapes

Illustrated opposite page 65.

A very welcome trend in modern cuisine has been the use of flavoured wines, such as vermouth, as a cooking medium. The delicate balance of wine and herb is often far more subtle than would normally be used in a dish. The Maître d'Hôtel of Maxim's in Paris created the famous Sole Albert around the combination of this fish with vermouth, and it is a most successful partnership of flavours. I recall once being entertained by two distinguished chefs of the *Société des Cuisiniers de Paris* — amongst the other guests, and seated next to me, was the late Duchess of Windsor — and the dish being served was Sole Maxime. It was baked in the oven and brought to the table on the bone. The Head Waiter had to fillet it and present it to each guest, finishing the sauce as it was served, in front of the guest and before it could get cold. It was a wonderful demonstration of skill, and I wish we had more such waiters everywhere. I will not demand such a technical skill from my readers, so here sole fillets are served rolled around a light fish mousse and coated with a piquant sauce flavoured with vermouth.

Imperial (Metric)	American
1 large sole (approx. 1½ lbs/700g), skinned, boned and filleted	1 large sole (approx. 1½ pounds), skinned, boned and filleted
8 oz (225g) smoked trout fillets	2 cups smoked trout fillets
1 egg white	1 egg white
2 fl oz (60ml) double cream	¼ cup heavy cream
1 tablespoon chopped parsley	1 tablespoon chopped parsley
1 pint (600ml) fish stock, made with the bones from the sole (page 170)	2½ cups fish stock, made with the bones from the sole (page 170)
2 fl oz (60ml) Noilly Prat vermouth	¼ cup Noilly Prat vermouth
3 fl oz (70ml) sour cream	⅓ cup sour cream
1 egg yolk	1 egg yolk
½ teaspoon cornflour	½ teaspoon cornstarch
Sea salt and freshly ground black pepper	Sea salt and freshly ground black pepper
Pinch cayenne pepper	Pinch cayenne pepper
Juice of ½ lemon	Juice of ½ lemon
3 oz (75g) butter	⅓ cup butter

For decoration:	For decoration:
8 oz (225g) *duchesse* potatoes (page 88)	8 ounces *duchesse* potatoes (page 88)
8 oz (225g) seedless white grapes in small bunches	1⅓ cups seedless white grapes in small bunches
1 lemon, studded with pieces of radish	1 lemon, studded with pieces of radish

1 Beat the fillets gently to flatten and break up their fibres.
2 Blend or process the smoked trout with the egg white, cream and parsley to make a smooth paste.
3 Spread each fillet with some of the trout mixture, roll up carefully and place on end in a baking dish. Either choose a dish just big enough to hold the *paupiettes* standing up, or wrap each round with a little foil so that they cannot unroll during cooking.
4 Boil the fish stock fiercely to reduce to ¼ pint (150ml/⅔ cup). Cool and mix with the vermouth. Pour this mixture over the fillets.
5 Bake the *paupiettes* for 10 to 15 minutes in a preheated oven at 400°F/200°C (Gas Mark 6).
6 Collect the juices from the fish and keep the *paupiettes* warm. Pour the juices into a pan and boil for 5 minutes.

7　In a bowl, blend together the cream, egg yolk and cornflour (cornstarch). Add gradually to the fish juices, stirring to produce a smooth sauce. Season with salt, pepper and cayenne, add the lemon juice and lastly beat in the butter.

8　Pour half the sauce onto a serving dish. Pipe a semi-circle, or other decorative pattern, of *duchesse* potatoes. Arrange the *paupiettes* on the sauce, decorate with grapes and, if you like, spoon a little more sauce over each *paupiette*. Decorate the dish with the lemon, and serve with the remaining sauce offered separately.

Note: If the *paupiettes* are quite large, a pretty effect, such as illustrated opposite page 65, can be achieved by slicing them in half and arranging them cut-side upward on the plate.

Darne de Colin en Papillote
Hake Baked in a Parcel

Hake is a superb fish, with a subtle yet rich flavour, and firm yet tender flesh. It is considered by many, myself included, to be second only to salmon in terms both of cooking and eating. The papillote style of cooking which we shall be using in this recipe was originally developed around a wrapping of greaseproof paper, and the fish has usually been pre-fried, so the parcel element was more a method of presentation than anything. Yet this way of cooking is ideally suited to the good qualities of fish — the natural oils need no supplement and do not overwhelm the dish, and the essential juices, which keep the fish moist, are retained in all their aromatic glory. The fish bakes in its own juices, and its natural texture remains unspoilt, since it stays in its parcel from beginning to end of the cooking process. Foil has replaced paper in the method and is more robust, and so better able to withstand even the handling of the most inexperienced or hurried cook.

Imperial (Metric)	American
4 skinned fillets of hake (6 oz/175g each)	4 skinned fillets of hake (6 ounces each)
Sea salt and freshly ground black pepper	Sea salt and freshly ground black pepper
8 large green cabbage leaves, blanched	8 large green cabbage leaves, blanched
4 oz (100g) *julienne* of carrot	⅔ cup *julienne* of carrot
4 oz (100g) *julienne* of leek	⅔ cup *julienne* of leek
4 oz (100g) *julienne* of preserved ginger	½ cup *julienne* of preserved ginger
4 oz (100g) butter	½ cup butter
4 sprigs fresh thyme	4 sprigs fresh thyme

1　Cut a sheet of foil four times the size of an individual fillet. Fold in half and cut a half-heart shape from the foil, easily large enough to parcel up the fillet in. Unfold to form a complete heart shape. Repeat for the remaining fillets and set the foil aside.

2　Season each fillet with salt and pepper. Lay each fillet on a blanched cabbage leaf.

3　Mix together the *julienne* ingredients and divide the mixture evenly between each fillet, laying it neatly on top of each.

4　Cover each fillet with another blanched cabbage leaf and wrap the leaves around to form a neat parcel.

5　Butter the foil 'hearts' and lay a fillet on one side of each. Fold the empty half over the fish and crimp the edges tightly to completely seal the parcel.

6　Place the parcels on a baking tray and bake at 400°F/200°C (Gas Mark 6) for 12 to 15 minutes. Serve the sealed parcels to your guests, allowing them to open them to catch the full cloud of deliciously-scented steam which escapes as the parcel is undone.

Truite Farcie Duxelles en Chemise
Baked Rainbow Trout with a Mushroom Stuffing, Wrapped in Leaves

Serves 2
Illustrated inside front cover.

When serving a stuffed and wrapped fish, it is a courtesy to your guests to make sure that all the bones have been removed before the dish is prepared. That way fish, stuffing and wrapping can all be enjoyed without the meal becoming a fiddly, time-consuming affair, or a risky business with the danger of swallowing an unseen fish bone. For this dish you could also skin the fish, since it will not be on view, but it is perfectly harmless to leave it on. But do bear in mind that some people find dark fish skin unpalatable, and decide accordingly.

Imperial (Metric)	American
2 rainbow trout (approx. 8 oz/225g each)	2 rainbow trout (approx. 8 ounces each)
Sea salt and freshly ground black pepper	Sea salt and freshly ground black pepper
For the filling:	For the filling:
6 oz (175g) button mushrooms	3 cups button mushrooms
2 oz (50g) butter	¼ cup butter
1 oz (25g) finely chopped onion	¼ cup finely chopped onion
1 oz (25g) wholemeal breadcrumbs	½ cup whole wheat breadcrumbs
1 egg, beaten	1 egg, beaten
1 tablespoon fresh chopped herbs (parsley, mint, basil and tarragon are best)	1 tablespoon fresh chopped herbs (parsley, mint, basil and tarragon are best)
For the wrapping:	For the wrapping:
4 large chard leaves	4 large chard leaves
2 oz (50g) melted butter	¼ cup melted butter
For the garnish:	For the garnish:
1 carrot	1 carrot
4 oz (100g) button mushrooms	2 cups button mushrooms
1 oz (50g) butter	2 tablespoons butter
Juice of ½ lemon	Juice of ½ lemon
Sprigs of tarragon	Sprigs of tarragon

1 Carefully bone the fish or, if this has been done for you, check to ensure all bones have been removed. Skin the fish, according to taste. Season.

2 Finely chop the mushrooms for the filling. Heat the butter in a pan and sauté the mushrooms and chopped onion for 2 minutes. Remove from the heat and stir in the breadcrumbs. Beat in the egg and herbs. Season.

3 Allow the filling mixture to cool, then stuff the fish, shaping them firmly around the filling into their original form.

4 Brush the chard leaves with hot melted butter to soften them, then wrap two leaves around each fish.

5 Lay the fish in an earthenware dish, greased with a little more butter, cover with foil and bake in a preheated oven at 400°F/200°C (Gas Mark 6) for 20 minutes.

6 Cut one-third of the carrot into fine *julienne* and blanch for 1 minute. Cut grooves in the sides of the remaining carrot, then cut on the diagonal to form attractive leaf-like shapes. Blanch for 2 minutes.

7 Wash and trim the mushrooms for the garnish. Slice and sauté in butter for 1 minute, then add lemon juice.
8 Lay each fish on a warm serving dish and garnish attractively with mushrooms, carrot 'leaves' and *julienne* and leaves or sprigs of fresh tarragon.

Casserole de Poisson en Croûte Feuilletée
Mediterranean Layered Fish Pie

Serves 8 to 10

The regions of France which border on the Mediterranean Sea have an unequalled heritage of culinary styles, brought to their shores by traders over the centuries. The pastas of Italy and the paellas of Spain, of course, would have come by land trade routes to be adapted and evolved into the local cuisine, but some styles and ingredients were carried by ship from farther climes. Couscous from North Africa is one example, but this dish reflects the influence of Hellenic trade on the region. Just as the vineyards of Provence were the result of strong Greek influence, so the use of translucent sheets of pastry — known in Greece as *filo* — can be found in this part of France alone. Once almost unobtainable outside very specialist shops, *filo* is fast becoming widely stocked by good food shops, so here is an opportunity to try it in a simple, versatile dish which will do justice to picnic, buffet or dinner party alike.

Imperial (Metric)	American
4 fl oz (120ml) melted butter	½ cup melted butter
10 sheets *filo* pastry, covered with a damp cloth until required	10 sheets *filo* pastry, covered with a damp cloth until required
1 large onion, thinly sliced	1 large onion, thinly sliced
8 oz (225g) filleted cod, cut into small cubes	1⅓ cups filleted cod, cut into small cubes
6 oz (150g) tomatoes, skinned, seeded and chopped	1 cup skinned, seeded and chopped tomato
1 red pepper, seeded and diced	1 red pepper, seeded and diced
8 oz (225g) cooked and drained spinach	1⅓ cups cooked and drained spinach
2 oz (50g) tinned anchovies, rinsed and chopped	¼ cup canned anchovies, drained and chopped
2 cloves garlic, crushed	2 cloves garlic, crushed
Sea salt and freshly ground black pepper	Sea salt and freshly ground black pepper
Freshly grated nutmeg	Freshly grated nutmeg

1 Brush the base and sides of an earthenware oven dish (12×6×3 inches/30×15×7.5cm) with melted butter. Lay four sheets of *filo* pastry in the base, brushing each layer with a little butter.
2 Onto the pastry base, place a layer of sliced onion and diced fish, using half of each. Follow with a layer of half the tomato and pepper, then one of spinach, anchovy and garlic. Season with salt, pepper and nutmeg, then repeat the layers, using the remaining ingredients. Fold loose filo pastry edges over the filling.
3 Lay the remaining *filo* leaves over the top of the pie, brushing lightly with butter at each layer. Tuck the loose edges down the inside of the dish. Brush the top with butter and bake at 400°F/200°C (Gas Mark 6) for 25 minutes, until golden and crisp. Serve at once.

Paupiettes de Plie Princesse

Parcels of Plaice (Flounder) with Asparagus

The family of flat fish which includes plaice (flounder) sole and dab has the shared characteristic of very soft fibres which are easily broken upon cooking, resulting in a messy dish — though not, of course, affecting the flavour. Still, this method of rolling the fillets of fish around a stuffing before cooking ensures an attractive as well as appetizing dish. Here the fish are poached but for a richer dish they could be coated in flour, eggwash and breadcrumbs and deep-fried for 4 minutes. But this recipe is just as tasty and far healthier for you and your guests.

Imperial (Metric)	American
4 large fillets of plaice	4 large fillets of flounder
Sea salt and freshly ground black pepper	Sea salt and freshly ground black pepper
2 oz (50g) butter	¼ cup butter
4 oz (100g) mushrooms, finely chopped	½ cup finely chopped mushrooms
2 oz (50g) finely chopped onion	⅓ cup finely chopped onion
2 oz (50g) wholemeal breadcrumbs	1 cup whole wheat breadcrumbs
4 oz (100g) raw minced plaice fillet	½ cup raw minced flounder fillet
1 tablespoon chopped fresh tarragon	1 tablespoon chopped fresh tarragon
1 tablespoon chopped fresh parsley	1 tablespoon chopped fresh parsley
¼ pint fish stock (page 170)	⅔ cup fish stock (page 170)
¼ pint (150ml) dry white wine	⅔ cup dry white wine
1 oz (25g) wholemeal flour	¼ cup whole wheat flour
2 oz (50g) Gruyère cheese, grated	½ cup grated Gruyère cheese
2 fl oz (60ml) double cream	¼ cup heavy cream
1 lb (450g) steamed asparagus spears	1 pound steamed asparagus spears

1 Skin the fillets. Lay, skinned side uppermost, on a board and season with salt and pepper.

2 Melt half the butter in a pan and sauté the mushrooms and onion for 2 minutes. Remove from the heat and stir in the breadcrumbs and minced fish. Season and beat in the herbs. The mixture should form a smooth paste. Cool.

3 Spread the cold paste over the fillets and roll up carefully. Secure with cocktail sticks, or wrap in foil.

4 In a small shallow pan place both liquids. Place the *paupiettes* in the pan, cover and poach for 6 minutes. Remove the fish and keep warm. Reserve the liquid.

5 In a saucepan, make a *roux* with the remaining butter and the flour, then whisk in ½ pint (300ml/1⅓ cups) of the fish juices. Bring to the boil, whisking continuously until the sauce is thick and smooth.

6 Stir in the cheese and cream and stir until smooth. Check seasoning.

7 Arrange the freshly-steamed asparagus spears, tips outwards, on a warmed serving dish. Lay the fillets over this and coat with sauce. Glaze quickly under a hot grill (broiler) and serve.

Opposite: *Couronne Néptune aux Deux Poissons* (page 68).

Darne de Truite Saumonée aux Épinards et Pâte-Nouilles Tricolores
Salmon Trout with Noodles and Spinach

Serves 1
Illustrated opposite.

The presentation of fish in a bell dish is always spectacular, but is usually only done in restaurants, first because not many people own bell dishes and second because the true purpose of the bell dish is to keep the food sealed within a vacuum of warmth until the customer is ready to eat it. However, if you can obtain one large or four small bell dishes, this presentation makes for a memorable dinner party to amaze or amuse your friends. If you are not using a bell dish, complete the cooking under a dome of foil and serve at once.

Imperial (Metric)	American
1 large salmon trout steak	1 large salmon trout steak
Sea salt and freshly ground black pepper	Sea salt and freshly ground black pepper
1 lb (450g) fresh raw spinach, washed	1 pound fresh raw spinach, washed
2 oz (50g) butter	¼ cup butter
1 carrot	1 carrot
½ mooli radish	½ mooli radish
3 oz (75g) multicoloured pasta, cooked	1 cup multicolored pasta, cooked
3 fl oz (90ml) natural yogurt	⅓ cup plain yogurt
Juice of ½ lemon	Juice of ½ lemon

1 Remove the central bone from the fish, thus dividing in two. Remove the skin. Season with salt and pepper.

2 Select several small, perfect spinach leaves and blanch for a few seconds in boiling water. Reserve.

3 Shred the remaining spinach and simmer with half the butter — no water is necessary — for 4 minutes. Drain and squeeze out as much moisture as possible.

4 Cut half the carrot and radish into *julienne* strips.

5 Place an attractive mound of spinach on the base of the bell dish (or on an ovenproof serving plate) and lay the *darnes* of fish over this. Beside them arrange a sprinkling of cooked pasta. Last, sprinkle some of the *julienne* vegetables over the fish.

6 Cover the dish with the bell, or make a dome of foil and crimp this into place over the plate. Place in a preheated oven at 400°F/200°C (Gas Mark 6) for 10 minutes.

7 Blend the yogurt with the lemon juice and the remaining butter to make a sauce.

8 When the fish is ready, uncover the dish before your guest and spoon a little sauce beside the pasta. Serve the remaining pasta and sauce separately. If the dish is being covered with foil, use the reserved spinach leaves to decorate the edge of the plate. The remaining carrot and radish could be cut into thin oval slices and then trimmed into leaf shapes to decorate either the dish or the sauce and pasta.

Lotte Cressonière Hermitage
Monkfish (Anglerfish) with Watercress Purée

My first encounter with this, my favourite recipe for monkfish, was when I worked for a season at the Hermitage Hotel at Le Touquet, one of the most prestigious and palatial hotels in Northern France whose culinary reputation was on a par with the Carlton in Cannes and the Savoy in London. The head chef was M. Brulé, one of the most respected chefs of his day and the only one I ever knew who actually turned down the position of Head Chef at the Savoy. He gave me this recipe to try one afternoon, and it was so successful that we featured it that same evening at a glittering royal function.

Imperial (Metric)	American
1 pint (600ml) fish stock (page 170)	2½ cups fish stock (page 170)
2 oz (50g) butter	¼ cup butter
2 shallots, chopped	2 shallots, chopped
1 lb (450g) filleted monkfish	1 pound filleted anglerfish
4 fl oz (120ml) dry Alsace wine	½ cup dry Alsace wine
8 puff pastry 'moons' (see opposite)	8 puff pastry 'moons' (see opposite)

For the sauce:	For the sauce:
2 egg yolks	2 egg yolks
1 teaspoon cornflour	1 teaspoon cornstarch
4 fl oz (120ml) sour cream	½ cup sour cream
2 oz (50g) butter	¼ cup butter
2 shallots, chopped	2 shallots, chopped
8 oz (225g) tomatoes, skinned, seeded and diced	2 tomatoes, skinned, seeded and diced
6 leaves fresh tarragon, chopped	6 leaves fresh tarragon, chopped
Sea salt and freshly ground black pepper	Sea salt and freshly ground black pepper

For the purée:	For the purée:
1 oz (25g) butter	2 tablespoons butter
3 bunches watercress, chopped leaves only	3 bunches watercress, chopped leaves only
3 leeks, white parts only, sliced	3 leeks, white parts only, sliced
3 fl oz (90ml) fish stock (page 170)	⅓ cup fish stock (page 170)
¼ lemon	¼ lemon
Nutmeg	Nutmeg

1   Boil the fish stock until reduced to one-quarter of its original volume.
2   Heat the butter in a sauté pan and lightly sauté the shallots for 2 minutes.
3   Cut the fish into four equal pieces. Add to the sauté pan with the reduced stock and the wine. Cover and poach for 5 minutes. Drain the liquid into another pan and reserve the fish while preparing the rest of the dish.
4   Bake the pastry moons as instructed below, and reserve.
5   Boil down the fish juices for 4 minutes.
6   In a bowl, beat together the egg yolks and cornflour (cornstarch), then stir in the sour cream. Stir this mixture gradually into the fish juices, bring back to the boil, stirring, and simmer for 4 minutes.
7   In another pan, heat the butter and sauté the shallots for 1 minute, then add the diced tomato and tarragon. Cook for 1 minute, then add this mixture to the sauce. Season to taste.

8 To prepare the purée, heat the butter in a saucepan and sauté the watercress and leeks for 1 minute, then stir in the fish stock and cook down to a purée. Drain and press out any excess liquid. Season to taste and add a squeeze of lemon juice and a twist of freshly grated nutmeg.

9 On individual serving plates, spoon an attractive mound of watercress purée and lay a piece of monkfish fillet over this. Spoon on a little of the sauce, to coat attractively, and decorate with two 'moons' of puff pastry. Serve at once with a selection of vegetables.

Note:
Puff Pastry Moons
Roll out 8 ounces (225g) wholemeal (whole wheat) puff pastry (see page 58) to a thickness of ⅛-inch (4mm). Cut into small sickle-moon shapes about 1½ inches (4cm) long. Brush with beaten egg and bake for 12 minutes at 400°F/200°C (Gas Mark 6).

Gratin de Flétan à la Nantaise

Baked Halibut Fillets with a Rich Trout Mousse

Halibut is a fish which can grow to an enormous size and so is often to be found cut into steaks, but fillets taken from smaller fish are worth seeking out, since the texture and flavour are especially good. Its mild flavour is enhanced by a rich accompaniment, such as in this recipe, where it is balanced by a mousse of rainbow trout enriched with nuts.

Imperial (Metric)	American
4 fillets of halibut (approx. 6 oz/150g each)	4 fillets of halibut (approx. 6 ounces each)
For the sauce:	*For the sauce:*
Head, bones and skin from the halibut	Head, bones and skin from the halibut
1 onion, sliced	1 onion, sliced
1 carrot, sliced	1 carrot, sliced
1 stick celery, sliced	1 stalk celery, sliced
1 stick fennel, sliced	1 stalk fennel, sliced
1 sprig thyme	1 sprig thyme
6 black peppercorns	6 black peppercorns
3 fl oz (90ml) Noilly Prat vermouth	⅓ cup Noilly Prat vermouth
¼ pint (150ml) water	⅔ cup water
1 fl oz (30ml) gin	2 tablespoons gin
4 fl oz (120ml) double cream	½ cup heavy cream
2 egg yolks	2 egg yolks
½ level teaspoon cornflour	½ level teaspoon cornstarch
Sea salt and freshly ground black pepper	Sea salt and freshly ground black pepper
Pinch cayenne pepper	Pinch cayenne pepper
Juice of ½ lemon	Juice of ½ lemon
For the mousse:	*For the mousse:*
8 oz (225g) minced rainbow trout	1 cup minced rainbow trout
1 egg white	1 egg white
4 fl oz (120ml) double cream	½ cup heavy cream
1 dessertspoon tomato purée	2 teaspoons tomato paste
4 oz (100g) button mushrooms, finely chopped	2 cups button mushrooms, finely chopped
4 oz (100g) walnuts, finely chopped	⅔ cup English walnuts, finely chopped
1 teaspoon chopped chives	1 teaspoon chopped chives
1 teaspoon chopped tarragon	1 teaspoon chopped tarragon
Sea salt and freshly ground black pepper	Sea salt and freshly ground black pepper

1 When buying your halibut fillets, ask for the offcuts which you will need to make the fish *fumet* which will be the base of your sauce. (If this is not possible, other fish trimmings will have to be substituted — you will need about 1 pound/500g).

2 Wash the fish head, bones and skin and place in a large pan with the vegetables, thyme and peppercorns. Cover with the water, vermouth and gin, bring to the boil and simmer for 35 minutes to reduce the volume of the *fumet* by half.

3 Strain the stock into a clean pan and reheat to boiling point.

4 In a bowl, beat together the cream, egg yolks and cornflour. Add this slowly to the pan, stirring constantly, until you have a smooth, creamy sauce. Simmer for 3 minutes, then season and stir in the lemon juice.

5 While the *fumet* is cooking you can prepare the mousse. In a bowl, beat together the minced fish, egg white, cream and tomato purée (paste). Freeze this mixture for 20 minutes, then beat in the chopped mushrooms and walnuts. Add the herbs and seasoning, and mix well.

6 Place the halibut fillets in a lightly-oiled earthenware dish.

7 Fit a piping bag with a ½ inch (1cm) nozzle, fill with mousse and pipe a zig-zag pattern onto each fillet to cover it.

8 Place the baking dish in a preheated oven at 400°F/200°C (Gas Mark 6) for 15 to 20 minutes, until the fish is cooked and the mousse is just starting to brown.

9 Spoon a little hot sauce onto individual, warmed serving plates and lay a fillet of fish neatly over it. Decorate with the garnish of your choice and serve at once.

Cassoulet de Cabillaud Carcassonnaise
A Rich Cod and Bean Stew

To most people who love good French food, the name cassoulet is synonymous with the rich and hearty stew of beans, pork, saucisson and preserved goose which, according to most authorities, takes several days to prepare. Yet the region around Carcassonne has produced many variations on this theme over the centuries — some with meat, some with poultry, some with just the goodness of the pulses and vegetables, and some with fish of all sorts, whether sea or river; salted, smoked or fresh; cut into chunks or minced into *quenelles*. Here I have chosen to make tasty little dumplings of smoked fish. The smoky flavour is perfect with the traditional white beans which form the basis for this dish, and the dumplings give an interesting variety in texture which is always enjoyed.

Imperial (Metric)	American
For the beans:	For the beans:
8 oz (225g) haricot beans, soaked overnight	1 cup navy beans, soaked overnight
1 small onion	1 small onion
3 cloves	3 cloves
1 sprig thyme	1 sprig thyme
1 carrot	1 carrot
1 stick celery	1 stalk celery
For the fish dumplings:	For the fish dumplings:
1 lb (450g) smoked *or* haddock fillets (fresh)	1 pound smoked *or* haddock fillets (fresh)
2 egg whites	2 egg whites
2 fl oz (60ml) olive oil	¼ cup olive oil
3 cloves garlic, chopped	3 cloves garlic, chopped
1 teaspoon fresh chopped basil	1 teaspoon fresh chopped basil
1 teaspoon fresh chopped tarragon	1 teaspoon fresh chopped tarragon
3 oz (75g) mashed, cooked potato	½ cup mashed, cooked potato
Sea salt and freshly ground black pepper	Sea salt and freshly ground black pepper
Seasoned wholemeal flour	Seasoned whole wheat flour
½ pint (300ml) fish stock (page 170)	1⅓ cups fish stock (page 170)
For the sauce:	For the sauce:
2 fl oz (60ml) olive oil	¼ cup olive oil
1 red onion, sliced	1 red onion, sliced
1 clove garlic, crushed	1 clove garlic, crushed
1 large red pepper, seeded and chopped	1 large red pepper, seeded and chopped
1 lb (450g) tomatoes, skinned, seeded and chopped	1 pound tomatoes, skinned, seeded and chopped
2 tablepoons tomato purée	2 tablespoons tomato paste
½ pint (300ml) fish stock (page 170)	1⅓ cups fish stock (page 170)
¼ pint (150ml) French red wine	⅔ cup French red wine
1 red and 1 green chilli, seeded and sliced	1 red and 1 green chili, seeded and sliced
Sea salt and freshly ground black pepper	Sea salt and freshly ground black pepper
Parsley	Parsley

1 Drain the soaked beans and place in a large flameproof casserole with plenty of fresh water (spring or distilled water is a good choice for both this and the soaking, since it prevents the skins of the beans from becoming tough).

2 Peel the onion and stud it with the cloves. Add it to the cooking water with the thyme and the roughly chopped carrot and celery.

3 Bring the water to the boil and simmer for 15 minutes, skimming off any scum which rises to the top. Then cover the casserole with a lid and place in the oven at 350°F/180°C (Gas Mark 4) for 2½ to 3 hours.

4 When the beans are cooked, drain off most of the cooking liquid, discard the herbs and vegetables, and reserve the beans.

5 To prepare the fish dumplings, first soak the fish in water for 1 hour to reduce the salt. Then skin the fillets and mince them finely.

6 Place the fish in a bowl with the egg whites. Blend the oil, garlic and herbs and stir this into the mixture. Beat in the mashed potato and seasoning.

7 Shape the fish mixture into little dumplings about the size of an egg. Roll in seasoned flour and place in a greased baking tin. Add just enough stock to come half-way up the dumplings. Bake at 400°F/200°C (Gas Mark 6) for 10 minutes.

8 For the sauce, heat the olive oil in a pan and sauté the onion, garlic and pepper for 5 minutes, then stir in the tomatoes and the tomato purée (paste). Add the stock and wine, and simmer gently for 15 minutes. Add the sliced chillies and check the seasoning. Simmer until thickened and reduced.

9 Stir the beans into the sauce to reheat and absorb the flavours. Spoon some of the bean stew into individual earthenware pots, float fish dumplings on top and sprinkle with chopped fresh parsley. Serve at once.

Filet de Sole Dieppoise
Sole with a Creamy Seafood Sauce

Here is a classic dish of French fish cookery which is so good, yet so simple, that it really should not be forgotten by professional or amateur cooks. Throughout my years as a professional chef it has been featured on many a menu, always to be greeted with praise and delight by diners whether they are tasting it for the first time or greeting it as a familiar favourite.

Imperial (Metric)	American
18 oz (500g) fresh mussels	18 ounces fresh mussels
¼ pint (150ml) dry white wine *or* cider	⅔ cup dry white wine *or* cider
2 tablespoons cider vinegar	2 tablespoons cider vinegar
2 oz (50g) chopped onion *or* shallot	⅓ cup chopped onion *or* shallot
1 sprig thyme	1 sprig thyme
2 oz (50g) butter	¼ cup butter
8 fillets of sole (approx. 3 oz/75g each)	8 fillets of sole (approx. 3 ounces each)
½ pint (300ml) Sauce Normande (page 177)	1⅓ cups Sauce Normande (page 177)
Juice of ½ lemon	Juice of ½ lemon
Pinch cayenne pepper	Pinch cayenne pepper
4 oz (100g) cooked, peeled shrimps	⅔ cup cooked, peeled shrimps
Sea salt and freshly ground black pepper	Sea salt and freshly ground black pepper
1 lb (450g) *duchesse* potato (see below)	2 cups *duchesse* potato (see below)

1   Clean and scrape the mussel shells thoroughly.

2   In a pan, heat the wine or cider with the vinegar. Boil the chopped onion for 2 minutes, then add the mussels and herbs. Cover and cook for 5 minutes. Discard any mussels which are still closed and reserve the rest. Strain and reserve the cooking liquid.

3   Use the butter to grease a shallow baking dish and a sheet of greaseproof (parchment) paper. Lightly beat the fillets of sole with a rolling pin. This will prevent them from curling up during cooking. Lay them in the baking dish.

4   Cover the fish with cooking juices from the mussels, lay the buttered paper over the top, and bake at 400°F/200°C (Gas Mark 6) for 15 minutes.

5   Remove the baking dish from the oven and drain off the fish juices into a pan. Stir in the Sauce Normande and mix well. Add lemon juice and a pinch of cayenne. Heat to boiling point, then stir in the cooked shrimps and shelled mussels. Simmer for a few minutes until the sauce is creamy. Check the seasoning.

6   Place the fillets neatly in the baking dish and pipe or spoon *duchesse* potato around the edge. Pour the sauce over the fish and return the dish to the oven for a few minutes to brown the potato and glaze the sauce. Serve at once.

Note:
Duchesse Potatoes
Peel and boil 1 pound (450g) potatoes until cooked. Mash in a bowl with seasoning, the yolk of 1 egg and 1 ounce (25g) butter. This dryish mixture is good for decorative borders since it holds its shape well, tastes delicious, and browns attractively if placed briefly in the oven or under a grill (broiler).

Blanc de Turbot Champs-Elysées

Fillet of Turbot with Mushrooms and Loire Wine

The story traditionally told about turbot is that the great chef Vatel flung himself on his sword when the turbot failed to arrive on time at a royal banquet which he had prepared. It was the last straw in a series of culinary mishaps during a visit by the French king, and I think that any cook who has ever experienced a disastrous dinner party, when the soufflé collapses or the main course burns or the sorbet refuses to freeze, will identify with Monsieur Vatel and wish they had had access to a ready means of doing away with themselves rather than having to soldier on to the end of the evening!

Imperial (Metric)	American
3 lb (1.35 kilos) turbot, skinned and filleted	3 pound turbot, skinned and filleted
1 pint (600ml) stock (page 170) made with the head and bones of the turbot and ½ pint (300ml) sparkling Loire wine	2½ cups stock (page 170) made with the head and bones of the turbot and 1⅓ cups sparkling Loire wine
2 eggs yolks	2 eggs yolks
¼ pint (150ml) sour cream	⅔ cup sour cream
Pinch cayenne pepper	Pinch cayenne pepper
Sea salt and freshly ground black pepper	Sea salt and freshly ground black pepper
1 lb (450g) button mushrooms	1 pound button mushrooms
½ oz (15g) butter	1 tablespoon butter
Juice of ½ lemon	Juice of ½ lemon
8 oz (225g) *duchesse* potatoes (page 88)	1 cup *duchesse* potatoes (page 88)
1 sliced tinned truffle, for garnish	1 sliced canned truffle, for garnish
1 piece preserved ginger, cut into *julienne*, for garnish	1 piece preserved ginger, cut into *julienne*, for garnish

1 Make sure, if your fishmonger is preparing the turbot for you, to ask for the bones and head for the stock.

2 Prepare a stock as described on page 170, using the turbot offcuts and substituting wine for the same amount of other liquid. Then boil 1 pint of this stock for 35 minutes to reduce.

3 Season the turbot fillets and place them in a shallow dish. Cover level with cooled stock. Cover the top with greaseproof (parchment) paper and bake for 10 to 15 minutes, depending on the thickness of the fillets, at 400°F/200°C (Gas Mark 6). Remove the paper and strain the juices into a pan. Keep the turbot warm while you prepare the sauce.

4 Boil the juices fiercely for 5 minutes. In a bowl, beat together the egg yolks, cream and seasoning. Whisk this into the fish liquid to make a creamy sauce. Strain and reserve, keeping warm.

5 Remove the stalks from the mushrooms (these can be used in another dish) and sauté the caps in the butter for 2 minutes. Add the lemon juice and 3 fl oz (90ml/⅓ cup) of the sauce. Season to taste.

6 On individual serving plates pipe a decorative border of *duchesse* potato. Spoon on a couple of tablespoons of sauce, place a fillet of turbot along side or over the sauce and arrange two spoonsful of mushroom garnish on the other side of the fish. Decorate the top of the fish with truffle and ginger and serve at once with sparkling Saumur to drink. Light green vegetables make a perfect accompaniment.

Note:
Brill or halibut would be excellent in this recipe, too.

5 Les Plats de Poissons Froids

Cold Main Courses

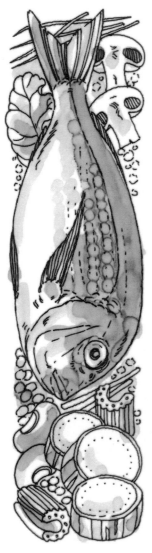

There are good cooks who are not artistically minded, just as there are great artists who cannot boil an egg. The science of cookery can be taught, just as can technical drawing and the principles of fine art, but it is the spark of creativity which makes a true chef, just as it does a true artist. When these skills come together, then we are in the presence of culinary greatness — an Escoffier, a Carème . . . Yet cookery, without this balance of art, is as sterile as a blueprint, a diagram; for all great dishes rely on artistic as well as culinary appeal. They must first entice in an intensely visual and tactile way. Colour, line and form call to the eye just as strongly as aroma does to the nostril — the classic adage 'we eat with our eyes' is very true. The most delicious aroma emanating from a heap of hideous stodge simply cannot tempt our tastebuds. And texture — so beloved of the artist, sculptor, potter, weaver — is surely as important in that crucial first bite as is the flavour of the dish.

But here we are in a quandary. For just as healthy food need not be beautiful, so beautiful food need not be healthy. Must one be sacrificed for the other? Some will say it is worth it — worth consuming unappealing food for the sake of health or conscience; worth embracing heart disease, gout, obesity and other more dreadful prospects for the sake of hedonism and gluttony. I say there is a balance to be struck just as clearly as that between art and cookery. The balance of culinary delight and vibrant good health is just as closely woven, for without good health our food becomes unpalatable — indeed our digestion may no longer be able to cope with anything other than 'invalid food' — and without the pleasure of good food one of the great savours of life is lost. Whatever you see as good food, from the crisp, clean first bite into an apple to the most delicate and subtle mouthful of salmon mousse or the spark and delight of a sorbet of wild strawberries and the luscious smoothness of a ripe French cheese, each has its merits, each its place and each is a colour on the palette of a master chef and a wise diner. They can be chosen or rejected, blended in the pattern of a meal or a day's eating to provide all that is needed for a healthy body and a fit and energetic life, while also meeting the aesthetic needs of our complex species with a wealth of flavour, texture, colour, aroma and style.

So how does the modern chef satisfy this infinitely interwoven demand for beauty, skill, vitality, pleasure? Food historians will show you a background as complicated and intricate as a detective story, and even now we are still witnessing new clues, new solutions, new . . . red herrings? We have seen the swing from the rich and heavy sauces of yesteryear, with their emphasis on taste and complicated presentation and their abandonment of health and simplicity, to the exquisite beauty of a creation of the *nouvelle cuisine*, when every dish was a work of art yet diners left the table empty

of pocket and of stomach! The answer may lie in this idea of balance, of harmony. Now our ingredients complement our seasons just as our themes have always done. Chefs have always chosen to select their palette of colour from the seasons — festive greens and reds at Christmas time; golden-yellow and chocolate brown at Easter; berry-reds and nut-browns for the autumn — and now a more healthy approach to food is bringing a welcome return to food served in its season, not frozen, freeze-dried or preserved but freshly harvested. And the fine work being done by researchers and writers in all areas of health and food technology means that we are better informed, better able to pick and choose what is good *and* tasty. The asceticism of the past has been swept away by the imagination and expertise of a new generation of cooks, who have embraced our knowledge of healthy eating as a welcome liberation from old rules, while carrying with them what is good and wise from the past as a firm foundation for the cookery of the latter years of this century, and the infancy of the next.

The region of Provence has a quality of light — a richness and clarity — which has always drawn artists to it, from Cézanne (my great-great uncle!) and Van Gogh to the beach-side portrait painters who make a hand-to-mouth living off the tourists all along the coast from Hyères and Le Lavandou to Saint-Tropez and Fréjus. The food of that part of France, too, seems to me to epitomize much that I have just discussed. Armed with a marvellous palette of colours, aromas and flavours, and perhaps inspired by the wealth of natural beauty around them just as are more conventional artists, the people of Provence have developed a style of cookery as unique and distinctive as that of any school of painting. Take, for example, the marinade of mullet and mackerel on page 94 — cooked and presented with care, who could deny it its place as a work of art?

Here you will find, I hope, a reflection of some of these ideas. Food which tastes wonderful; which looks beautiful; which has texture and character; which makes you feel as if you have been treated to a taste of luxury; which reflects what is worthy from cuisines of the past; which balances simple, healthy ingredients with some special treats for the suitably special occasion. Take the opportunity to use your kitchen as an artist's studio — it is a revelation and it is the very essence of being a cook!

Galantine de Brochet Princesse Marie-Louise
Pike Loaf with Salmon and Pistachios

Serves 8

Pike is a scavenger — it is sometimes called the shark of the river — but its flesh is tender and delicately flavoured, and is acknowledged as the best for quenelles and mousses. I created this luxurious galantine for a great lady who used to come and see me often when I was at Fortnum and Mason. She was a great-grand-daughter of Queen Victoria, and her love of France was equalled by her appreciation of good food and wine. We enjoyed many splendid lunches together, but this one was especially memorable — just after the coronation of Queen Elizabeth II we dined like royalty on this exquisite galantine, accompanied by plenty of my favourite Lanson champagne.

Imperial (Metric)	American
For the panada:	For the panada:
4 oz (100g) unsalted French butter	½ cup unsalted French butter
4 oz (100g) wholemeal flour	1 cup whole wheat flour
½ pint (300ml) milk	1⅓ cups milk
4 egg yolks	4 egg yolks
Sea salt and freshly ground black pepper	Sea salt and freshly ground black pepper
For the fish mousse filling:	For the fish mousse filling:
1½ lb (680g) pike flesh, skinned and finely minced	1½ pounds pike flesh, skinned and finely minced
4 egg whites	4 egg whites
½ pint (300ml) natural yogurt	1⅓ cups plain yogurt
2 tablespoons chopped tarragon	2 tablespoons chopped tarragon
2 tablespoons chopped parsley	2 tablespoons chopped parsley
1 teaspoon raw cane sugar	1 teaspoon raw cane sugar
Generous pinch mace	Generous pinch mace
For the decorative filling:	For the decorative filling:
2 oz (50g) butter	¼ cup butter
2 shallots, chopped	2 shallots, chopped
2 cloves garlic, crushed	2 cloves garlic, crushed
8 oz (225g) button mushrooms, quartered	4 cups button mushrooms, quartered
8 oz (225g) salmon trout fillets, cut into ¼ inch (5mm) squares	1⅓ cups salmon trout fillets, cut into ¼ inch squares
¼ pint (150ml) champagne	⅔ cup champagne
3 oz (75g) skinned pistachio nuts	½ cup skinned pistachio nuts
12 tinned green peppercorns	12 canned green peppercorns
3 oz (75g) softened butter, for mould	⅓ cup softened butter, for mold

1 Prepare the panada by heating the butter in a pan and then beating in the flour to form a roux. Cook for 1 minute, stirring continuously, without browning.

2 Remove the pan from the heat and gradually stir in the milk to form a smooth mixture. Heat gently, stirring, until the sauce is thickened. Remove the pan from the heat once again and beat in the egg yolks. Cool and season the paste.

3 In a large bowl, beat together the pike and the egg whites. Gradually stir in the yogurt to form a smooth, soft mixture. Then beat in the cold panada until the whole thing is smooth and creamy. Add the herbs, sugar and mace, and check the seasoning.

4 Place the bowl, covered, in the freezer for 10 minutes to firm, while you prepare the decorative filling.

5 Heat the butter in a large sauté pan and gently cook the shallots and garlic for 1 minute only. Then add the mushrooms and cook for a further minute.

6 Add the salmon and the champagne to the pan. Bring to the boil and cook for 2 minutes. Strain the juices into another pan and boil fiercely for 5 minutes to reduce by one-third. Cool the salmon mixture and the liquid.

7 Remove the pike paste from the freezer. Beat into it the liquid, the salmon mixture, the pistachios and peppercorns. Check the seasoning.

8 Butter a large oblong mould (about 5½lb/2.5 kilos/11 cup capacity) and spoon in the mousse. Place in a baking tray half-filled with hot water and bake at 350°F/180°C (Gas Mark 4) for 1¼ hours. Remove from the oven and cool completely before turning out.

9 Serve garnished with a selection of salad leaves. Slice quite thickly to avoid portions crumbling unattractively.

Marinade de Rouget et Maquereau à l'Orange

Red Mullet (Snapper) and Mackerel Fillets, Marinated in Grand Marnier and Vermouth

This sort of marinated fish dish is typical of the South of France, where it may be served as a luncheon or supper dish. Marinated fish keeps well in the refrigerator, so as long as you have fresh salad ingredients to hand you can be sure of a refreshingly piquant treat at the end of a hot summer's day, whether it has been spent at the office, in the garden or on the beach. I have chosen mackerel and mullet (snapper) for this dish because of the contrast both in flavour and texture and in skin colour — the unusual orange-red of the mullet (snapper) looks wonderful alongside the striking blue-silver of the mackerel.

Imperial (Metric)	American
For the fish:	For the fish:
4 red mullet fillets	4 red snapper fillets
4 mackerel fillets	4 mackerel fillets
3 oz (75g) seasoned wholemeal flour	¾ cup seasoned whole wheat flour
3 fl oz (90ml) vegetable oil	⅔ cup vegetable oil
For the marinade:	For the marinade:
½ pint (300ml) mixture of *Noilly Prat* vermouth and water	1⅓ cups mixture of *Noilly Prat* vermouth and water
Juice and finely grated rind 1 orange	Juice and finely grated rind 1 orange
2 tablespoons Grand Marnier	2 tablespoons Grand Marnier
2 tablespoons white wine vinegar	2 tablespoons white wine vinegar
Sea salt and freshly ground black pepper	Sea salt and freshly ground black pepper
4 bay leaves	4 bay leaves
1 stick fennel, finely sliced	1 stalk fennel, finely sliced
1 onion, sliced	1 onion, sliced
1 carrot, grooved lengthways, then sliced	1 carrot, grooved lengthways, then sliced
2 chillies, sliced	2 chilies, sliced
6 coriander seeds, crushed	6 coriander seeds, crushed
6 black peppercorns, crushed	6 black peppercorns, crushed
8 stoned black olives	8 pitted black olives
For decoration:	For decoration:
4 crisp lettuce leaves	4 crisp lettuce leaves
2 oranges, peeled and segmented	2 oranges, peeled and segmented
2 sprigs basil	2 sprigs basil
Blanched *julienne* strips of orange skin	Blanched *julienne* strips of orange skin

1 Clean the fillets. Lightly scrape the mackerel skins to remove scales, but leave the skins of both fish intact. Pat dry and coat each side in seasoned flour.

2 Heat the oil in a shallow pan and sauté the fish fillets for 6 minutes, turning once. Remove from the pan and drain on kitchen paper towels, then place in a dish large enough to take all the fillets in a single layer and allow to cool.

3 Meanwhile, place all the marinade ingredients, except the olives, in a pan, bring to the boil and simmer for 10 minutes. Remove from the heat, add the black olives, allow the mixture to cool until just tepid then pour over the fish.

4 Cover the fish and chill. The fish should now be left to marinate for 2 days for the best flavour.

5 When ready to serve, remove the fish from the marinade. Place a lettuce leaf on each of four serving plates and then lay one of each type of fillet on each leaf. Place the fillets skin-side upwards, to contrast the colours. Garnish with orange segments and black olives, slices of carrots and basil leaves, sprinkle lightly with *julienne* strips of orange skin and pour a little of the marinade over the fish.

Charentais aux Rondelles de Soles Venus
Charentais Melon Filled with Tiny Poached Fish Spirals and Strawberries

This piquant blend of fruit and fish is a great favourite for a light supper party. Charentais melon is perfectly suited to this dish, but any other small, scented melon such as ogen, cantaloup, musk or netted melon will also provide a delightful dish combined with the subtle accent of fish and the fresh, summery taste of strawberries. I feel this dish represents the sort of contribution the cookery of the 'new world' is making to gourmet cuisine — light, exciting and healthy.

Imperial (Metric)	American
2 ripe charentais melons	2 ripe charentais melons
3 fl oz (90ml) natural yogurt	⅓ cup plain yogurt
Juice of 1 orange	Juice of 1 orange
Juice of 2 lemons	Juice of 2 lemons
4 small fillets of sole	4 small fillets of sole
Sea salt and freshly ground black pepper	Sea salt and freshly ground black pepper
4 oz (100g) minced cod *or* whiting	½ cup minced cod *or* whiting
1 egg white	1 egg white
4 fl oz (120ml) double cream	½ cup heavy cream
8 shredded lettuce leaves	8 shredded lettuce leaves
4 chopped mint leaves	4 chopped mint leaves
¼ pint (150ml) white port	⅔ cup white port
8 oz (225g) fresh strawberries	2 cups fresh strawberries

1 Halve the melons and remove the seeds. With a Parisienne cutter, scoop out small balls of melon. Cut out about half the melon flesh in this way and scoop out the rest roughly, leaving just the shells.

2 Place the roughly-cut melon flesh in a blender and add the yogurt, orange and half of the lemon juice. Season and blend to a smooth cream. This is your dressing: set aside for the flavours to develop.

3 Gently beat the sole fillets, without breaking the fibres.

4 In a bowl combine the minced fish, egg white, cream, half the lettuce and mint. Season lightly.

5 Spread the sole fillets on the skin side with the minced fish cream, roll up carefully and secure with cocktail sticks. Place in a small, deep dish and cover with 3 fl oz (90ml/⅓ cup) water, the port wine and the remaining lemon juice, plus a little seasoning. Poach gently for 15 minutes and cool in the liquid.

6 When the fillets are cold, slice thinly into pretty spirals.

7 Line each melon shell with the remaining lettuce, then carefully arrange the melon balls and the fish spirals in the melon cups. Drizzle with a little dressing and decorate with strawberries. Serve the melons in chilled glass bowls, with the remaining sauce served separately.

Truite Arc en Ciel aux Groseilles Rouges
Rainbow Trout Poached in a Vermouth Stock, with Redcurrants

Serves 6

There are few finer flavours than a carefully cooked, cold rainbow trout and I am delighted that modern cookery has abandoned the idea that it is necessary to coat such a dish in a heavy sauce, or decorate it with complicated garnishes. Far better is this concept of using a few fresh fruits and vegetables as a decoration, and serving as a side dish a sauce which is as light and refreshing as the fish itself, and which guests can choose to help themselves to. My presentation of the trout itself makes this dish a very special visual delight. If you find it fiddly to accomplish, enlist the help of a friend to assist in the preparation — they will be glad to oblige in return for a portion of the finished feast!

Imperial (Metric)	American
1 large rainbow trout (approx. 3 lb/1.5 kilos), cleaned and gutted	1 large rainbow trout (approx. 3 pounds), cleaned and gutted
3 pints (1.7 litres) fish stock (page 170) made with *Noilly Prat* vermouth instead of wine	7¾ cups fish stock (page 170) made with *Noilly Prat* vermouth instead of wine
2 pints (1.15 litres) aspic	5 cups aspic
8 oz (225g) redcurrants	1⅓ cups redcurrants
½ oz (15g) chives	Small bunch chives
1 bunch fresh coriander	1 bunch fresh coriander
¼ pint (150ml) natural yogurt	⅔ cup plain yogurt
5 mint leaves, finely chopped	5 mint leaves, finely chopped
1 teaspoon finely chopped chives	1 teaspoon finely chopped chives
¼ pint (150ml) mayonnaise (page 179) *or* fish velouté (page 176) made with stock from the trout	⅔ cup mayonnaise (page 179) *or* fish velouté (page 176) made with stock from the trout

1 To cook the trout so that it 'sets' in a swimming motion, you must wrap both head and tail securely in a band of greaseproof (parchment) paper, then tie with a loop of string around head and tail so that the fish is held in an 'S'shape.

2 Place the fish in a large pan, just big enough to hold the trout, and pour in the court bouillon. The trout should be covered by the liquid.

3 Cover the pan, bring the liquid just to a boil and simmer very gently for 15 minutes. Alternatively, bake at 375°F/190°C (Gas Mark 5) for 15-20 minutes. Allow the fish to cool in the liquid.

4 When the fish is completely cold, remove from the pan. Discard the string and paper and carefully peel off the skin, leaving head and tail intact.

5 Place the trout on a flat dish and put this in the freezer for 15 minutes. Then remove and brush the trout with a layer of aspic (freezing the fish for just this brief period helps the aspic set more quickly).

6 When the first layer of aspic is set, split the chives into thin strands and arrange like stems and leaves along the body of the fish. Brush very carefully with another layer of aspic to hold the chives in place.

7 Select a flat, oval serving dish for your trout, and pour about 1 pint (600ml/2½ cups) aspic onto this. When it has set firm, place the trout on the plate.

8 Arrange sprigs of redcurrants and coriander leaves decoratively on and around the trout.

9 For the sauce, combine the yogurt with the mint and chives, then beat in the mayonnaise or velouté sauce.

10 Serve the fish with side dishes or garnishes of lettuce, corn salad or watercress. Feathery leaves of dill look attractive with the redcurrants, too. The sauce makes a good accompaniment to hot new potatoes or sliced, peeled cucumber. If redcurrants are not available, substitute cranberries or fresh raspberries.

Galette de Poisson Levantine

Cracked Wheat and Fish Loaf with Pine Nuts

Serves 6

The Lebanon was a French protectorate in the years after World War I, and this dish is typical of the cuisine which develops when two cultures combine gastronomical styles and ingredients — a gateau or galette which uses Middle-Eastern ingredients in an imaginative and delicious way. How sad to reflect that a dish which embodies culinary harmony should stem from such a troubled and war-torn region.

Imperial (Metric)	American
1 lb (450g) cracked wheat *or* bulgur	2²/₃ cups cracked wheat *or* bulgur
2 lb (900g) fish fillets (cod, red mullet *or* trout)	2 pounds fish fillets (cod, red snapper *or* trout)
5 oz (125g) chopped onion	1¼ cups chopped onion
4 large cloves garlic, chopped	4 large cloves garlic, chopped
Juice of 1 orange	Juice of 1 orange
Juice and grated rind of 1 lemon	Juice and grated rind of 1 lemon
1 green chilli, chopped	1 green chili, chopped
1 oz (25g) fresh coriander leaves, chopped	½ cup fresh coriander leaves, chopped
Sea salt and freshly ground black pepper	Sea salt and freshly ground black pepper
2 eggs, beaten	2 eggs, beaten

For the topping:	For the topping:
2 fl oz (60ml) olive oil	¼ cup olive oil
1 large onion, sliced	1 large onion, sliced
3 oz (75g) pine nuts	½ cups pignoli

For the garnish:	For the garnish:
Shredded crisp lettuce leaves	Shredded crisp lettuce leaves
2 oz (50g) soaked raisins	¼ cup soaked raisins
Lime slices	Lime slices

1 Soak the wheat in boiling water for 10 minutes, then strain and squeeze out excess water.

2 Blend or process together the fish, onion and garlic.

3 In a bowl, beat together the wheat with the fish mixture. Add the orange and lemon, chilli, coriander and seasoning, then bind the mixture with egg.

4 Lightly oil a shallow baking dish and press the mixture evenly into the base, levelling it with a palette knife.

5 Heat the olive oil in a pan and gently sauté the onion for 3 minutes, then add the pine nuts (pignoli) and cook for a further minute.

6 Spread the nut and onion mixture over the wheat base. Place in a preheated oven at 400°F/200°C (Gas Mark 6) and bake for 25 minutes, basting occasionally with olive oil, until golden brown.

7 Leave the galette in its dish to cool, then cut into diamond shapes and serve with shredded lettuce sprinkled with raisins and offer slices of lime to squeeze over the dish.

Croustade de Lotte et Crevettes

Pastry Boats Filled with Fish in a Cucumber Mayonnaise

Serves 6

This is a perfect dish for a summer buffet party, along with a selection of other chilled food. It is light, refreshing and appetizing, simple to make once the initial preparation of ingredients has been done, and of course is prepared in advance — no last minute work in a hot kitchen when you could be mingling with your guests, sipping a glass of chilled Muscadet or Saumur.

Imperial (Metric)	American
For the puff pastry:	For the puff pastry:
½ lb (225g) wholemeal bread flour	2 cups whole wheat bread flour
Pinch sea salt	Pinch sea salt
½ lb (225g) butter	1 cup butter
4 fl oz (120ml) water	½ cup water
1 tablespoon lemon juice	1 tablespoon lemon juice
Extra wholemeal flour for dusting	Extra wholewheat flour for dusting
1 egg, beaten, for glazing	1 egg, beaten, for glazing
For the filling:	For the filling:
8 oz (225g) peeled, cooked shrimps	1⅓ cups peeled, cooked shrimp
8 oz (225g) cooked, diced monkfish	1⅓ cups cooked, diced monkfish
4 fl oz (120ml) mayonnaise	½ cup mayonnaise
2 oz (50g) finely chopped cucumber	½ cup finely chopped cucumber
1 tablespoon tomato purée (optional)	1 tablespoon tomato paste (optional)
2 oz (50g) sliced button mushrooms, marinated in lemon juice and vermouth	1 cup sliced button mushrooms, marinated in lemon juice and vermouth
Cooked asparagus tips to garnish	Cooked asparagus tips to garnish

1 Sift the flour and salt into a large bowl. Reserve the bran for some other dish.

2 Rub a quarter of the butter into the flour.

3 Make a well in the mixture and add the water and lemon juice. Knead the mixture to a dough and roll into a ball.

4 Slash the top of the dough in a cross shape, cover with a damp cloth and leave to rest for 30 minutes.

5 While the dough is resting, knead the butter until it is the same consistency as the pastry dough, and then roll it out on a floured board to a neat oblong ⅛ inch (3mm) thick. You will need to flour the butter and the rolling pin, as well as the board, very carefully so that the butter does not stick.

6 Roll out the dough to the same thickness as the butter. Place the butter piece on top of the dough and fold the two layers three times. Roll again into an oblong, fold into three again and rest the dough for 20 minutes.

7 Repeat this procedure twice more, then wrap in clingfilm and chill for 10 minutes.

8 Roll the pastry out to a depth of ⅙ inch (4mm) and cut 6 oval 'boats', 4 inches (10cm) long. Use a small oval cutter (or a steady hand and a sharp knife) to indent an inner oval which will form an optional lid when the vol-au-vent is cooked. Rest for 1 hour.

9 Place the pastry boats on a greased baking sheet, glaze with egg, and bake at 400°F/200°C (Gas Mark 6) for 15-20 minutes, until risen and golden. Leave to cool before removing the inner oval and scooping out the soft centres.

10 Place the shrimps and fish in a bowl. Gently stir in the mayonnaise and cucumber. Add tomato purée (paste) if you wish a rosy pink effect. Stir in the well-drained mushrooms and pile into the boats. Alternatively, the mushrooms could form a separate layer under or over the fish mayonnaise. Serve garnished with asparagus tips. The golden pastry 'lids' can be replaced at an attractive angle if wished.

Variation:
For an even lighter dish, well-seasoned yogurt could replace the mayonnaise.

Le Poupeton de la Cannebière
A Chilled Fish Charlotte

Here is an easy way of stretching a small quantity of fish, which is a little more elegant than, say, a kedgeree or fish cakes, and more original than a mousse. This dish is based on the *ménagères* of southern France and can be as simple or as luxurious as you care to make it, simply by varying the ingredients. Leftover fish can be used — provided you are careful to observe storage rules to keep it fresh and moist — or a small portion can be cooked especially. Or a high quality canned fish, such as salmon or tuna, can make this a standby dish for short-notice entertaining.

Imperial (Metric)	American
8 oz (225g) poached haddock fillets *or* tinned fish *or* fish of choice	1⅓ cups poached haddock fillets *or* canned fish *or* fish of choice
4 oz (100g) fresh wholemeal breadcrumbs	2 cups fresh whole wheat breadcrumbs
½ pint (300ml) cream	1⅓ cup cream
5 eggs, beaten	5 eggs, beaten
Sea salt and freshly ground black pepper	Sea salt and freshly ground black pepper
2 cloves garlic	2 cloves garlic
2 fl oz (50ml) dry white wine	¼ cup dry white wine
2 oz (50g) grated cheese, preferably Gruyère	½ cup grated cheese, preferably Gruyère
2 oz (50g) butter	¼ cup butter
1 tablespoon chopped fresh basil	1 tablespoon chopped fresh basil
Lightly cooked vegetables of choice, to garnish	Lightly cooked vegetables of choice, to garnish
Black olives, to garnish	Black olives, to garnish

1 Flake the fish into a bowl. Stir in the breadcrumbs, then add the cream and beaten eggs and mix thoroughly. Season.
2 Place the peeled garlic in a blender with the white wine and purée to a smooth cream. Stir this into the fish mixture. Add the grated cheese and mix well.
3 Choose an attractive mould (2 lb/1 litre/5 cup size). Butter it liberally, and sprinkle the buttered inside with chopped basil. Pour in the fish custard mixture.
4 Place the mould in a baking tray and pour in hot water to come halfway up the side of the mould. Bake in a preheated oven at 325°F/170°C (Gas Mark 3) for about 45 minutes. Allow to cool for 10 minutes.
5 Turn the mould out onto a serving dish. Leave to finish cooling then decorate with vegetables of your choice — tomatoes stuffed with vegetable mayonnaise are good — and black olives. Serve lightly chilled.

Darne de Colin à l'Ailoli

Hake with a Garlic and Nut Mayonnaise

Serves 6

The fish known as hake in English is called *colin* in Paris, *saumon blanc* — white salmon — in Boulogne, and *merluche* in Dunkerque. It has a firm but tender white flesh with a delicate flavour enjoyed by gourmets. If unobtainable, cod or haddock can be substituted, but for this dish it is worth seeking out the genuine article with which to treat your guests.

Imperial (Metric)	American
6 hake fillets, approx. 8 oz (225g) each	6 hake fillets, approx. 8 ounces each
2 pints (1.15 litres) court bouillon (page 170)	5 cups court bouillon (page 170)
For the aioli:	For the aioli:
8 oz (225g) fresh wholemeal breadcrumbs	4 cups fresh whole wheat breadcrumbs
2 fl oz (60ml) boiling milk	¼ cup boiling milk
Juice of 1 lemon	Juice of 1 lemon
4 walnut kernels	4 walnut kernels
12 blanched almonds	12 blanched almonds
1 oz (25g) pine nuts *or* cashews	2 tablespoons pignoli *or* cashews
6 hazelnuts	6 filberts
2 egg yolks	2 egg yolks
6 cloves garlic	6 cloves garlic
1 tablespoon white wine vinegar	1 tablespoon white wine vinegar
⅓ pint (200ml) olive oil	¾ cup olive oil
Sea salt and freshly ground black pepper	Sea salt and freshly ground black pepper
Pinch ground cumin	Pinch ground cumin
6 hard-boiled eggs	6 hard-cooked eggs
For garnish:	For garnish:
2 oz (50g) salmon caviar	¼ cup salmon caviar
4 tomatoes	4 tomatoes
4 oz (100g) green olives, stoned	1 cup green olives, pitted
Sprigs lamb's lettuce and radicchio	Sprigs lamb's lettuce and radicchio
1 lemon	1 lemon

1 Place the hake fillets in a shallow flameproof dish and cover with cold stock. Bring to a very gentle simmer and poach for 15 minutes.

2 Remove the fish from the court bouillon. Remove large bones and skin and set aside to cool.

3 Place the breadcrumbs in a bowl and soak with the boiling milk. Add the lemon juice and beat to a paste.

4 Place the nuts in a blender with the egg yolks, garlic, vinegar and oil, and blend to a smooth cream.

5 Stir the nut cream into the breadcrumb mixture, season to taste with salt, pepper and cumin. Beat the mixture to a thick paste.

6 Halve the eggs. Push the yolks through a sieve (strainer) and beat them into the aioli.

7 Fill the egg whites with salmon caviar.

8 Place the fish fillets on individual serving plates. Decorate with the eggs, slices of tomato, olives, lettuce and lemon wedges. Place a spoonful of aioli on each plate and serve the rest separately.

Roulade d'Épinard au Poisson Fumé
Spinach and Smoked Trout Roll

This dish is a particular favourite of members of the Arts Club, and I often receive requests for it when creating the menu for a special dinner or other function. It is very versatile — the spinach roulade can be filled with many different mixtures, and I usually include at least one version without fish to provide a very tasty and elegant vegetarian dish. In this recipe, smoked trout and anchovies give a smoky, piquant flavour which goes beautifully with the fluffy spinach roulade.

Imperial (Metric)	American
1½ lb (675g) fresh spinach	1½ pounds fresh spinach
2 oz (50g) butter *or* vegetable oil	¼ cup butter *or* vegetable oil
1 chopped onion	1 chopped onion
Juice of ½ lemon	Juice of ½ lemon
5 eggs, separated	5 eggs, separated
2 fl oz (60ml) double *or* sour cream	¼ cup heavy *or* sour cream
1 fl oz (30ml) yogurt	2 tablespoons yogurt
Sea salt and freshly ground black pepper	Sea salt and freshly ground black pepper
Freshly grated nutmeg	Freshly grated nutmeg
1 oz (25g) wholemeal flour	¼ cup whole wheat flour
1 oz (25g) diced cucumber	2 tablespoons diced cucumber
1 oz (25g) sweetcorn kernels	2 tablespoons corn kernels
1 oz (25g) diced red pepper	2 tablespoons diced red pepper
1 oz (25g) chopped spring onion	¼ cup chopped scallions
1 oz (25g) sliced mushrooms	½ cup sliced mushrooms
2 oz (50g) anchovy fillets, rinsed, dried and chopped	¼ cup anchovy fillets, rinsed, dried and chopped
4 oz (100g) smoked trout, flaked	1 cup flaked smoked trout
8 oz (225g) curd *or* cream cheese	1 cup curd *or* cream cheese
1 fl oz (30ml) sour cream	¼ cup sour cream

1 Wash the spinach thoroughly, removing any coarse stems. Place in a large pan with just the water which clings to the leaves, cover with a lid and cook for 3 minutes until softened. Drain and squeeze out as much water as possible. Chop the spinach and reserve in a large bowl.

2 Heat half the butter or oil and sauté the onion until soft. Stir into the spinach and add the lemon juice.

3 Lightly beat the egg yolks and stir into the spinach mixture. Add the cream and yogurt and mix well. Season to taste with salt, pepper and nutmeg.

4 Beat the egg whites until stiff and gently fold into the spinach mixture.

5 Grease an oblong tin 12×8 inches (30×20cm) with the remaining butter and dust with flour, shaking off any excess. Line with greaseproof (parchment) paper, grease and flour again.

6 Pour the spinach mixture into the tin and bake at 375°F/190°C (Gas Mark 5) for 10 minutes.

7 While the roulade is cooking, prepare the filling. Place all the chopped vegetables in a bowl, along with the anchovies and trout. Lightly beat in the cheese, adding sour cream to thin the mixture to a spreadable cream.

8 When the roulade is cooked, remove it from the oven, turn it out onto a clean work surface and, while it is still warm and flexible, roll it up very gently, with the silicon (parchment) paper on the inside. Leave for 2 minutes, then unroll, peel off the paper and spread the inside of the roll with filling and re-roll. Leave to cool. Slice and serve with a garnish of radicchio leaves and asparagus tips.

Une Pastorale Arcadienne de Turbot Vert Pré
Turbot on a Bed of Lemon-Scented Spinach Purée

Serves 6

When creating a dish for a special occasion it is always easy for the artistically-minded cook to overstep the point where the beauty of the dish suits the occasion and the result is a fussy, overcomplicated — if delicious — work of art. Sometimes it is the very simplicity of presentation which strikes the right note. This dish is one of my favourite creations and needs little embellishment to do it justice. The fish used is turbot, the 'King of the Ocean', and it is appropriate that it was developed to delight a princess — which it duly did.

Imperial (Metric)	American
1 turbot (approx. 4 lb/1.8 kilos), filleted, skinned and divided into 6 portions	1 turbot (approx. 4 pounds), filleted, skinned and divided into 6 portions
3 pints (1.7 litres) fish stock, made with the head and bones of the turbot (page 170)	7½ cups fish stock, made with the head and bones of the turbot (page 170)
For the sauce:	**For the sauce:**
¼ pint (150ml) fish stock, reduced (see point 2)	⅔ cup fish stock, reduced (see point 2)
2 hard-boiled eggs, sieved to a paste	2 hard-cooked eggs, strained to a paste
1 tablespoon chopped chives	1 tablespoon chopped chives
4 tablespoons natural yogurt	4 tablespoons plain yogurt
Juice of 2 lemons	Juice of 2 lemons
Sea salt and freshly ground black pepper	Sea salt and freshly ground black pepper
For the spinach purée:	**For the spinach purée:**
2 lb (1.8 kilos) fresh spinach	2 pounds fresh spinach
4 fl oz (120ml) natural yogurt	½ cup plain yogurt
3 shallots, chopped	3 shallots, chopped
Juice and finely grated rind of 2 lemons	Juice and finely grated rind of 2 lemons
For the decoration:	**For the decoration:**
1 carrot, cut into *julienne* strips	1 carrot, cut into *julienne* strips
1 small leek, cut into *julienne* strips	1 small leek, cut into *julienne* strips
1 truffle, tinned, cut into *julienne* strips	1 truffle, canned, cut into *julienne* strips
1 piece preserved ginger, cut into *julienne* strips	1 piece preserved ginger, cut into *julienne* strips

1 Place the turbot fillets in the boiling stock and cook for 4 to 6 minutes only. Remove from the heat and allow the fish to cool in the stock. This latent heat process, as it is called, will produce perfectly cooked fish by the time the stock is cool.

2 When cool, drain off ¼ pint (150ml/⅔ cup) stock and boil it for 3 minutes to reduce its volume.

3 In a bowl, beat the stock with the egg paste, chives, yogurt and lemon juice. Leave to cool, then season to taste.

4 Rinse the spinach thoroughly and place in a pan with a further ¼ pint (150ml/⅔ cup) of the fish stock. Cook the spinach briefly until soft. Drain well and squeeze to press out any excess moisture. Place the spinach in a blender with the yogurt, shallots and lemon juice and rind. Blend to a purée, which should be the texture of whipped cream. Season to taste.

5 Blanch the *julienne* of carrot and leek in a little of the remaining fish stock for just 30 seconds. Drain well and cool.

6 On individual serving plates arrange two spoonsful of spinach purée and gently lay the turbot fillets on top of this. Sprinkle with a mixture of all the *julienne* ingredients and decorate the plate with a salad leaf such as endive or chicory. Serve the sauce separately, to be spooned on to the fish by your guests.

Macédoine de Légumes au Fumet de Truite en Croûte
Wholemeal Loaf Stuffed with a Fish and Vegetable Mousse

Serves 6

This is a very versatile dish — easy to transport on a picnic; pretty enough to serve as a delightful appetizer for a dinner party; convenient to prepare ahead of time for a buffet meal; flexible, in that you can substitute many different types of fish and vegetables for the ones suggested — choose the occasion and you are sure to find this recipe of use!

Imperial (Metric)	American
1 wholemeal loaf (approx. 2 lb/900g)	1 whole wheat loaf (approx. 2 pounds)
½ oz (15g) agar-agar	1 tablespoon agar-agar
3 fl oz (90ml) dry white wine	⅓ cup dry white wine
½ pint (300ml) fish velouté (page 176)	1⅓ cups fish velouté (page 176)
Sea salt and freshly ground black pepper	Sea salt and freshly ground black pepper
5 oz (125g) cooked *or* canned fish	⅔ cup cooked *or* canned fish
4 skinned and boned smoked trout	4 skinned and boned smoked trout
Juice of 1 lemon	Juice of 1 lemon
1 oz (25g) capers	2 tablespoons capers
1 oz (25g) chopped gherkins	2 tablespoons chopped dill pickles
2 oz (50g) cooked peas	⅓ cup cooked peas
2 oz (50g) cooked sweetcorn kernels	⅓ cup cooked corn kernels
2 oz (50g) diced red pepper	⅓ cup diced red pepper
2 oz (50g) diced cooked potato	⅓ cup diced cooked potato
2 oz (50g) chopped cooked French beans	⅓ cup chopped cooked snap beans
2 oz (50g) cooked flageolet beans	⅓ cup cooked flageolet beans
¼ pint (150ml) natural yogurt	⅔ cup plain yogurt

1 Place the fresh wholemeal (whole wheat) loaf in the refrigerator for 24 hours, then cut off one end and reserve. Carefully scoop out the soft crumb filling (this can be used in other dishes, and freezes well).

2 Dissolve the agar-agar in the wine, then bring the velouté sauce to a boil and beat in the dissolved agar-agar. Boil gently for 10 minutes. Season to taste.

3 Mash the fish with a fork, then add this to the sauce. Stir in the lemon juice, capers and gherkins (pickles), and all the vegetables. Allow the mixture to cool.

4 When the mixture is quite cold, beat in the yogurt.

5 Fill the loaf 'shell' with the filling mixture, then replace the sliced end. Hold in place with a strip of foil if necessary and refrigerate until the filling is firm and sliceable. Slice with a warmed bread knife and serve with cucumber and curly lettuce.

Saint-Pierre au Châteauneuf-du-Pape

Saint Peter's Fish Baked in Fine Red Wine

Serves 8-10

I find it rather apposite that the fish John Dory, which we in France name after St Peter, should be cooked in a wine whose literal translation is 'the new castle of the Pope'. The name of the fish stems from it supposedly bearing the thumb print of the fisherman Apostle (and, incidentally, its flatness is attributed to its ancestors having been split in two when the Red Sea was parted). The wine, on the other hand, is so-called because its vineyards were founded by the medieval Popes of Avignon. John Dory is becoming more readily available than it once was, but you could substitute plaice (flounder) or sole. Do not be tempted, however, to substitute a cheap red wine in which to cook it — a wine of quality is needed to produce the rich, full flavour of this delicious dish.

Imperial (Metric)	American
1 large onion, sliced	1 large onion, sliced
2 sticks celery, sliced	2 stalks celery, sliced
2 stems fennel, sliced	2 stems fennel, sliced
1 green pepper, seeded and sliced	1 green pepper, seeded and sliced
2 cloves garlic, crushed	2 cloves garlic, crushed
2 bay leaves	2 bay leaves
2 sprigs thyme	2 sprigs thyme
6 lb (2.7 kilos) John Dory *or* other flat fish, gutted, scaled and washed	6 pounds John Dory *or* other flat fish, gutted, scaled and washed
2 lb (900g) tomatoes, skinned, seeded and chopped	2 pounds tomatoes, skinned, seeded and chopped
3 tablespoons tomato purée	3 tablespoons tomato paste
½ pint (300ml) Châteauneuf-du-Pape	1⅓ cups Châteauneuf-du-Pape
½ pint (300ml) water	1⅓ cups water
Sea salt and freshly ground black pepper	Sea salt and freshly ground black pepper
Pinch saffron strands	Pinch saffron strands
8 stoned black olives	8 pitted black olives
1 teaspoon each chopped fresh mint, basil and marjoram	1 teaspoon each chopped fresh mint, basil and marjoram

1 Place half the chopped onion, celery, fennel, pepper, garlic and herbs in the base of a large, shallow earthenware dish.
2 Lay the fish on top of the vegetable mixture.
3 Cover the fish with the remaining chopped vegetables, tomatoes and tomato purée (paste). Gently pour on the wine and water and add seasoning, the saffron strands and the olives.
4 Cover the dish with greaseproof (parchment) paper and bake at 375°F/190°C (Gas Mark 5) for 25 to 30 minutes, basting every 10 minutes with the liquid.
5 When the fish is cooked, remove the dish from the oven and chill in its own stock.
6 Serve sprinkled with the chopped fresh herbs, with a side salad of curly lettuce or French (snap) beans in a light vinaigrette.

Variation:

This dish is good served hot, too, with new potatoes or a rice pilaff. Serve with the rich wine stock.

6 *Les Salades*

Salads

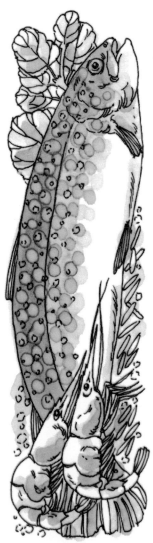

Famous menus of the past often disappoint the discerning taste of the modern gourmet. The banquets of bygone Versailles might very well stick in our throat, so glutinous were the sauces needed to cloak the tang of poorly cooked — or even bad — meat. And any photograph of an Edwardian feast will reveal the drooping eyelid and heavy jowl of the gouty *bon viveur*.

Haute cuisine, then, has usually been the high temple of cholesterol and calories, with excess taking the place of judicious elegance in far too many instances. The latter-day trend towards lightly and simply cooked food has been a welcome and healthy release for us all.

I need not explain to you about *nouvelle cuisine* — a phrase coined by the 1973 *Gault Millau Guide*. The genre is epitomized by the now-familiar style of diet-conscious cuisine where the ingredients are ascetic and only the presentation hedonistic. Yet the foundations of this 'new' cookery are older than it would seem . . .

In the 1950s my career brought me into the circle of some of the loveliest of the great international beauties — Dietrich and Darrieux, Princess Marina and Margot Fonteyn. Now, fine dishes have been dedicated to great ladies since time immemorial — but I have always wondered how these fabulous creatures could ever have remained so beautiful if they lived on a diet of the sort of sweet and sickly concoctions supposedly created in their honour. It was common at that time for the Hollywood stars in particular to be kept by their studios on the strictest of diets. Yet my whole training as a chef had been founded on the concept that love thrives on a diet of fine food (Escoffier once boasted to my father of his huge popularity with the ladies of the *belle époque* — that certainly influenced my ideas!).

And so I developed something very like the current style of 'new' cookery, for the time-honoured purpose of pleasing the fair sex. Dishes which were beautiful enough to justify the names attached to them — dishes which were a delight to the palate just as much as to the eye — but dishes which would not leave a slender form bloated, just replete with health-giving, balanced food to make the hair glossy, the eyes shine, the skin even more radiant than before. Little did I realize, in the Fifties, that I was taking the first steps towards the healthy diet which would become so fantastically popular almost thirty years later — although it is really no surprise, when you look at the facts, that it is an idea whose time has come.

Of course, crucial to the success of my approach was my belief that a healthy salad meal should not be one of abstinence, denying the pleasures of appetizing and luxurious ingredients in favour of the pursuit of health. That in itself was quite novel, and it was especially popular with the more wealthy of my patrons, whose love of good food

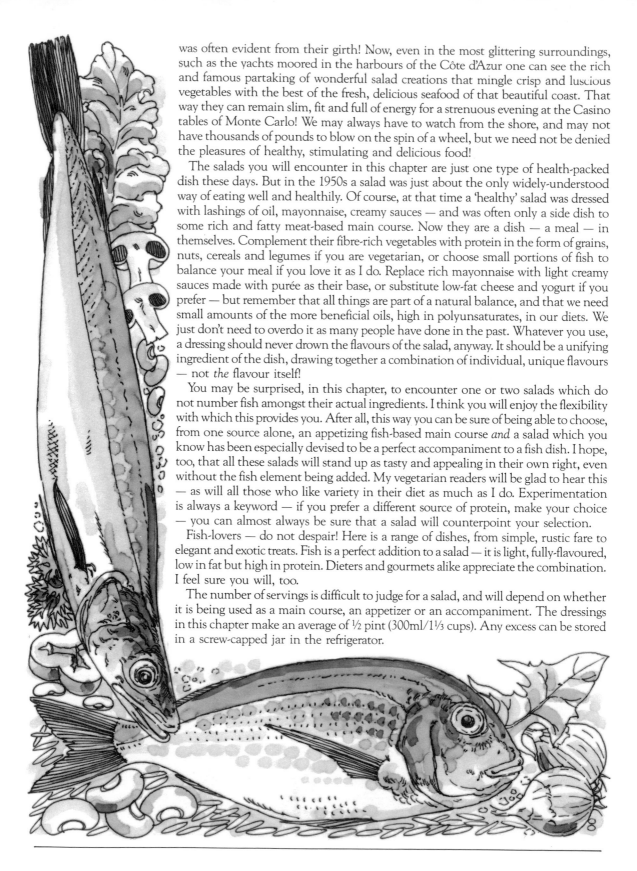

was often evident from their girth! Now, even in the most glittering surroundings, such as the yachts moored in the harbours of the Côte d'Azur one can see the rich and famous partaking of wonderful salad creations that mingle crisp and luscious vegetables with the best of the fresh, delicious seafood of that beautiful coast. That way they can remain slim, fit and full of energy for a strenuous evening at the Casino tables of Monte Carlo! We may always have to watch from the shore, and may not have thousands of pounds to blow on the spin of a wheel, but we need not be denied the pleasures of healthy, stimulating and delicious food!

The salads you will encounter in this chapter are just one type of health-packed dish these days. But in the 1950s a salad was just about the only widely-understood way of eating well and healthily. Of course, at that time a 'healthy' salad was dressed with lashings of oil, mayonnaise, creamy sauces — and was often only a side dish to some rich and fatty meat-based main course. Now they are a dish — a meal — in themselves. Complement their fibre-rich vegetables with protein in the form of grains, nuts, cereals and legumes if you are vegetarian, or choose small portions of fish to balance your meal if you love it as I do. Replace rich mayonnaise with light creamy sauces made with purée as their base, or substitute low-fat cheese and yogurt if you prefer — but remember that all things are part of a natural balance, and that we need small amounts of the more beneficial oils, high in polyunsaturates, in our diets. We just don't need to overdo it as many people have done in the past. Whatever you use, a dressing should never drown the flavours of the salad, anyway. It should be a unifying ingredient of the dish, drawing together a combination of individual, unique flavours — not *the* flavour itself!

You may be surprised, in this chapter, to encounter one or two salads which do not number fish amongst their actual ingredients. I think you will enjoy the flexibility with which this provides you. After all, this way you can be sure of being able to choose, from one source alone, an appetizing fish-based main course *and* a salad which you know has been especially devised to be a perfect accompaniment to a fish dish. I hope, too, that all these salads will stand up as tasty and appealing in their own right, even without the fish element being added. My vegetarian readers will be glad to hear this — as will all those who like variety in their diet as much as I do. Experimentation is always a keyword — if you prefer a different source of protein, make your choice — you can almost always be sure that a salad will counterpoint your selection.

Fish-lovers — do not despair! Here is a range of dishes, from simple, rustic fare to elegant and exotic treats. Fish is a perfect addition to a salad — it is light, fully-flavoured, low in fat but high in protein. Dieters and gourmets alike appreciate the combination. I feel sure you will, too.

The number of servings is difficult to judge for a salad, and will depend on whether it is being used as a main course, an appetizer or an accompaniment. The dressings in this chapter make an average of ½ pint (300ml/1⅓ cups). Any excess can be stored in a screw-capped jar in the refrigerator.

La Salade de Thon au Goût de Pernod
Tuna and Rice Salad, with a Hint of Pernod

When I ran my restaurant at the Athenaeum Hotel in Park Lane, in the Fifties, one of the most popular dishes was *Langoustine au Pernod*, an extremely rich and luxurious dish featuring a heady sauce based on the classic French aperitif with its wonderful aroma of aniseed. As I have said, this dish — or rather, this sauce — was very popular indeed, not just with my guests but, as it turned out, with my chefs, too. This was because more of the Pernod was going into the cooks than in the sauce! One evening I came into the kitchen to find it in uproar. My sauce cook had drunk a whole bottle and then collapsed under a table. Since then I have always carefully supervised the preparation of such tempting dishes!

Imperial (Metric)	American
6 oz (150g) *Uncle Ben's* wholegrain rice	¾ cup *Uncle Ben's* wholegrain rice
Sea salt and freshly ground black pepper	Sea salt and freshly ground black pepper
1 tin (*or* 6 oz/150g fresh) tuna fish *or* salmon	1 can (*or* 1 cup fresh) tuna fish *or* salmon
2 heads fennel, thinly sliced	2 heads fennel, thinly sliced
4 oz (100g) stoned black olives	1 cup pitted black olives
1 tablespoon Pernod	1 tablespoon Pernod
¼ pint (150ml) mayonnaise (page 179) *or* yogurt	⅔ cup mayonnaise (page 179) *or* yogurt
6 spring onions	6 scallions
3 hard-boiled eggs	3 hard-cooked eggs

1 Cook the rice until tender, then season with salt and pepper and place in a large wooden salad bowl.

2 Drain the fish of oil or brine and flake with a fork into the rice. Toss gently.

3 Lightly mix the sliced fennel and the olives into the salad bowl.

4 Stir the Pernod into the mayonnaise or yogurt, then fold half this mixture into the salad. Chill for 30 minutes.

5 Before serving, slice the spring onions (scallions) lengthways and peel and slice the eggs. Decorate the salad with these and lastly drizzle the remaining Pernod mayonnaise or yogurt over the salad. Serve at once.

La Salade de Saumon Fumé et d'Avocat Monégasque

Smoked Salmon and Avocado Pasta Salad

How could anyone with a taste for luxury resist this sublime combination of ingredients — smoked salmon, prawns (shrimp) and avocado, balanced with the nutty taste of wholewheat pasta and the tang of a mustardy, lemony dressing. It would not seem out of place on the decks of the millionaires' yachts in the harbour at Monte Carlo, served with correctly chilled *Dom Perignon* champagne to set you up for an exciting evening at the casino tables. Ah well ... one can dream, and this elegant salad will make you feel like a millionaire without having to spend like one!

Imperial (Metric)	American
For the salad:	For the salad:
8 oz (225g) wholewheat pasta shells	4 cups whole wheat pasta shells
Sea salt	Sea salt
2 oz (50g) smoked salmon	3 medium slices smoked salmon
1 ripe avocado	1 ripe avocado
6 spring onions	6 scallions
1 bunch radishes	1 bunch radishes
4 oz (100g) peeled prawns	1 cup peeled shrimp
1 tablespoon fresh chopped parsley	1 tablespoon fresh chopped parsley
1 pinch fresh chopped dill	1 pinch fresh chopped dill
Freshly ground black pepper	Freshly ground black pepper
For the dressing:	For the dressing:
3 tablespoons lemon juice	3 tablespoons lemon juice
2 tablespoons olive oil	2 tablespoons olive oil
1 tablespoon natural yogurt	1 tablespoon plain yogurt
½ teaspoon French mustard	½ teaspoon French mustard
Sea salt and freshly ground black pepper	Sea salt and freshly ground black pepper

1 Place all the dressing ingredients in a blender or food processor and blend to a smooth emulsion.
2 Cook the pasta shells in plenty of boiling, salted water until just tender — *al dente* as the Italians put it. Drain well, place in a bowl and toss in the dressing while still warm, so that the pasta absorbs some of the flavour.
3 Slice the smoked salmon into very thin strips.
4 Halve the avocado and remove the stone. Either scoop into tiny balls with a melon scoop, or peel and thinly slice.
5 Chop the spring onions (scallions) finely.
6 Toss the salmon, avocado, onions, radishes and prawns lightly with the dressed pasta.
7 Transfer to a glass bowl or a plate lined with crisp lettuce. Sprinkle with the herbs and a little black pepper to taste. Serve.

Variations:
Extra strips of smoked salmon could be used as a garnish, as could whole cooked king prawns (jumbo shrimp). Melon or pawpaw (papaya) could be substituted for the avocado. Other smoked fish, such as trout, could replace the salmon, or you could replace it with seafood such as scallops or oysters. Flakes of fresh fish would be a pleasant change, too. The variations are many — you just need to think of your favourite savoury ingredients and I am sure you could find they would adapt well to this 'dream' salad.

Salade Marinée Tonkinoise

Marinated Coley Salad with a Tofu Dressing

Here is another dish which reflects the exchange of valuable influences between Vietnamese cuisine and the traditional cookery of France. It pairs a deceptively simple salad of assorted attractive leaves, dotted with walnuts and white mushrooms, with a piquant marinade of finely sliced raw coley. The final touch is an exotic dressing of fresh fruits in tofu. Tofu is the correct name for bean curd, which is becoming more readily available in health stores and delicatessens around the world. It is rich in protein and its bland flavour absorbs that of other ingredients. It is low in calories, making it an ideal substitute for mayonnaise when you wish to avoid the tang of yogurt in your dressing.

Imperial (Metric)	American
Juice and finely grated rind of 3 limes	Juice and finely grated rind of 3 limes
Juice and finely grated rind of 2 lemons	Juice and finely grated rind of 2 lemons
3 coriander seeds, lightly crushed	3 coriander seeds, lightly crushed
3 black peppercorns, lightly crushed	3 black peppercorns, lightly crushed
Sea salt	Sea salt
2 lb (900g) very fresh coley fillet, very finely sliced	2 pounds very fresh coley fillet, very finely sliced
4 oz (100g) silken tofu	½ cup silken tofu
4 oz (100g) mixed finely diced fresh pineapple, pawpaw and watermelon	⅔ cup mixed finely diced fresh pineapple, pawpaw and watermelon
4 crisp lettuce leaves	4 crisp lettuce leaves
4 leaves radicchio	4 leaves radicchio
4 leaves oak lettuce	4 leaves oak lettuce
8 oz (225g) beansprouts	4 cups beansprouts
2 oz (50g) chopped walnuts	⅓ cup chopped walnuts
4 oz (100g) sliced white mushrooms	1½ cups sliced white mushrooms
Fresh chopped herbs, to taste	Fresh chopped herbs, to taste
Sea salt and freshly ground black pepper	Sea salt and freshly ground black pepper

1 Mix the juice and rind of the limes and lemons in a bowl with the coriander, peppercorns and a little salt. Toss the slivers of coley in this, cover and leave to marinate for 2 hours.

2 In another bowl, beat together the tofu and the chopped fruit. Leave for the tofu to absorb the flavour of the fruit.

3 Arrange the salad leaves and beansprouts prettily on four serving plates, keeping the centre of each clear. Over the salad, lay slivers of marinated fish and sprinkle with nuts, mushrooms, herbs and seasoning.

4 Spoon some dressing into four individuals small bowls (tiny Oriental ones with matching china spoons are ideal for this) and place them in the centre of each dish. Serve at once, allowing guests to spoon sauce over the fish themselves.

L'Anchoyade Arlésienne aux Haricots Verts

French Bean, Anchovy and Caper Salad

This is perhaps one of the tastiest of all bean salads, combining freshly cooked French (snap) beans with the classic southern French flavours of anchovies, capers, olives and garlic, and full-flavoured ripe tomatoes. Again, we make use of the counterbalance of hot and cold. In just the same way as children (or children at heart) adore the combination of ice-cream with hot chocolate sauce, so the gourmet appreciates the sensation of the still-warm beans in a cold dressing — this is known as a *salade tiède*.

Imperial (Metric)	American
For the dressing:	For the dressing:
3 tablespoons natural yogurt	3 tablespoons plain yogurt
Juice of 1 lemon	Juice of 1 lemon
Sea salt and freshly ground black pepper	Sea salt and freshly ground black pepper
Pinch cayenne pepper *or* 1 fresh green chilli, sliced	Pinch cayenne pepper *or* 1 fresh green chili, sliced
2 hard-boiled eggs	2 hard-boiled eggs
For the salad:	For the salad:
1 lb (450g) French beans	1 pound snap beans
2 oz (50g) anchovy fillets (desalted)	2 ounces anchovy fillets (desalted)
2 cloves garlic	2 cloves garlic
1 oz (25g) capers	2 tablespoons capers
8 black olives, stoned	8 black olives, pitted
4 large, ribbed tomatoes	4 large, ribbed tomatoes
4 triangles fried wholewheat bread	4 triangles fried whole wheat bread

1 Blend together the yogurt and lemon juice with the seasoning and chilli, if used.

2 Peel the eggs, separate white from yolk, and chop the egg white. Push the yolks through a sieve (strainer). Stir both white and yolk into the dressing.

3 Top and tail the beans and cook in lightly salted water for 8 to 10 minutes only, then drain. Place them in a bowl while still hot.

4 Chop the anchovy fillets and the garlic cloves. Stir them into the beans along with the capers.

5 Spoon on the dressing and stir well so that everything is evenly coated.

6 On individual plates, arrange the bean salad attractively, and decorate around the edge with olives, slices of tomato and triangles of bread. Serve at once, while the beans are still warm.

La Salade de Poireaux du Tréport aux Filets de Maquereau
Leek and Mackerel Salad

Le Tréport is a seaside resort in France, much frequented by the natives of Picardy. We often visited it in my youth, making it a whole day's outing for all the family. We would take a picnic lunch sufficient for us all, in a huge basket. It is a charming place, but the beach is rather stony and, as I recall it, probably the windiest place on that coast! So a substantial salad, making use of ingredients for which the region is famous, seems an ideal reminder of those summer picnics. I have combined fillets of mackerel, one of the specialities of Le Tréport, with leeks such as are grown to perfection in the rich farmlands of Normandy and Picardy. With a loaf of good French bread, a slice of Maroilles — perhaps the best of the local cheeses — and a bottle of Normandy cider, you would have a perfect picnic, whatever the location and whatever the weather.

Imperial (Metric)	American
8 small leeks	8 small leeks
2 fresh mackerel, filleted	2 fresh mackerel, filleted
¼ pint (150ml) dry white wine	⅔ cup dry white wine
1 large red onion, thinly sliced	1 large red onion, thinly sliced
1 carrot, thinly sliced	1 carrot, thinly sliced
For the dressing:	For the dressing:
2 teaspoons Dijon mustard	2 teaspoons Dijon mustard
1 tablespoon cream	1 tablespoon cream
4 tablespoons cider vinegar	4 tablespoons cider vinegar
Sea salt and freshly ground black pepper	Sea salt and freshly ground black pepper
2 oz (50g) chopped walnuts	½ cup chopped English walnuts
1 hard-boiled egg	1 hard-cooked egg
1 lemon, sliced, for garnish	1 lemon, sliced, for garnish
1 tablespoon chopped parsley, for garnish	1 tablespoon chopped parsley, for garnish

1 Trim the ends of the leeks and split the green part of each to allow dirt to be washed away. Clean thoroughly under cold running water.
2 Tie the leeks in bundles and boil in salted water for 5 minutes. Drain and refresh in cold water. Then drain again and squeeze gently to remove any excess water. Lay the leeks on a dish.
3 Rinse the mackerel fillets and place them in a shallow pan with the wine, onion and carrot. Bring to the boil, then lower the heat and simmer for 10 minutes. Allow the mackerel to cool in the liquid, then drain, reserving a tablespoon of the liquor, and the sliced carrot and onion.
4 Place the reserved liquor in a bowl with the mustard, cream, vinegar and a little seasoning. Beat to form a smooth emulsion.
5 Place the walnuts and the peeled egg in a blender or food processor, along with the dressing. Blend until creamy.
6 Arrange the mackerel fillets decoratively with the leeks and pour the dressing over. Decorate with slices of carrot and onion rings, arrange lemon slices around the dish and sprinkle with the parsley.
7 Serve onto crisp lettuce leaves — cos would be ideal — with two leeks and one mackerel fillet per person. New potatoes would be a good accompaniment if you are not picnicking.

Chiquetaille de Légumes des Corsaires
Caribbean-style Spicy Salad

Illustrated opposite.

I always like a salad to have some 'bite', and I confess that if I am preparing one for myself I will almost always add some chopped green chilli. You may think my taste too peppery, but this is just my preference for salads — I don't, for example, like strawberries sprinkled with black pepper, which so many chefs favour at the moment. *Chacun a son goût!*

Now, you may be surprised that, in a book of fish cookery, this salad has fish only as an optional ingredient. Well, this is because I feel a salad should always contain the very finest vegetable ingredients which, by themselves, make a delicious dish. So this salad can be enjoyed as a dish in itself by vegetarians, or — since its ingredients have been chosen to complement fish — as an accompaniment to a wide range of fish dishes, or with the optional tang of tuna as a fish dish.

Imperial (Metric)	American
For the dressing:	For the dressing:
4 fl oz (120ml) nut oil	½ cup nut oil
2 cloves garlic	2 cloves garlic
Juice of 2 limes	Juice of 2 limes
3 fl oz (90ml) natural yogurt	⅓ cup plain yogurt
2 fl oz (60ml) fresh pineapple juice	¼ cup fresh pineapple juice
½ oz (15g) desiccated coconut, toasted	2 tablespoons desiccated coconut, toasted
1 green chilli, chopped	1 green chili, chopped
1 small piece fresh ginger	1 small piece fresh ginger
For the salad:	For the salad:
3 oz (75g) French beans	3 ounces snap beans
3 oz (75g) thinly sliced red onion rings	3 ounces thinly sliced red onion rings
3 oz (75g) thin strips red pepper	3 ounces thin strips red pepper
3 oz (75g) cooked black beans	½ cup cooked black beans
3 oz (75g) celery, cut into thin strips	3 ounces celery, cut into thin strips
3 oz (75g) ripe banana, sliced	3 ounces ripe banana, sliced
3 oz (75g) fresh pineapple, cubed *or* shredded	⅔ cup fresh pineapple, cubed *or* shredded
3 oz (75g) toasted peanuts	⅓ cup toasted peanuts
4 oz (100g) drained tinned tuna (optional)	½ cup drained canned tuna (optional)
Stoned black olives (optional)	Pitted black olives (optional)

1 Put all the dressing ingredients into a blender or processor and blend to a perfect emulsion. Leave to one side for the flavours to develop.

2 Top and tail the fresh beans and blanch in lightly salted water for 3 minutes only, then refresh under cold running water.

3 For an informal salad, toss all the ingredients in a large bowl with the dressing, and serve, if liked, on a bed of crisp lettuce or Chinese leaves. For a more formal dinner party dish, arrange the various ingredients into beautiful displays on individual plates or a large platter, either drizzled with the dressing, or with it served separately. (If serving your salad in this way, the banana should be tossed in a little lemon juice to prevent discoloration.)

Variation:
Different types of bean could be substituted for the black beans, to vary flavour, texture and especially colour. More tuna fish can be served according to taste.

L'Éffeuillé de la Marée Côte de l'Émeraude

A Salad of White Fish on Potatoes and Chives in a Light Yogurt Dressing

One of the great attractions of the *salade tiède*, as it is known, is that it combines the physiological effects of both hot and cold, to enhance the flavours of all the ingredients used. In this recipe a little diced raw fish is sautéed in butter with shallots and served on a bed of potato salad — but, since new potatoes make a delicious hot salad, you could equally well reverse the technique and serve a hot potato salad, in a vinaigrette dressing, with slivers of cold fish. Either way will be delicious.

Imperial (Metric)	American
For the dressing:	For the dressing:
4 fl oz (120ml) natural yogurt	½ cup plain yogurt
1 tablespoon chopped chives	1 tablespoon chopped chives
1 tablespoon chopped parsley	1 tablespoon chopped parsley
Sea salt and freshly ground black pepper	Sea salt and freshly ground black pepper
Pinch cayenne pepper	Pinch cayenne pepper
1 raw egg yolk (optional)	1 raw egg yolk (optional)
For the salad:	For the salad:
8 oz (225g) new potatoes	8 ounces new potatoes
8 oz (225g) cod fillet	8 ounces cod fillet
2 oz (50g) butter	¼ cup butter
1 shallot, chopped	1 shallot, chopped
4 large lettuce leaves	4 large lettuce leaves
2 heads chicory	2 Belgian endives

1   In a bowl, stir together the yogurt, herbs and seasoning. If you prefer a thinner dressing, or a richer one, add lightly beaten egg yolk to taste.

2   Boil the new potatoes and, when cool enough to handle, skin if wished and slice or cube. Stir carefully into the dressing.

3   Cube or slice the cod fillet. Just before you wish to serve the salad, heat the butter in a pan and sauté the fish and shallots, turning carefully so that the fish does not break up.

4   Pile the potato salad onto a serving dish, with shredded lettuce leaves and fanned-out chicory (endive) leaves surrounding it, and arrange the fish mixture over the potatoes. Alternatively, divide the potato salad between the four lettuce leaves, with some fish on top of each, and then surround with chicory (endive).

Opposite: *Coquilles Saint-Jacques aux Salicornes* (page 140).

La Salade Catalane au Riz
Rice Salad from the South of France

Rice-based salads and other dishes are very popular in southern France, no doubt due to the infleunce of Spanish cooking in that region. The traditional paella-type dish is, of course, classic country food, using the freshest fish from the local port with nothing wasted. For the more fastidious palate, which might prefer to forego the bones and shells which are part and parcel of many a seafood and rice creation, here is a slightly more exotic adaptation which can be varied according to taste and availability of ingredients.

Imperial (Metric)	American
4 oz (100g) brown rice	½ cup brown rice
4 fl oz (120ml) mayonnaise (page 179)	½ cup mayonnaise (page 179)
2 tablespoons natural yogurt	2 tablespoons plain yogurt
1 clove garlic, crushed	1 clove garlic, crushed
1 small red onion, chopped	1 small red onion, chopped
Sea salt and freshly ground black pepper	Sea salt and freshly ground black pepper
1 slice pineapple, cubed	1 slice pineapple, cubed
2 oz (50g) seeded grapes	2 ounces seeded grapes
1 oz (25g) pine nuts *or* chopped cashews	¼ cup pine nuts *or* chopped cashews
1 head radicchio	1 head radicchio
8 leaves endive	8 leaves curly chicory
6 oz (150g) shelled, cooked prawns *or* peeled, cooked scampi *or* flaked white fish	1 cup shelled, cooked prawns *or* peeled, cooked scampi *or* flaked white fish
1 lemon, sliced, to garnish	1 lemon, sliced, to garnish
Sprigs dill, to garnish	Sprigs dill, to garnish

1 Cook the brown rice in 3 times its volume of water until tender. Drain and refresh under cold running water and drain again.

2 In a bowl mix the rice with the mayonnaise, yogurt, garlic and chopped onion. Season to taste.

3 Stir the fruit and nuts gently into the mixture.

4 Arrange constrasting-coloured leaves of lettuce on your serving plate or plates, and place spoonsful of the mixture carefully onto the leaves.

5 Lay your chosen fish decoratively on top of the rice salad and garnish with sprigs of dill and twists of lemon.

La Salade de Hareng Saur aux Oranges

Marinated Kipper, Potato and Onion Salad with Oranges

This is a rich and tangy country supper dish, such as the type my grandmother Mathilde was apt to serve, using naturally smoked herrings and boiled potatoes to make an inexpensive yet substantial meal. I have embellished the good flavours of the kipper by marinating it in spices and cider, and added watercress and orange to give the dish an attractive and different note. Serve with fresh wholewheat bread for a very hearty feast.

Imperial (Metric)	American
4 undyed kipper fillets	4 undyed kipper fillets
1 tablespoon pickling spices	1 tablespoon pickling spices
4 fl oz (120ml) cider vinegar	½ cup cider vinegar
4 fl oz (120ml) water	½ cup water
1 lb (450g) new potatoes	1 pound new potatoes
1 small onion, sliced	1 small onion, sliced
2 oranges, peeled and segmented	2 oranges, peeled and segmented
4 large crisp lettuce leaves	4 large crisp lettuce leaves
4 radicchio leaves	4 radicchio leaves
Leaves from 1 small bunch watercress	Leaves from 1 small bunch watercress

1   Cut the kipper fillets into 1-inch (2.5cm) squares. Mix together the spices, cider vinegar and water in a bowl. Add the kipper pieces, stirring gently to coat them all. Cover and leave for anything from 12 hours to 1 week, refrigerated.

2   Boil the new potatoes in lightly salted water. Drain and slice.

3   Drain the kipper pieces. In a bowl, mix gently together the potatoes, kippers and onion.

4   Arrange the mixture on a serving platter. Decorate around it with the orange segments and the salad leaves — lay each red leaf in the hollow of a green one for a most attractive contrast. Arrange the watercress leaves in the centre of the dish.

La Salade de Langouste aux Mangues
Langouste (Rock Lobster) Salad with Exotic Fruit

It is more and more the case these days that wherever in the world you can buy exotic fruit, so you can also purchase more unusual fish. Fruit which, in my younger days, were only to be found in the regions in which they grew, are now displayed in abundance in markets everywhere. And those which might only have been offered as an exotic and costly dessert now act as a garnish to a wealth of savoury dishes. Acid fruit combined with protein creates a well-balanced meal, and the enzyme papayin in the pawpaw (papaya) aids the digestion of protein in this rich but healthy salad.

Imperial (Metric)	American
2 lb (900g) cooked, cooled langouste	2 pounds cooked, cooled rock lobster
1 pawpaw	1 papaya
1 mango	1 mango
4 slices fresh pineapple	4 slices fresh pineapple
2 heads radicchio	2 heads radicchio
1 round lettuce	1 Bibb lettuce
8 oz (225g) bean sprouts	4 cups bean sprouts
1 red pepper	1 red pepper
1 green pepper	1 green pepper
3 slices fresh ginger	3 slices fresh ginger
For the dressing:	For the dressing:
4 fl oz (120ml) natural yogurt	½ cup plain yogurt
3 tablespoons mango chutney	3 tablespoons mango chutney
3 eggs yolks	3 eggs yolks
4 oz (100g) pecan nuts	1 cup pecans
Sea salt and freshly ground black pepper	Sea salt and freshly ground black pepper

1 Split the langouste (rock lobster) in two, discard the intestinal cord and carefuly remove the tail meat from each one. Slice thinly and reserve.

2 Halve the pawpaw (papaya) and remove the seeds. Halve the mango and remove the stone. Peel and thinly slice both fruit.

3 Cut the pineapple into small wedges.

4 Wash and drain the two types of lettuce, and the bean sprouts.

5 On individual serving plates, arrange the lettuce leaves with red on one side, green on the other, and a thin band of bean sprouts down the centre.

6 Arrange the pieces of langouste (rock lobster) over the green lettuce, and slices of fruit over the radicchio.

7 Cut the two peppers into very fine *julienne* strips. Cut the ginger slices into thin slivers.

8 Arrange slices of red pepper over the langouste (rock lobster) green over the fruit, and ginger over the bean sprouts.

9 Blend or process all the dressing ingredients together and serve separately, allowing guests to add as much to their salad as they choose.

Les Deux Chicorées Dunquerkoise

Chicory and Endive Salad with Trout

The bitter taste of both chicory and endive is very popular with gourmets. It is often said to be an acquired taste, but this is not always the case — most Nordic and North European races love both bitter beers and bitter vegetables. In Northern France, where German and Flemish influence is strong, a salad of endive, chicory and smoked fish is very popular, served with a good tankard of cold beer.

Imperial (Metric)	American
For the dressing:	For the dressing:
4 fl oz (120ml) natural yogurt	½ cup plain yogurt
Juice and finely grated rind of 2 lemons	Juice and finely grated rind of 2 lemons
1 red onion, chopped	1 red onion, chopped
2 tablespoons cream of horseradish	2 tablespoons cream of horseradish
For the salad:	For the salad:
4 heads chicory	4 heads Belgian endive
1 curly endive	1 head curly chicory
4 smoked trout	4 smoked trout
8 oz (225g) cooked sweetcorn kernels	1⅓ cups cooked corn kernels
1 red pepper	1 red pepper
½ cucumber	½ cucumber
1 tablespoon chopped fresh parsley	1 tablespoon chopped fresh parsley
1 tablespoon chopped fresh mint	1 tablespoon chopped fresh mint

1　In a blender, combine the dressing ingredients to form a thick sauce. Leave for the flavours to develop, while you prepare the salad.
2　Separate the salad leaves, wash and shred finely. Drain very thoroughly.
3　Skin, bone and flake the trout. Stir into the corn, then mix the dressing into this mixture carefully.
4　Seed and chop the pepper, and cut the cucumber into matchstick-sized sticks.
5　Arrange a bed of salad on a serving plate. Onto this lay the fish and corn mixture. Arrange the chopped pepper and sliced cucumber decoratively around this, and finally sprinkle with chopped herbs.

Variation:
Other vegetables could be added for further decoration, such as blanched mangetout (snow) peas, carrots, radishes or tomatoes cut decoratively — use your imagination to make this salad as pretty as you wish, or keep it plain and simple, it will taste as good either way!

Aspergio de Homard Annette

Asparagus and Lobster Salad

During the sultry month of June 1938 I was in Cherbourg, doing my conscripted service in the French Navy, so you can perhaps imagine my delight at being invited to dinner by a most charming and beautiful Countess! However, this clever hostess knew that I was the cook for the Officers' Mess — my Captain was invited too, and I prepared the dinner as usual! One of the dishes we served was this salad, using small lobsters known, for some reason, as the *Demoiselles de Cherbourg*. The eggs and coral from these hen lobsters make a rich and elegant sauce. For me, the flavours of this salad always conjure up images of that time — the last few tastes of luxury before long years of deprivation. This is a very special dish, for a very special occasion.

Imperial (Metric)	American
For the court bouillon:	For the court bouillon:
2 carrots	2 carrots
1 onion	1 onion
2 slices fennel	2 slices fennel
2 pints (1.15 litres) water	5 cups water
2 tablespoons wine vinegar	2 tablespoons wine vinegar
For the salad:	For the salad:
4 small (12 oz/350g) female lobsters	4 small (12 ounce) lobsters
2 lb (450g) green asparagus spears	2 pounds green asparagus spears
4 leaves radicchio	4 leaves radicchio
4 green lettuce leaves	4 green lettuce leaves
1 tinned truffle	1 canned truffle
4 large white mushrooms	4 large white mushrooms
1 piece preserved ginger	1 piece preserved ginger
For the dressing:	For the dressing:
Reserved eggs and coral from lobsters (see below)	Reserved eggs and coral from lobsters (see below)
4 fl oz (120ml) natural yogurt	½ cup plain yogurt
1 shallot, chopped	1 shallot, chopped
2 egg yolks	2 egg yolks
3 rinsed anchovy fillets	3 rinsed anchovy fillets
2 small pickled gherkins	2 small dill pickles
2 tablespoons tomato purée	2 tablespoons tomato paste
1 teaspoon honey	1 teaspoon honey
2 tablespoons port	2 tablespoons port
Sea salt and freshly ground black pepper	Sea salt and freshly ground black pepper

1 Prepare the court bouillon by cleaning and slicing the vegetables and bringing to the boil in the water and vinegar. (Remember, if you were serving lobsters in their shell, you should not be using vinegar, as it bleaches the colour from the shell — but in this dish it is the benefits of the vinegar's flavour which count as the shell is discarded.)

2 Wash the lobsters very well and poach in the boiling *bouillon* for 15 minutes. Allow to cool slowly in the liquid.

3 Carefully remove the meat from the lobster, reserving the eggs and coral for the dressing. Crack the claws and remove the white meat without breaking it up.

4 Scrape the woody stems of the asparagus, tie into bundles of eight, and boil for 10 minutes, with the tips above the water level covered in a dome of foil if necessary. Drain, refresh in iced water, and drain again. Leave to cool.

5 While both lobster and asparagus are cooling, carefully wash your eight perfect salad leaves and drain well. Also, slice the truffle, mushrooms and ginger into the finest *julienne* strips.

6 Blend all the dressing ingredients together, checking the seasoning before adding further salt and pepper. Allow the flavours to mingle while you assemble the salad.

7 Place one of each type of lettuce leaf on each plate. Lay spears of asparagus prettily over the red leaf, so that the colours contrast nicely. Place pieces of lobster over the green leaf, once again allowing the colours to contrast.

8 Sprinkle *julienne* strips of truffle, mushroom and ginger over the salads, spoon on just the smallest amount of dressing, serving the rest in a sauce boat for guests to add themselves. Serve with a bottle of Chablis — choosing a *cru* to match the occasion!

Variations:
Poached scampi or red mullet (snapper) fillets could be served instead of the lobster.

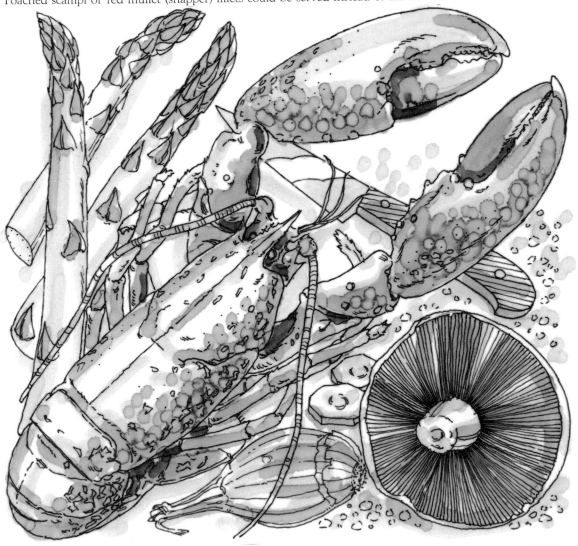

La Salade Marseillaise aux Coquillettes
Aromatic Pasta Salad

Here is another salad designed to accompany your fish instead of including it. This flavoursome salad from the South of France would be an ideal dish to serve with freshly-caught and barbecued fish, or perhaps your favourite shellfish. The simple flavour of the pasta is balanced by the spicy tang of the dressing, which uses the type of Eastern flavourings that have been brought to Marseilles by sea for centuries, and which have influenced the cooking of the port and the region in a very special way.

Imperial (Metric)	American
For the dressing:	For the dressing:
2 tablespoons vegetable oil	2 tablespoons vegetable oil
1 tablespoon chopped raw onion	1 tablespoon chopped raw onion
½ teaspoon curry powder	½ teaspoon curry powder
3 fl oz (90ml) natural yogurt	⅓ cup plain yogurt
1 tablespoon tomato purée	1 tablespoon tomato paste
2 teaspoons mango chutney	2 teaspoons mango chutney
Juice of ½ lemon	Juice of ½ lemon
Sea salt	Sea salt

Imperial (Metric)	American
For the salad:	For the salad:
6 oz (150g) cooked wholewheat pasta shells	3 cups cooked whole wheat pasta shells
3 sticks celery, chopped	3 stalks celery, chopped
4 oz (100g) raw mushrooms, sliced	2 cups raw sliced mushrooms
2 tablespoons chopped raw onion	2 tablespoons chopped raw onion
1 crisp lettuce	1 crisp lettuce
1 tablespoon chopped parsley	1 tablespoon chopped parsley
4 oz (100g) prawns	1 cup shrimp

1 Heat the oil in a small pan and sauté the chopped onion with the curry powder for 1 minute. Allow to cool.

2 In a bowl, blend the cooled curry mixture with the yogurt, tomato purée (paste), mango chutney and lemon juice. Taste and add salt if necessary.

3 Mix together the pasta, celery, mushrooms and raw onion, and stir in the dressing.

4 Arrange crisp lettuce leaves on individual plates and top with pasta salad. Sprinkle with parsley and decorate with prawns (shrimp).

Variations:
Garlic could be added to the dressing by blending two chopped cloves with 2 tablespoons red wine and stirring together with the dressing mixture. The chopped parsley could be replaced by chopped mint.

La Salade aux Champignons Saint Raphaël
Marinated Mushroom Salad

Mushrooms Saint Raphaël will enliven your summer lunch with their tangy flavours of lemon, capers and tarragon. They are ideal served with a very simple fish dish such as trout poached in a delicate *court bouillon*, served on a bed of spinach leaves, or the evocative Mediterranean flavour of freshly barbecued sardines or small red mullet (snapper) — but even an easy supper of kipper and boiled new potatoes will become quite special when this salad is served alongside.

Imperial (Metric)	American
1 lb (450g) white button mushrooms	8 cups white button mushrooms
4 cloves garlic, crushed	4 cloves garlic, crushed
1 small red onion *or* 1 shallot, chopped	1 small red onion *or* 1 shallot, chopped
2 tablespoons olive oil	2 tablespoons olive oil
1 teaspoon Dijon mustard	1 teaspoon French mustard
Juice and finely grated rind of 1 lemon	Juice and finely grated rind of 1 lemon
2 tablespoons natural yogurt	2 tablespoons plain yogurt
Sea salt and freshly ground black pepper	Sea salt and freshly ground black pepper
2 slices wholemeal bread	2 slices whole wheat bread
Radicchio *or* green lettuce leaves of choice	Radicchio *or* green lettuce leaves of choice
1 tablespoon chopped fresh tarragon	1 tablespoon chopped fresh tarragon
1 tablespoon chopped fresh parsley	1 tablespoon chopped fresh parsley
2 hard-boiled eggs, chopped finely	2 hard-cooked eggs, chopped finely
2 tablespoons capers	2 tablespoons capers

1 Wash and drain the mushrooms well. Remove the stalks — these can be used in another dish. Slice the mushroom caps and place in a large bowl with the garlic and onion.
2 Beat together half the oil with the mustard, lemon rind and juice, yogurt and seasoning. Stir this mixture into the mushrooms so that everything is evenly coated, and leave to marinate.
3 Cut the bread into croûtons and sauté in the remaining oil until crisp and golden. Drain on paper towels.
4 Arrange a bed of salad leaves on a serving platter or individual dishes.
5 Spoon mushrooms over the leaves. Sprinkle with herbs, chopped egg, capers and croûtons, and serve with the fish of your choice.

Variation:
Sliced, blanched fennel is equally delicious in this marinade.

7

Le Déjeuner sur l'Herbe

Outdoor Cooking

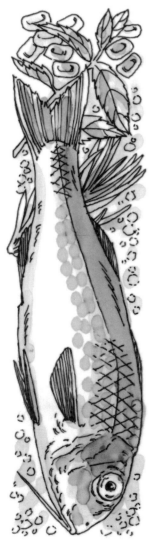

I remember once we had a Conil family gathering, of some thirty people, among the sand dunes at the edge of the famous Sables-d'Olonne. What a party that was! Anyone coming upon the event unexpectedly would have thought we had brought a whole kitchen with us — we had huge *friture* pans, other pans for boiling, barrels, huge trestle tables, and the whole household was bustling about helping prepare the feast to come. Men, women and children were all busily involved, some peeling potatoes, others making up the great sixteen-foot-long buffet tables, some preparing bowls of salad or putting taps to the barrels of cider. And others were carefully preparing the splendid array of fish which had been fetched from the boats that morning, or stoking the fire ready to cook this tasty harvest of the local waters. Morning-baked bread was arrayed along the table with golden slabs of local butter to spread on it, and huge bowls of fresh fruit made a perfect finish to the meal, both visually and gastronomically. Music was played by some talented members of the family, and the revelry went on long into the evening, despite our early start that morning getting everything prepared.

So you see, your outdoor meal can be as simple or as splendid as you like. Perhaps it is a dim memory of when our ancestors first learnt the magical powers of fire for cooking that makes this simple method so special for us. Even in the days of the most sophisticated cookers — with fans, or microwave, or ceramic hobs — everyone longs for the fine weather and even the smallest of gardens (and even balconies) sports a barbecue.

Fish lends itself splendidly to this style of cooking — oily fish can be laid straight onto the bars over the hot coals, much as our ancestors would have cooked them fresh from the stream, and dried, delicate fish can make use of the technique of wrapping, either in the classic protection of leaves or the modern sophistication of aluminium foil. But, as you might expect, I have created one or two special treats for this chapter, a little different from usual barbecue fare, such as my delicious little minced cod morsels which everyone loves. I have also developed a collection of sauces and dressings which can be prepared in advance and taken to your chosen picnic place in tightly sealed tubs. I have not forgotten that most proficient of outdoor chefs, either, the camper with only fire or camping stove on which to cook a satisfying meal for a hungry family, and at the end of the chapter you will find a few one-pan dishes which will suit a simple supper or a special feast.

Even if you live hundreds of miles away from the nearest sea or ocean, I hope you will at some time have the opportunity of trying out these dishes with fish bought at the harbourside, but even if your fish is of the frozen variety you will find that my sauces and marinades will bring you the flavours of the Mediterranean, the Atlantic, the Caribbean, or any ocean your imagination chooses!

Of course, outdoor meals need not always involve a fire or a barbecue. I have kept the dishes in this chapter to that central theme, but scattered throughout this book you will find many dishes which have provided superb picnic fare for my family and friends in the past, or which I have created for this book with long summer days in mind — or even picnics on a windy beach when the sun refuses to shine! For instance, several of the soups would provide a welcome touch of warmth if taken along on your picnic in a vacuum flask, whereas almost all the salads can easily be packed into boxes to serve alongside other picnic fare, be it cooked over red-hot coals or not. At the very end of this chapter you will find a selection of dishes to give you some ideas of other outdoor fare either for campfire and barbecue cooking, or to make your picnics even more of a treat than ever.

Turbot Grillé Sauce Paloise

Grilled Turbot with a Mint Mayonnaise

The turbot is one of the most delicious fish in the ocean. A fully-grown turbot can reach 20 pounds (9 kilos), but they are more often found at around 5 to 10 pounds (2.25 to 4.5 kilos). Small turbot or *turbotin* can be obtained, and are wonderful when carefully boned and stuffed with a soufflé mixture but this is a tricky manoeuvre for the non-professional, so let your introduction to turbot be a simple one — ask your fishmonger to cut you four turbot steaks and serve them simply grilled (broiled) with a light sauce which will enhance rather than swamp the true flavour of the fish.

Imperial (Metric)	American
4 turbot steaks (approx. 10 oz/300g each)	4 turbot steaks (approx. 10 ounces each)
2 oz (50g) seasoned wholemeal flour	½ cup seasoned whole wheat flour
3 fl oz (90ml) olive oil	⅓ cup olive oil
1 teaspoon soya *or* Worcestershire sauce	1 teaspoon soy *or* Worcestershire sauce
Juice and finely grated rind of 1 lemon	Juice and finely grated rind of 1 lemon
½ teaspoon ground ginger	½ teaspoon ground ginger
¼ pint (150ml) Mayonnaise sauce (page 182)	⅔ cup of Mayonnaise sauce (page 182)
1 tablespoon fresh mint, finely chopped	1 tablespoon fresh mint, finely chopped

1 Turn the steaks in the seasoned flour.
2 Blend together the olive oil, sauce, lemon juice and rind and ground ginger and coat the fish in this mixture.
3 Place the fish on the barbecue and cook for 7 to 8 minutes on each side, basting with extra marinade if necessary.
4 Blend the Mayonnaise with the mint and serve with the freshly-cooked fish.

Note: Barbecued vegetables are delicious with this dish — courgettes (zucchini) sliced lengthways, aubergines (eggplants), flat mushrooms are all good. Yogurt could be substituted for the Mayonnaise if you prefer.

Poisson Rouge aux Amandes
Red Mullet (Snapper) with Almonds

This colourful fish is plentiful in the Mediterranean and is ideally suited to all sorts of barbecue cooking, whether placed straight onto the bars of the grill (broil) or, as in this recipe, wrapped in constrasting green cabbage leaves and then in foil to hold in all the delicious flavour. This is an easy dish to take on a barbecue picnic, since the foil parcels can be prepared in advance and simply placed on the grill (broiler) when you are ready. I have used a stuffing which I learned for this fish when in the Navy and our ship docked at Casablanca for two weeks. The combination of dried fruits, spices, almonds and mint is far more novel than a more common bread-based stuffing for fish, and gives your meal an exotic flavour well suited to the lovely colour of the food. Serve it with a cucumber, garlic and yogurt sauce for an especially Mediterranean feel.

Imperial (Metric)	American
4 red mullet (approx. 10 oz /300g each) cleaned and boned	4 red snapper (approx. 10 ounces each) cleaned and boned
Sea salt and freshly ground black pepper	Sea salt and freshly ground black pepper
1 teaspoon ground cumin	1 teaspoon ground cumin
1 teaspoon ground ginger	1 teaspoon ground ginger
Juice of 2 limes	Juice of 2 limes
8 oz (225g) toasted flaked almonds, coarsely ground	2 cups toasted slivered almonds, coarsely ground
2 eggs, beaten	2 eggs, beaten
4 leaves mint, chopped	4 leaves mint, chopped
2 tablespoons sultanas *or* dates, roughly chopped	2 tablespoons golden seedless raisins *or* dates, roughly chopped
Pinch crushed saffron threads	Pinch crushed saffron threads
4 large cabbage leaves, blanched	4 large cabbage leaves, blanched
Vegetable oil	Vegetable oil

1 Lay the fish skin downwards and season with salt and pepper. Sprinkle with the spices and squeeze the lime juice all over. Leave to marinate.
2 In a bowl, mix together the almonds, eggs, mint, fruit and saffron. Beat to a paste.
3 Fill the cavity of each fish with an equal portion of the mixture and reshape the fish firmly around the stuffing.
4 Wrap each fish tightly in a cabbage leaf. Oil 4 large squares of foil and place a fish on each. Wrap in a parcel of foil, crimping the edges together so that no steam will escape during cooking.
5 Cook the fish over hot charcoal for 8 minutes on each side of the parcel. Serve with a crisp green salad and the sauce described above.

Variation:
Bream or John Dory could be substituted for the red mullet (snapper).

Truite Saumonée Grillée aux Herbes Paul Cézanne

Salmon Trout with a Juicy Herb Stuffing

Salmon trout has a delicate pale pink flesh which I have chosen to contrast in this recipe with a stuffing of white haddock minced with green lettuce and herbs, creating a delightful harmony of colours. This is another dish which is cooked in foil, and thus is easy to transport to your chosen picnic place — it also means the bars of your barbecue grill (broiler) are untainted by fishy flavours, so you could serve barbecued fresh fruit kebabs as a dessert.

Imperial (Metric)	American
3½ lb (1.6 kilo) salmon trout *or* rainbow trout cleaned, boned and prepared in a 'butterfly' cut	3½ pounds salmon trout *or* rainbow trout cleaned, boned and prepared in a 'butterfly' cut
Sea salt and freshly ground black pepper	Sea salt and freshly ground black pepper
8 oz (225g) fresh haddock fillets, minced	1⅓ cups minced fresh haddock fillets
2 eggs, lightly beaten	2 eggs, lightly beaten
2 oz (50g) wholemeal breadcrumbs	1 cup whole wheat breadcrumbs
2 oz (50g) shredded lettuce	1 cup shredded lettuce
2 oz (50g) spring onions, chopped	½ cup chopped scallions
2 oz (50g) shredded raw spinach	1 cup shredded raw spinach
1 sprig tarragon, chopped	1 sprig tarragon, chopped
3 fl oz (90ml) double cream	⅓ cup heavy cream
2 fl oz (60ml) sherry	¼ cup sherry
Vegetable oil	Vegetable oil

1. If the fish has been professionally prepared, check to make sure that *all* bones have been removed. Remove any fins which have been left. (All the bones, plus the head once the dish has been eaten, can be used to make fish stock — see page 170.)

2. Dry the inside of the fish, lay it on a board skin side down and season the flesh with salt and pepper.

3. In a bowl, mix together the minced haddock, beaten egg, breadcrumbs, lettuce, onions, spinach and herbs. Season well with salt and pepper, then beat in the cream and, last, enough sherry to make a smooth but firm stuffing mixture.

4. Spoon this mixture onto one side of the flattened fish, shaping it into a neat, firm shape, then fold the other side of the fish over it, pressing with your hands to reshape the fish neatly into its original form.

5. Brush the fish with oil, place it on a large sheet of foil and seal it up tightly, crimping the edges so that no steam can escape during cooking. This way, the fish cooks in its natural juices and remains beautifully moist.

6. Cook on a high rack over hot charcoal for 20 minutes, turning the parcel every 5 minutes.

7. To serve, place the unopened parcel on a serving plate so that your guests can savour the wonderful aroma when the foil is undone. Cut slices of fish for each person — you can peel off the skin before serving or leave this for each guest to do. A simple mayonnaise, flavoured with tarragon or mint, is the best accompanying sauce for this dish. Pitta breads and a crisp lettuce salad are the only other side dishes needed. Serve chilled dry vermouth instead of wine to drink.

Loup de Mer au Pastis

Sea Bass in a Liqueur Marinade with Avocado Sauce

Serves 4 to 6

Sea bass is a well-flavoured fish much sought by gourmets. When poached, it is not scraped of its scales, but this should be done for a grilled (broiled) dish. It is complemented here by one of the two classic French aperitifs — Ricard, the liquorice-scented *pastis*, or Pernod, with its aroma of aniseed. They are similar in flavour and both develop wonderfully in cooking to create a delightful accent to the flavour of the fish, adding a fennel-like scent and flavour to the dish.

Imperial (Metric)	American
1 sea bass (approx. 2½-3 lb/1.2-1.4 kilos), scaled and gutted	1 sea bass (approx. 2½-3 pounds), scaled and gutted
For the marinade:	**For the marinade:**
3 fl oz (90ml) Ricard *or* Pernod	⅓ cup Ricard *or* Pernod
Juice of 1 lemon	Juice of 1 lemon
3 fl oz (90ml) olive oil	⅓ cup olive oil
Sea salt and freshly ground black pepper	Sea salt and freshly ground black pepper
4 sprigs fresh dill	4 sprigs fresh dill
2 oz (50g) butter	¼ cup butter
For the sauce and garnish:	**For the sauce and garnish:**
2 avocados	2 avocados
2 tomatoes, skinned, seeded and chopped	2 tomatoes, skinned, seeded and chopped
2 cloves garlic, crushed	2 cloves garlic, crushed
Juice of 1 lemon	Juice of 1 lemon
Sea salt and freshly ground black pepper	Sea salt and freshly ground black pepper
1 shallot, finely chopped	1 shallot, finely chopped
1 tablespoon Pernod *or* Ricard	1 tablespoon Pernod *or* Ricard
4 lemon wedges	4 lemon wedges
4 sprigs dill	4 sprigs dill

1 Place the fish in a shallow dish and cover with a mixture of the liqueur, lemon juice, oil and seasoning. Cover and refrigerate for at least 4 hours.

2 Remove the fish and insert the sprigs of dill in the cavity. Make a few slashes at the broadset part of the fish to allow even cooking on both sides.

3 Place the fish in an oiled fish clamp and lay it on the barbecue. Cook for 8 to 10 minutes each side, basting with butter from time to time.

4 For the sauce, peel and dice the avocados, and place in a bowl with the tomato flesh. Mix in the garlic, lemon juice, seasoning, shallot and liqueur. (This sauce could be blended very briefly as a raw *coulis* if preferred.)

5 Serve portions of the cooked fish with a garnish of sauce, lemon wedges and fresh dill. A few crisp lettuce leaves also make a perfect match.

Les Rougets aux Feuilles de Vigne
Red Mullet (Snapper) in Vine Leaves

Here is another recipe making use of this elegant little red fish. Once again it is wrapped in leaves to keep in all the moisture and flavour, but this time the leaves used are not cabbage but vine leaves, which impart a delicate lemony flavour to the fish. Since the leaves themselves are not eaten in this recipe, there is no need to wrap the whole thing in foil. Just place the fish in their wrapping of leaves straight on the barbecue so that the leaves form a protection for the fish. Fresh, blanched vine leaves are best for this dish, but canned ones are an acceptable substitute if you are unable to find a handy grapevine!

Imperial (Metric)	American
For the marinade:	For the marinade:
4 tablespoons olive oil	4 tablespoons olive oil
1 clove garlic, chopped	1 clove garlic, chopped
Juice of 1 lemon	Juice of 1 lemon
Sea salt and freshly ground black pepper	Sea salt and freshly ground black pepper
Good pinch cayenne pepper	Good pinch cayenne pepper
For the fish:	For the fish:
4 red mullet (approx. 8 oz/225g each)	4 red snappers (approx. 8 ounces each)
4 large sprigs fresh dill	4 large sprigs fresh dill
12 blanched vine leaves	12 blanched vine leaves
1 lemon, quartered	1 lemon, quartered

1 Liquidize all the ingredients for the marinade.

2 Wash the fish thoroughly, but there is no need to gut or scrape them. Place them in a shallow dish, pour on the marinade and leave for 1 hour so that the fish absorbs plenty of flavour.

3 Remove the fish from the marinade, lay a sprig of dill on each one, then wrap carefully in vine leaves. Keep them with the loose edges of the leaves on the underside until ready to cook, so that they do not unfold.

4 Place the fish on the grill (broiler) over hot charcoal and cook for 3 to 4 minutes on each side, brushing frequently with marinade. When the leaves are starting to char, the fish is ready. Serve in their leaves, for guests to peel away, with lemon to sprinkle over the fish. Vegetable kebabs — mushrooms, chunks of aubergine (eggplant), tomatoes, slices of courgette (zucchini), and slices of onion and pepper threaded onto skewers — make a good side dish, as do potatoes, wrapped in foil and baked in amongst the coals themselves.

Les Sardines Grillées au Beurre d'Ail

Grilled Sardines with Garlic Butter

This may sound like a very simple dish — as indeed it is — but if you can buy fresh sardines, as is so often the case if you holiday by the sea, there is hardly a barbecue meal to beat it. Although I have suggested garlic butter as the main choice for this meal, there are many others which are just as tasty. I have listed some other combinations at the end of the recipe — why not serve a choice, then even garlic-haters will be happy. Wrap the butters in foil or greaseproof (parchment) paper and freeze. Then you can cut slices as you need them or, if taking them on a picnic with you, they can be packed into your coolbox without fear of arriving at the beach with pools of melted butter dripping from your hamper. It is best to use a fish clamp when cooking small fish such as sardines, to prevent them falling down between the bars of your barbecue — they are too good to waste.

Imperial (Metric)	American
16 sardines	16 sardines
4 oz (100g) garlic cloves, skinned and chopped	⅔ cup garlic cloves, skinned and chopped
2 tablespoons water	2 tablespoons water
Juice of ½ lemon	Juice of ½ lemon
10 oz (300g) butter	1¼ cups butter
Sea salt and freshly ground black pepper	Sea salt and freshly ground black pepper
2 tablespoons olive oil	2 tablespoons olive oil
Seasoned wholemeal flour	Seasoned whole wheat flour

1 Remove the heads from the sardines, but do not scrape or gut them. Wash and pat dry.

2 Boil the garlic in the water for 3 minutes, or until the moisture is almost evaporated and the garlic softened.

3 Blend the garlic, lemon juice, butter and seasoning together in a blender or food processor. Form it into a sausage shape, wrap completely in foil or greaseproof (parchment) paper and freeze.

4 Brush the sardines with oil, dip in seasoned flour, place in a fish clamp and barbecue for just 2 minutes on each side. Serve with slices of butter (paper or foil removed!) laid on each sardine to melt.

Variations:
Anchovy Butter: To the garlic butter add ½ ounce (15g) anchovy fillets, pounded to a paste. Use unsalted butter and do not add extra salt.
Cod's Roe Butter: Process together 4 oz (100g) smoked cod's roe, 8 oz (225g/1 cup) butter, the juice of ½ a lemon and 1 clove chopped garlic.
Colbert Butter: To 8 oz (225g/1 cup) butter, add 1 teaspoon each chopped shallot, parsley, tarragon and chives.
Lobster Butter: To 8 oz (225g/1 cup) butter add the coral or eggs of 1 lobster, pounded.
Oriental Butter: To 8 oz (225g/1 cup) butter add the juice of 1 lemon, ½ oz (15g) fresh ginger, 1 clove garlic and 1 tablespoon soya sauce, liquidized with ½ oz (15g) fresh pineapple.
Curry Butter: To 8 oz (225g/1 cup) butter, add 4 oz (100g/½ cup) finely chopped onion, sautéd in 1 tablespoon vegetable oil with 1 teaspoon curry powder. Process the entire mixture before rolling and freezing.
Pernod Butter: To the garlic butter mixture, add 1 tablespoon *Pernod* and blend well.
Mint Butter: Follow the instructions for Colbert Butter, but replace the tarragon with mint.

Note: If the sardines are especially large, they may take a little longer to cook — about 6 minutes in all — and you and your guests may wish to discard the central bones. You may also wish to scrape them of scales before cooking.
 The barbecued sardines look particularly attractive when served on crisp lettuce leaves or blanched cabbage leaves.

Opposite: *Civet de Langouste au Martini Rosé* (page 157).

Filet de Saumon d'Écosse en Escabèche à la Papaye

Grilled Fillet of Salmon with a Piquant Sauce and Pawpaw (Papaya) Garnish

Illustrated opposite.

This is a delightful dish for a hot Summer's day, combining the clean and subtle taste of fresh salmon with a tropical sauce and the refreshing fruitiness of pawpaw. It is an intriguing combination, certainly, marrying a fish from the northern streams and lakes of the world — Scottish salmon is my very favourite — with the scents and flavours of fruits from the southern hemisphere, but it is a successful partnership, I feel sure you will agree.

Imperial (Metric)	American
For the marinade:	For the marinade:
6 tablespoons dry white wine	6 tablespoons dry white wine
1 tablespoon white wine vinegar	1 tablespoon white wine vinegar
1 tablespoon gin	1 tablespoon gin
Juice of 1 lime	Juice of 1 lime
½ peeled ripe pawpaw	½ peeled ripe papaya
1 teaspoon sweet Dijon mustard	1 teaspoon sweet Dijon mustard
2 fl oz (60ml) natural yogurt	¼ cup plain yogurt
Sea salt and freshly ground black pepper	Sea salt and freshly ground black pepper
Pinch raw cane sugar	Pinch raw cane sugar
For the fish:	For the fish:
4 small fillets salmon (approx. 7 oz/200g each)	4 small fillets salmon (approx. 7 ounces each)
2 tablespoons wholemeal flour	2 tablespoons whole wheat flour
1 fl oz (30ml) vegetable oil	2 tablespoons vegetable oil
For the garnish:	For the garnish:
1 ripe pawpaw, peeled and thinly sliced *or* diced	1 ripe papaya, peeled and thinly sliced *or* diced
½ cucumber, cut in small dice	½ cucumber, cut in small dice
2 diced tomatoes	2 diced tomatoes
1 lime, segmented	1 lime, segmented
2 sprigs dill	2 sprigs dill
Green peppercorns	Green peppercorns

1 Place all the ingredients for the marinade in a blender and process to a smooth cream.

2 Lay the salmon fillets on a shallow dish, cover with the marinade and then with greaseproof (parchment) paper. Marinate for at least 8 hours, turning several times during this period.

3 When ready to cook, wipe the fish dry, dust with flour and then brush with oil. Grill (broil) for 4 minutes on each side, brushing with excess marinade if necessary.

4 Serve hot, with the remaining marinade as a dressing, and garnish the plate with the various fruits, herbs and vegetables, making an attractive presentation.

Les Brochettes de Lotte Dinardaise
Monkfish (Anglerfish) Kebabs with Tarragon Sauce

The monkfish (anglerfish) is as horrible to look at as it is delicious to eat! So outlandish is its appearance that you may find it hard to obtain in all but the best fish markets — and even then it will usually be minus its head — because many fishermen throw it back into the ocean. However, it is highly prized in France for its firm and tasty flesh. It is this firmness which makes it so useful for kebabs, since it will not fall off the skewer as it cooks. However, well-marinated cod will provide a good substitute if your first choice is unobtainable. Fresh tuna, too, is quite superb barbecued on *brochettes*. You could vary your kebabs by alternating white fish with large prawns, scallops or minced fish boulettes (see page 86 for the recipe). But if you want to keep things simple, just a handful of fresh summer vegetables can be cut into chunks and threaded on skewers for a classic barbecue feast.

Imperial (Metric)	American
For the sauce:	For the sauce:
3 fl oz (90ml) fish velouté (page 176) *or* mayonnaise	⅓ cup fish velouté (page 176) *or* mayonnaise
3 fl oz (90ml) sour cream	⅓ cup sour cream
1 tomato, skinned, seeded and chopped	1 tomato, skinned, seeded and chopped
1 teaspoon chopped tarragon	1 teaspoon chopped tarragon
1 teaspoon chopped parsley	1 teaspoon chopped parsley
1 tablespoon tarragon vinegar	1 tablespoon tarragon vinegar
Sea salt and freshly ground black pepper	Sea salt and freshly ground black pepper
For the brochettes:	For the brochettes:
1 lb (450g) monkfish *or* cod fillets	1 pound anglerfish *or* cod fillets
3 fl oz (90ml) olive oil	⅓ cup olive oil
Juice of 1 lemon	Juice of 1 lemon
2 teaspoons Worcestershire sauce *or* 2 teaspoons chopped tarragon	2 teaspoons Worcestershire sauce *or* 2 teaspoons chopped tarragon
Sea salt and freshly ground black pepper	Sea salt and freshly ground black pepper
8 small onions	8 small onions
8 button mushrooms	8 button mushrooms
1 red pepper, seeded and cut into 1-inch (3cm) squares	1 red pepper, seeded and cut into 1-inch squares
1 green pepper, seeded and cut into 1-inch (3cm) squares	1 green pepper, seeded and cut into 1-inch squares
4 small, firm tomatoes, halved	4 small, firm tomatoes, halved
1 lemon, quartered	1 lemon, quartered

1 Blend together all the sauce ingredients and leave for the flavours to develop.
2 Cut the fish fillets into 1-inch (2.5cm) cubes and place in a bowl.
3 Cover them with a mixture of the oil, lemon juice, Worcestershire sauce if using, and seasoning. Leave to marinate for 30 minutes or more.
4 Blanch the onions in boiling water for 1 minute.
5 Select 4 skewers at least 7 inches (18cm) long and spear the fish, alternating with onions, mushrooms, pieces of pepper and tomato.
6 Place on a rack over hot charcoal and cook for 6 to 8 minutes, turning and brushing with marinade frequently.

7   If using tarragon instead of Worcestershire sauce, sprinkle this onto the *brochettes* just before serving.

8   Serve with slices of lemon to squeeze over the fish and vegetables, and the sauce as a dip for the pieces of barbecued food and a choice of *crudités*.

Raie aux Courgettes Provençale

Skate with Courgettes (Zucchini)

Any filleted flat sea fish can be used in this recipe, which combines a simple, baked 'wing' of fish with a rich, hot dressing evocative of the South of France in its flavours and aroma. The dressing can be cooked in advance and reheated in a pan on the barbecue — you will need quite a large grill (broiler) area for this dish.

Imperial (Metric)	American
For the sauce:	For the sauce:
3 oz (75g) butter	⅓ cup butter
1 onion, thinly sliced	1 onion, thinly sliced
4 courgettes, cut into batons	4 zucchini, cut into batons
1 tin anchovies, drained, rinsed and chopped	1 can anchovies, drained, rinsed and chopped
1 clove garlic, crushed	1 clove garlic, crushed
1 tablespoon capers	1 tablespoon capers
Freshly ground black pepper	Freshly ground black pepper
Pinch mixed herbs (optional)	Pinch mixed herbs (optional)
For the fish:	For the fish:
4 skate wings	4 skate wings
Vegetable oil	Vegetable oil
Juice of 1 lemon	Juice of 1 lemon
Sea salt and freshly ground black pepper	Sea salt and freshly ground black pepper
Lemon slices to garnish	Lemon slices to garnish

1   Melt the butter in a large pan. Sauté the onion, without browning, until soft.

2   Stir in the courgettes (zucchini) and cook gently for about 5 minutes.

3   Add the anchovies, garlic and capers. Season with black pepper and add herbs if using. Cook for a minute or two, then remove from heat and allow to cool unless serving the dish immediately.

4   Wash and dry the fish. Lightly oil a large sheet of foil and lay the fish in a single layer on this. Sprinkle with lemon juice and seasoning. Cover with another sheet of oiled foil and crimp the edges tightly. Place this on the barbecue and cook for 7 minutes on each side.

5   When ready to serve, reheat the sauce. Remove the fish from the foil and place on a serving dish. Pour any juices from the fish into the sauce and spoon this over the fish. Serve with slices of lemon.

Variation:
If cooking this dish indoors, the fish in its foil can be baked in the oven at 400°F/200°C (Gas Mark 6) for 20 minutes while the sauce is prepared.

Mignons de Cabillaud aux Champignons Marinés

Minced Cod Morsels with Marinated Mushrooms

These delicate little cakes of raw minced cod, grilled (broiled) over charcoal, are at the other end of the gastronomic scale from the classic, dull fishcake of cooked leftover fish and mashed potato. Served with a piquant mushroom marinade and a tangy watercress dressing, these little morsels of fish bound with cream and onion will appeal to everyone — the sophisticated gourmet looking for something a bit novel from a barbecue meal; children for whom whole pieces of fish may be *too* unusual; and even hardened hamburger-addicts will be tempted into a change by the wonderful aromas wafting from the grill (broiler).

Imperial (Metric)	American
For the mignons:	For the mignons:
1 lb (450g) cod fillets, finely minced	1 pound cod fillets, finely minced
2 egg whites	2 egg whites
4 fl oz (120ml) double cream	½ cup heavy cream
2 oz (50g) onion, finely minced	⅓ cup onion, finely minced
2 oz (50g) wholemeal breadcrumbs	1 cup whole wheat breadcrumbs
2 oz (50g) blanched, chopped almonds	⅓ cup blanched, chopped almonds
Juice of ½ lemon	Juice of ½ lemon
Sea salt and freshly ground black pepper	Sea salt and freshly ground black pepper
Seasoned wholemeal flour	Seasoned whole wheat flour
For the mushrooms:	For the mushrooms:
1 lb (450g) button mushrooms	1 pound button mushrooms
2 tablespoons dry white wine	2 tablespoons dry white wine
Juice of 1 lemon	Juice of 1 lemon
3 tablespoons natural yogurt	3 tablespoons plain yogurt
1 teaspoon honey	1 teaspoon honey
Sea salt and roughly crushed black peppercorns	Sea salt and roughly crushed black peppercorns
For the watercress sauce:	For the watercress sauce:
2 oz (50g) watercress leaves	1 cup watercress leaves
3 fl oz (90ml) mayonnaise	⅓ cup mayonnaise
2 fl oz (60ml) natural yogurt	¼ cup plain yogurt
Sea salt and freshly ground black pepper	Sea salt and freshly ground black pepper
½ oz (15g) chopped gherkins	2 tablespoons chopped dill pickles
1 tablespoon chopped parsley	1 tablespoon chopped parsley

1 In a large bowl, beat together all the ingredients for the mignons (except the flour) until the mixture forms a fairly smooth, firm paste.

2 Sprinkle some seasoned flour onto a board and divide the mixture into 8 lumps of equal size, then flatten in the flour to form small cakes. Chill until required.

3 Clean the mushrooms and trim the stalks level with the caps (the offcuts may be used in another dish).

4 Stir together the ingredients for the mushroom marinade, add the mushrooms and stir well to coat. Leave the mushrooms to marinate for 2 hours.

5 Blend the watercress in a processor or blender with the mayonnaise, yogurt and seasoning. Stir in the chopped gherkin (dill pickle) and parsley.

6 Brush the mignons with a little oil, place them in a folding burger holder and grill (broil) over hot charcoal for 3 minutes on each side.

7 Serve 2 mignons per person, topping one with a spoonful of mushrooms, and the other with a spoonful of dressing. Wedges of tomato and sprigs of watercress make an attractive garnish. Serve with crusty French bread or wholewheat buns.

Cardine aux Graines de Maïs

Megrim and Sweetcorn Stew

This is a simple but substantial supper dish which any camper would be happy to devour in the dusk of a summer's evening after a busy day by the sea. *Cardine* or *limandelle* has a pleasant, bland flavour and pale-yellow colour similar, as one of its French names suggests, to lemon sole (*limande*). It is well suited to a creamy sauce and the milky-sweetness of corn. Other vegetables could be added, according to what is best in the market or what you have to hand — chopped red or green pepper would add a splash of colour, for instance, thinly sliced fennel a more sophisticated flavour and aroma — use your imagination for an infinitely varied meal.

Imperial (Metric)	American
1½ lbs (675g) skinned megrim fillets, sliced into strips	1½ pounds skinned megrim fillets, sliced into strips
2 oz (50g) seasoned wholemeal flour	½ cup seasoned whole wheat flour
2 oz (50g) butter	¼ cup butter
4 oz (100g) button mushrooms, washed	2 cups button mushrooms, washed
6 spring onions, chopped	6 scallions, chopped
6 oz (150g) sweetcorn kernels, fresh or tinned	1 cup corn kernels, fresh or canned
¼ pint (150ml) milk	⅔ cup milk
2 fl oz (60ml) sour cream	¼ cup sour cream
Sea salt and freshly ground black pepper	Sea salt and freshly ground black pepper

1 Toss the fish in seasoned flour.
2 Melt the butter in a large pan. Add the vegetables and cook briefly, stirring constantly.
3 Add the fish and cook for 2 minutes, stirring occasionally.
4 Stir in the milk and cream and season to taste.
5 Simmer gently for 5 minutes, stirring occasionally. Serve with baked potatoes if convenient, or with wholewheat bread and salad.

Maquereau à la Moutarde
Mustard-Grilled Mackerel with Gooseberry and Damson Sauce

Moutarde des Graines — wholegrain mustard — is perfect for this dish, adding piquancy as well as texture to the grilled fish. Choose a grainy mustard with dark seeds as well as light, as it is these which contain the essential oils that give both fire and flavour, much as black pepper is favoured by gourmets over white. Gooseberries and mackerel are a classic combination which I have mellowed with the addition of damsons and a little honey. Since this sauce is served cold it is easy to transport to the site of your barbecue, there to spoon it by the side of a sizzling fish.

Imperial (Metric)	American
For the marinade:	For the marinade:
2 fl oz (60ml) olive oil	¼ cup olive oil
Grated rind and juice of 1 lemon	Grated rind and juice of 1 lemon
1 tablespoon soya *or* Worcestershire sauce	1 tablespoon soy *or* Worcestershire sauce
1 clove garlic, chopped	1 clove garlic, chopped
1 small piece fresh ginger, chopped	1 small piece fresh ginger, chopped
For the sauce:	For the sauce:
8 oz (225g) gooseberries	2 cups gooseberries
4 oz (100g) stoned damsons	1 cup pitted damsons
1 apple, peeled and cored	1 apple, peeled and cored
2 fl oz (60ml) honey	2 tablespoons honey
1 sprig fresh mint	1 sprig fresh mint
Pinch cinnamon	Pinch cinnamon
¼ pint (150ml) water	⅔ cup water
½ oz (15g) cornflour mixed with 2½ fl oz water	½ ounce cornstarch mixed with ⅓ cup water
For the mackerel:	For the mackerel:
4 mackerel (8 oz/225g), cleaned, gutted and filleted butterfly-style	4 medium mackerel (approx. 8 ounces), cleaned, gutted and filleted butterfly-style
1 oz (25g) seasoned wholemeal flour	¼ cup seasoned whole wheat flour
2 oz (50g) wholegrain mustard	¼ cup wholegrain mustard
Vegetable oil	Vegetable oil
Chopped parsley to garnish	Chopped parsley to garnish
12 raw gooseberries to garnish	12 raw gooseberries to garnish
4 twists lemon to garnish	4 twists lemon to garnish

1 Place all the ingredients for the marinade in a blender and purée to a smooth liquid. Set aside.

2 Top and tail the gooseberries and place them in a pan with the damsons, chopped apple, honey, mint, cinnamon and water. Cook gently until the fruit is soft.

3 Blend the fruit very briefly to a rough purée, then return to the pan. Stir in the thickening mixture and reboil for 4 minutes to thicken the sauce and cook the flour. Leave the sauce to cool.

4 While the sauce is cooling, place the mackerel in the marinade and leave for 30 minutes.

5 Drain the mackerel, pat dry with paper towels, coat both sides in seasoned flour, then spread the insides of the fish with half the mustard. Splash each fish with a little oil.

6 Place the fish on the barbecue skin side down and cook for 3 to 4 minutes on each side.

7 Place a sizzling mackerel on each plate, spread with a little more mustard, sprinkle with parsley and

spoon a little sauce by the side of each fish. Decorate the sauce with the fresh gooseberries and the fish with a twist of lemon. Serve at once.

Royan au Boursin

Sprats Stuffed with Garlic Cheese

This dish makes a good 'campfire' supper, although you must take extra care when cooking out of doors — whether over an open fire or a sophisticated purpose-built camping stove — to ensure that your frying pan is stable and is not overfilled with oil. Served with sticks of crusty French bread this is a good, simple family meal, and even children who profess not to like garlic adore the creamy cheesy filling tucked inside these little fish.

Imperial (Metric)	American
1 lb (450g) sprats, cleaned, bones and heads removed	1 pound sprats, cleaned, bones and heads removed
Sea salt and freshly ground black pepper	Sea salt and freshly ground black pepper
6 oz (150g) softened *Boursin* cheese	¾ cup softened *Boursin* cheese
Seasoned wholemeal flour	Seasoned whole wheat flour
2 eggs, beaten	2 eggs, beaten
4 oz (100g) wholemeal breadcrumbs	2 cups whole wheat breadcrumbs
Vegetable oil for frying	Vegetable oil for frying

1 Wash and dry the sprats. Season the insides with salt and pepper.
2 Spread the cavities of the fish with cheese, then reshape around the stuffing.
3 Dust each fish with seasoned flour, then dip in beaten egg and coat in breadcrumbs. Chill until needed.
4 Heat several inches of oil in a deep saucepan. When the oil is hot add the sprats and cook for 4 minutes, until golden. Drain on paper towels and serve at once.

Variation:
Chopped peanuts could be added to the breadcrumbs for an even tastier coating. Small herrings could be used if sprats are unavailable.

  If *Boursin* is unavailable, just beat 1 crushed clove garlic, 1 tablespoon chopped parsley and a small pinch thyme to each 8 oz (225g/cup) of cream cheese — any left over from this recipe is sure to be finished up by your family or guests, spread onto crusty bread.

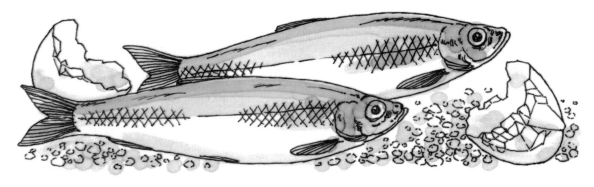

Truite Belle Meunière aux Aubergines et Amandes
Pan-fried Trout with Aubergines (Eggplants) and Almonds

This dish can be cooked in a pan over an open fire, a barbecue or a camping stove. Of course, it is equally good cooked indoors on a normal stove but, since it uses lovely summery ingredients, it is a pleasant outdoor dish. It involves rather more co-ordinating of preparation and cooking than most dishes in this chapter, so enlist a helper to keep things moving — it is certainly worth the little extra effort to prepare a sophisticated dish in less-than-sophisticated conditions!

Imperial (Metric)	American
1 small aubergine	1 small eggplant
2 tomatoes	2 tomatoes
½ cucumber	½ cucumber
4 rainbow trout (approx. 8 oz/225g each) cleaned and gutted	4 rainbow trout (approx. 8 ounces each) cleaned and gutted
2 oz (50g) seasoned wholemeal flour	½ cup seasoned whole wheat flour
4 oz (100g) butter	½ cup butter
2 fl oz (60ml) vegetable oil	¼ cup vegetable oil
1 clove garlic, crushed	1 clove garlic, crushed
½ lemon	½ lemon
2 oz (50g) toasted flaked almonds	⅓ cup toasted slivered almonds
Chopped fresh parsley to garnish	Chopped fresh parsley to garnish

1 Slice the aubergine (eggplant) thinly and sprinkle with plenty of sea salt. Leave for 20 minutes to exude bitter juices then wash well and drain.

2 Skin the tomatoes if your facilities permit, and peel the cucumber if wished. Slice both thinly.

3 Wash and dry the trout, then dust with seasoned flour.

4 Heat half the butter and all the oil in a large pan and sauté the fish for 4 to 5 minutes on each side until cooked. Remove from the pan, place on a warm serving dish and cover with foil to keep warm.

5 Immediately place the aubergine (eggplant) in the pan and cook for 1 minute. Add the tomato and cucumber and cook until just heated through. Spoon this mixture around the trout, aiming to vary the colours of the ingredients attractively. Cover tightly with the foil.

6 Add the rest of the butter to the pan, heat to sizzling point and add the garlic. Cook for 30 seconds then drizzle garlic butter over both fish and vegetables. Add a liberal squeeze of lemon, sprinkle with toasted almonds and chopped parsley, and serve at once. With a helper, this procedure should only take 3 minutes at most from the moment you remove the fish from the pan, so it will still be lovely and hot when it reaches the table.

Finally, here, as promised, is a selection of other dishes which seem particularly suited to outdoor cooking or eating. This list is by no means exhaustive, and depends very much upon your facilities when cooking outdoors or picnicking.

Chapter One:
Cartouches de Sardines Saint Jean de Luz
Rillettes de Maquereau Fumé au Beurre de Normandie
Petits Pains en Mosaique

Chapter Two:
Potage Paysanne Vallée de la Loire aux Truites Fumées
L'Assiette de Thon au Maïs Rochefort
Bisque de Crabe

Chapter Three:
Le Pâté d'Aiglefin au Cognac
Ratatouille de Sole à la Conil
Flamique d'Aiglefin aux Haricots Verts à la Boulonnaise

Chapter Four:
Casserole de Poisson en Croûte Feuilletée

Chapter Five:
Galette de Poisson Levantine
Macédoine de Légumes au Fumet de Truite en Croûte

Chapter Six:
Almost all the salads are suitable, with the possible exception of the *tiede* (warm) ones. You may also wish to save the especially luxurious ones for a formal occasion indoors. In most cases dressings can be taken on your picnic in screwcap jars and added at the last minute to salads transported in plastic containers. You will probably wish to forego the more sophisticated decorative arrangements suggested in the recipes for a simple mix of ingredients, too — don't worry, it will taste just as good!

Chapter Eight:
Moules Camarguaise
Palourdes Frites aux Noisettes
Coquilles Saint-Jacques Charentaise

Chapter Nine:
Brochettes de Fruits de Mer Vieille Bretagne
Omelette aux Crevettes à la Boulonnaise

8 *Les Coquillages*

Shellfish Dishes

I was born in the Vendée region of France in 1917 — my father had been wounded at the battle of the Somme and was convalescing at the military hospital where my mother was a nurse. Later, the family moved back to our homelands near Amiens, then my parents bought a hotel in Le Havre and later still, in 1923, ran a highly successful and acclaimed restaurant in Boulogne. You may think it sounds as though my family led something of a 'travelling circus' existence, and you would not be far wrong for my father ran many different restaurants all over the place during his lifetime. And of course, when I was fully grown my travels took me all over the world, but I have seldom spent too long away from the sea — from the port of La Rochelle near my birthplace, with its nearby islands renowned for their oysters and mussels, to the palm-fringed beaches of the tropics with their exotic harvest of seafood.

Yet I am always drawn back to the region of Poitou, in which lies the Vendée, and am always delighted afresh by the produce of the region, which gives an inventive chef so much scope for creativity — the sea with its clean, plump shellfish; the rivers with their varieties of crayfish, pike and eels; the land with its abundance of good fruit and vegetables, including artichokes, asparagus, cauliflowers and sweet yellow plums; and the dairies which provide thick cream and over twenty different types of butter! Who could resist bringing together the produce of the sea and the land in such a setting — you will find some of the results of this inspiration in this chapter.

Some words of advice may be useful before you begin to cook, however. The first, any good cook will be expecting — any shellfish you buy must be at the very peak of freshness. All shellfish should have a fresh, pleasant smell — do not buy any that smell of iodine or seaweed. They should be tightly shut in their shells or, if slightly open, they should snap shut when touched. Discard any which remain ajar. Conversely, when cooked they should open up — so discard any which remain closed. Never buy shellfish if you are in any doubt about the cleanness of the sea around the coast, but even if you are sure the waters are clean, always scrub the shells *very* thoroughly and remove all traces of seaweed or sand. A good soak in salted water overnight, followed by thorough rinsing, will ensure that you have got rid of all the sand and grit from closed shellfish. If you are opening raw shellfish, such as mussels or oysters, you will probably be using a special knife. Always hold the shellfish in a cloth, and prise the shell open slowly and carefully — you don't want to damage yourself *or* the shellfish! If you are very inexperienced in handling fresh shellfish, don't feel embarrassed to wear protective gloves — better to feel a little silly in the privacy of your own kitchen than to be rushed to hospital with a nasty cut, especially if you are on holiday in a strange country.

One last word of warning — many types of shellfish are seasonal in some, if not all, parts of the world. This may be just that they have a breeding season during which time they are unpalatable, but in some cases — such as with mussels — they are highly poisonous at some times of the year. Always check with your regular supplier at home, who is unlikely to supply you with 'out of season' produce anyway, and if you are on holiday in a different region or country — especially if you are by the sea — be guided by a reputable vendor. Look to see who the locals buy from, and what they are buying, if you cannot speak the language. And if you cannot find out what is good to eat locally at the time of year, *don't* gather shellfish from rocks around your nearest bay — you could at the very least ruin your holiday, at worst you might not be around to regret it.

I have stressed these points because I want you to enjoy the wonderful flavours and varieties of shellfish to the full, not because I want to scare you off them for good. When they are in season, fresh from the ocean into your kitchen, they are a real delight for any seafood enthusiast. Just a little care and forethought is all that is needed to sample this delicious food with no problems at all — and for any good cook or food-lover, care and forethought are all part of the fun. So *bon appetit!*

Moules Camarguaise

Mussels Stewed with Rosé Wine and Garlic

There are many different types of mussel — some small, some large; some tender, some tough. Around the shores of France, small, immature wild mussels are common, but if gathered from shallow-tidal waters they tend to be rather tough. When gathered from the deeper tidal regions, such as parts of Brittany, where the mussels are more permanently covered by water, they are fatter and more tender. But for general purposes the cultivated mussel is your best buy — indeed, this may be the only type you are offered — so do not look down on it just because it is not 'wild'.

Imperial (Metric)	American
1 oz (25g) butter	2 tablespoons butter
1 onion, finely chopped	1 onion, finely chopped
2 cloves garlic, crushed	2 cloves garlic, crushed
2 tablespoons tomato purée	2 tablespoons tomato paste
½ pint (300ml) dry rosé wine	1⅓ cups dry rosé wine
2 tablespoons lemon juice	2 tablespoons lemon juice
3 bayleaves	3 bayleaves
6 pints (3.5 litres) live mussels, cleaned	3½ quarts live mussels, cleaned
Sea salt and freshly ground black pepper	Sea salt and freshly ground black pepper
3 heaped tablespoons chopped fresh parsley	3 heaped tablespoons chopped fresh parsley

1 Melt the butter in a large pan and sauté the onion and garlic until soft, but not browned.

2 Stir in the tomato purée (paste), wine, lemon juice and bayleaves. Bring to the boil, then add the well-scrubbed mussels all at once.

3 Cover the pan and cook over a high heat, shaking the pan occasionally to ensure even cooking. When all the mussels have opened (discard any which remain tightly shut), transfer them to a heated serving dish to keep warm.

4 Reheat the sauce to boiling point, season to taste and pour over the mussels. Sprinkle with parsley and serve at once with hot French bread.

Coquilles Saint-Jacques aux Salicornes
Scallops with Samphire

Illustrated opposite page 113.

The combination of scallops and samphire is absolutely exquisite. Samphire has justly acquired its reputation as the gourmet sea vegetable. Its acid tang stimulates the palate so that any seafood which it is accompanying will be better enjoyed. It can be eaten as a garnish or as a vegetable, and only needs to be blanched for 30 seconds before it is ready to serve. It is still quite difficult to obtain in some places, but it is well worth searching out, so make a nuisance of yourself until you find a shop ready to supply it. Once you and your friends have tried samphire there will be a demand for it!

Imperial (Metric)	American
16 queen scallops	16 queen scallops
2 oz (50g) butter	¼ cup butter
2 oz (50g) chopped shallots	⅓ cup chopped shallots
2 cloves garlic, chopped	2 cloves garlic, chopped
2 tablespoons Noilly Prat vermouth	2 tablespoons Noilly Prat vermouth
4 sprigs fresh thyme	4 sprigs fresh thyme
4 small sprigs tarragon	4 small sprigs tarragon
10 oz (300g) tomatoes, skinned, seeded and diced	1⅔ cups skinned, seeded and diced tomatoes
¼ pint (150ml) sour cream	⅔ cup sour cream
½ teaspoon cornflour	½ teaspoon cornstarch
4 tablespoons double cream	4 tablespoons heavy cream
2 egg yolks	2 egg yolks
Sea salt and freshly ground black pepper	Sea salt and freshly ground black pepper
Pinch cayenne pepper	Pinch cayenne pepper
5 oz (125g) couscous	⅔ cup couscous
¼ pint (150ml) fish stock (page 170)	⅔ cup fish stock (page 170)
1 oz (25g) each of the following: seedless raisins; cooked peas; diced, blanched red peppers; glacé peel; skinned almonds	2 tablespoons each of the following: seedless raisins; cooked peas; diced, blanched red peppers; glacé peel; skinned almonds
1 lb (450g) fresh samphire	1 pound fresh samphire

1 Separate the white scallop meat from the coral. Slice the white laterally.

2 Heat half the butter in a sauté pan and cook the white scallop flesh gently for 1 minute. Remove and keep warm. Cook the corals for 30 seconds and remove. Keep with the white meat in a warm place. Reserve the butter for the couscous.

3 Stir-fry the shallots and garlic in the remaining butter. After 1 minute add the vermouth, herbs and half the diced tomato. Stir in the sour cream and bring back to the boil.

4 In a bowl, mix together the cornflour (cornstarch), double (heavy) cream and egg yolks. Add this mixture to the sauce, bring to the boil and season to taste. Simmer while you prepare the couscous.

5 Rub the couscous with the melted scallop butter, place in a pan with the fish stock and simmer for 3 minutes. Add the raisins, peas, peppers, peel and almonds and season to taste. Place in an ovenproof dish and set in a preheated oven at 400°F/200°C (Gas Mark 6) for 8 minutes to dry and fluff. Stir occasionally with a fork to avoid lumps.

6 On four warmed serving plates, spoon a small pool of sauce. Place a mould of fluffy couscous in the

centre. Surround with slices of white scallop, with a coral on each one. Between each scallop arrange little heaps of blanched samphire and a little diced tomato.

7   Serve the remaining sauce and couscous separately — everyone is sure to want more!

Note: My father and I served this dish at the first Fish Fair we organized jointly at the Buffet de la Halle in 1937. The fair was attended by 3,000 guests at ten successive dinners. Then the presentation of the dish was far more elaborate than it is now. It involved serving the scallops and sauce in their shells, with couscous in separate shells, all mounted on plates and saucers lined with napkins and half-filled with coarse sea salt tinted blue, and decorated with flowers carved from vegetables! You could adapt a little of this exotic presentation by serving the scallops and sauce in one shell and the couscous in another. You will probably be able to purchase scallop shells where you buy your fish — make sure they are well scrubbed before you use them to serve food in.

La Soupe Aux Palourdes Noirmoutier
Brittany-style Clam Soup

Serves 8

Clam soup is a traditional dish in many countries, from the classic clam chowders of New England to this good country recipe from Brittany. Try to obtain small clams for this dish, since they can then be left whole — if you are using large clams, they must either be cut into chunks, or the soup cooked longer. I have placed this soup into this chapter deliberately, since the shellfish are far and away the emphasis of this dish, and it can easily constitute a meal in itself — a sort of shellfish stew.

Imperial (Metric)	American
2 lb 2 oz (1 kilo) small clams	2 pounds small clams
2 oz (50g) butter	¼ cup butter
10 oz (300g) onions, chopped	2 cups chopped onions
2 sticks celery, chopped	2 stalks celery, chopped
1 lb (450g) potatoes, cut into small dice	1 pound potatoes, cut into small dice
2 cloves garlic, chopped	2 cloves garlic, chopped
2 pints (1.15 litres) fish stock (page 170)	5 cups fish stock (page 170)
6 fl oz (180ml) single cream	⅓ cup light cream
Sea salt and freshly ground black pepper	Sea salt and freshly ground black pepper

1   Wash the clams in plenty of water, then place them in a flameproof casserole over a low heat. Heat them, shaking the pan occasionally, until they have all opened.

2   Remove the pan from the heat and drain the clams in a muslin-lined colander, so that the juices are strained and collected.

3   Remove the clam meat and discard the shells.

4   Heat the butter in a large pan and sauté the onions and celery until soft but not browned — about 4 minutes.

5   Add the potatoes and garlic and give them a stir or two, then add the fish stock and strained clam juices.

6   Simmer the soup for about 20 to 25 minutes, or until the potatoes are just tender.

7   Add the clams to the soup and cook without boiling for a further 5 minutes.

8   Stir in the cream and reheat the soup, but do not allow it to boil.

9   Season to taste and serve at once, with plenty of fresh wholemeal (whole wheat) bread.

Coquilles Saint-Jacques Pignoli
Scallops with Pesto

This Southern French dish reflects the Italian influence on the cooking of that region, with its use of three colours of pasta and the classic sauce *pesto*, made with pine nuts, basil and anchovies. It is a simple dish to prepare, yet one which always makes a good impression on guests.

Imperial (Metric)	American
16 fresh scallops	16 fresh scallops
Sea salt and freshly ground black pepper	Sea salt and freshly ground black pepper
3 oz (75g) butter	⅓ cup butter
2 shallots, finely chopped	2 shallots, finely chopped
¼ pint (150ml) white Bordeaux *or* Muscadet	⅔ cup white Bordeaux *or* Muscadet
4 fl oz (120ml) double cream	½ cup heavy cream
4 tomatoes, skinned, seeded and chopped	4 tomatoes, skinned, seeded and chopped
5 oz (150g) dried shell pasta, green, red and wholemeal if possible, *or* all wholemeal	2 cups dried shell pasta — green, red and whole wheat if possible, *or* all whole wheat

For the pesto:	For the pesto:
10 large sprigs fresh basil, chopped	10 large sprigs fresh basil, chopped
2 oz (50g) pine nuts	½ cup pine nuts (pignoli)
1 clove garlic, chopped	1 clove garlic, chopped
2 anchovy fillets	2 anchovy fillets
2 fresh mint leaves, chopped	2 fresh mint leaves, chopped
Freshly ground black pepper	Freshly ground black pepper

1 Separate the white scallop meat from the corals, and cut the white in half laterally. Season with salt and pepper.

2 Heat one third of the butter in a pan and gently sauté the scallops for 4 minutes, then remove and keep warm.

3 In the same pan, heat the remaining butter and sauté the shallots for 2 minutes without browning. Add the wine and simmer for 5 minutes to reduce the liquid.

4 Stir in the cream and simmer for 3 more minutes. Season to taste and add the chopped tomatoes. Keep warm.

5 Bring a large pan of water to the boil and cook the pasta for 8 to 10 minutes, until just pleasantly tender.

6 While the pasta is cooking, place the *pesto* ingredients in a blender with 3 tablespoons of the sauce, and blend to a smooth cream. Add this mixture to the pan of sauce and reheat to boiling point. Check the seasoning — you may choose to add a little more pepper, but the anchovies should have added enough salt to the sauce.

7 Place the pasta shells in the centre of a serving dish. Around this spoon the sauce, and top this with the pieces of scallop. The pasta could be decorated with more chopped tomato and basil, if wished. Serve at once.

Huitres Portugaise au Champagne

Oysters Poached in Champagne with Ginger

This is a true gourmet dish, befitting the luxurious reputation of its two main ingredients, but oysters are remarkably versatile shellfish that can be adapted to make sauces, soups, *hors d'oeuvres*, fillings for *vol au vents*, and yet also can be served with just a simple garnish — or even just as they are, on a bed of crushed ice with no more than an accompaniment of lemon wedges — as an elegant appetizer. Serve this dish on special occasions, to make your guests feel truly indulged!

Imperial (Metric)	American
24 fresh Portuguese oysters	24 fresh flat oysters
2 oz (50g) unsalted butter	¼ cup unsalted butter
2 carrots, cut into thin *julienne*	2 carrots, cut into thin *julienne*
1 leek, cut into thin strips	1 leek, cut into thin strips
½ oz (15g) preserved ginger, cut into thin *julienne*	1 small piece preserved ginger, cut into thin *julienne*
1 spring onion, cut into thin *julienne*	1 scallion, cut into thin *julienne*
2 fl oz (60ml) raspberry vinegar (page 189)	¼ cup raspberry vinegar (page 189)
6 fl oz (180ml) Champagne	¾ cup Champagne
1 shallot, chopped	1 shallot, chopped
1 tablespoon chopped fresh mint	1 tablespoon chopped fresh mint
1 sprig thyme	1 sprig thyme
2 egg yolks	2 egg yolks
3 tablespoons sour cream	3 tablespoons sour cream
¼ teaspoon cornflour	¼ teaspoon cornstarch
Pinch cayenne pepper	Pinch cayenne pepper
Sea salt	Sea salt
4 sprigs chervil	4 sprigs chervil
Blanched samphire, to garnish	Blanched samphire, to garnish
Toasted wholemeal bread	Toasted whole wheat bread

1 Open the oysters over a muslin-lined bowl, so that you collect the strained juices. Place each oyster in a half-shell and arrange on a large serving plate. (The plate could be lined with coarse sea salt if wished, to hold the oysters steady.)

2 In a small pan, heat the butter and gently sauté the carrots, leek, ginger and spring onion (scallion) for 1 minute.

3 Remove the pan from the heat and lift the *julienne* onto a plate with a slotted spoon.

4 Place the pan back on a gentle heat and add the vinegar, Champagne, shallot and herbs. Boil quickly for 6 minutes to reduce the volume by half.

5 In a bowl, beat together the egg yolks, cream and cornflour (cornstarch). Beat this mixture into the boiling liquid and cook for 3 minutes, stirring, to produce a smooth, creamy sauce. Stir in the oyster juices, taste and season with cayenne and salt.

6 Place the oysters under a hot grill (broiler) for a minute to reheat, then spoon a little sauce over each one and place back under the grill (broiler) to glaze briefly.

7 Decorate the dish with the *julienne* of vegetables, sprigs of chervil and fronds of blanched samphire. Serve hot with toast to accompany this rich and delicious dish.

Pot-Pourri de Saint-Jacques à la Conil

A Medley of Scallops and Vegetables

Illustrated opposite page 176.

Saint James (*Saint Jacques*) was one of the fishermen who became apostles of Jesus. He was beheaded by King Herod and the story is that his remains were taken to Spain. He is the patron saint of shellfish and shellfishermen, and pilgrims to his shrine at Santiago de Compostela used to wear scallop shells as symbols of their journey. Now the connection with his patronage is best reflected by the use of his name in any French dish using scallops. I have called this dish a pot-pourri because its combination of pretty colours, and its wonderful aroma, make it almost an edible version of the traditional floral combinations used to decorate and scent a room.

Imperial (Metric)	American
8 oz (225g) rice vermicelli	2 cups rice vermicelli
16 scallops	16 scallops
2 fl oz (50ml) vegetable oil	¼ cup vegetable oil
3 oz (75g) onion, quartered and sliced	1 small onion, quartered and sliced
1 stick celery, chopped	1 stalk celery, chopped
2 sticks fennel, sliced	2 stalks fennel, sliced
2 cloves garlic, chopped	2 cloves garlic, chopped
½ oz (15g) fresh ginger, shredded	1 tablespoon fresh ginger, shredded
4 oz (100g) mangetout peas, trimmed	1 cup snow peas, trimmed
1 teaspoon cornflour	1 teaspoon cornstarch
3 fl oz (90ml) dry white wine	⅓ cup dry white wine
3 fl oz (90ml) fish stock (page 170)	⅓ cup fish stock (page 170)
3 oz (75g) white mushrooms, sliced	1½ cups sliced white mushrooms
8 oz (225g) baby corn cobs, tinned	1⅓ cups baby corn cobs, canned
Pinch saffron	Pinch saffron
Sea salt and freshly ground black pepper	Sea salt and freshly ground black pepper
Juice of 1 lemon	Juice of 1 lemon

1 Soak the rice vermicelli in boiling water for 15 minutes. Drain well, then stir-fry in a little vegetable oil. Keep warm until needed.

2 Shell and clean the scallops, separating the white meat from the coral and slicing the white part laterally. Set aside.

3 Heat the oil in a large pan or wok and stir-fry the onion, celery, fennel, garlic, ginger and peas for 1 minute.

4 In a bowl, combine the cornflour (cornstarch) with the wine and stock. Stir this into the pan and cook for 5 minutes, stirring constantly.

5 Add the scallops, mushrooms, corn, saffron and seasoning. Reheat for 3 or 4 minutes, sprinkle with lemon juice and serve over the vermicelli in individual bowls.

Variation:
To enhance the pot-pourri impression, the bowls could be decorated with a few nasturtium flowers — well-washed — which are good to eat.

Les Nouilles aux Praires Cap-Ferrat

Clam Sauce with Pasta

Clams and pasta is a classic match, to be found in many cuisines, and especially popular in America. This is a simple supper dish with a touch of class. The combination of colours and flavours evokes all the romance of the *Côte d'Azur*, and the high standard of canned clams means that you can recreate a summer mood any time of the year.

Imperial (Metric)	American
1 tablespoon olive oil	1 tablespoon olive oil
1 large onion, finely chopped	1 large onion, finely chopped
8 clams, fresh *or* tinned	8 clams, fresh *or* canned
10 oz (300g) tomato purée	1¼ cups tomato paste
1 teaspoon dried mixed herbs	1 teaspoon dried mixed herbs
4 fl oz (120ml) dry white wine	½ cup dry white wine
1 clove garlic, crushed	1 clove garlic, crushed
Pinch paprika	Pinch paprika
12 oz (350g) fresh green tagliatelle	3 cups fresh green tagliatelle
4 oz (100g) grated Gruyère cheese	1 cup grated Gruyère cheese

1 Heat the olive oil in a pan and sauté the chopped onion until translucent.

2 Add the clams, together with the tomato purée (paste), herbs, wine and garlic. Stir together well and season with salt, pepper and paprika. Simmer gently for 10 minutes.

3 While the sauce is cooking, bring a large pan of water to the boil and cook the pasta until it is just tender. Drain well.

4 By the time the pasta is cooked, the sauce should have cooked down to a medium-thick consistency. (If it is still too runny, you may wish to thicken it slightly with a slurry of 2 teaspoons cornflour (cornstarch) in 5 tablespoons water, stirred into the boiling sauce and cooked for 2 minutes.)

5 Serve the pasta on a serving dish or individual plates, topped with the sauce and a sprinkling of Gruyère cheese.

Moules au Saffran Méridional
Mussels in a Saffron and Martini Sauce

Serves 8

Mussels should always be bought alive, and care should be taken to clean their shells thoroughly of any sand, seaweed and 'beard' from the mussel. Some countries have seasonal mussels, outside which time they are unpleasant or even dangerous to eat — check with your supplier whether this applies to your region. *Moules Marinière* is the classic French dish using this plentiful and inexpensive shellfish, in which they are cooked in a simple sauce of white wine, shallots, parsley and butter, but each region has its special variations on this theme. *Boulonnaise* uses wine vinegar and a white sauce along with the herbs and shallots; *Dieppoise* amalgamates a cider-based cooking liquid with cream; *Provençale* adds garlic and a topping of toasted breadcrumbs. Here is my version of a *Méridional* style dish, from the *Midi* region of France.

Imperial (Metric)	American
4 pints (2 litres) mussels	12 cups mussels
2 oz (50g) butter	¼ cup butter
2 shallots, chopped	2 shallots, chopped
¼ pint (15ml) Martini rosé	1¼ cups Martini rosé
¼ pint (150ml) fish stock (page 170)	1¼ cups fish stock (page 170)
1 sprig thyme	1 sprig thyme
1 good pinch saffron threads	1 good pinch saffron threads
8 oz (225g) white mushrooms, sliced	3 cups sliced white mushrooms
2 egg yolks	2 egg yolks
¼ pint (150ml) double *or* sour cream	⅔ cup heavy *or* sour cream
½ teaspoon cornflour	½ teaspoon cornstarch
Sea salt and freshly ground black pepper	Sea salt and freshly ground black pepper
2 tablespoons chopped fresh parsley	2 tablespoons chopped fresh parsley
1 tablespoon chopped fresh tarragon	1 tablespoon chopped fresh tarragon

1 Clean the mussels thoroughly, as described above.

2 In a large pan, heat the butter and sauté the shallots for 3 minutes without browning. Add the wine, stock, thyme and saffron. Boil for 10 minutes.

3 Add the cleaned mussels and the mushrooms to the pan. Cook for 6 minutes, by which time all the mussels should have opened. Discard any that are still closed.

4 Strain the sauce into a smaller pan. Discard one shell from each mussel and place the full half-shells on warmed soup plates to keep warm.

5 Bring the sauce back to the boil. In a bowl, beat together the egg yolks, cream and cornflour (cornstarch); stir this into the boiling liquid and reheat and cook for 3 minutes, stirring, to produce a thick, creamy sauce. Season to taste. Strain the sauce.

6 Spoon the sauce over the mussels, sprinkle with the chopped herbs and serve at once, with lots of crusty French bread to mop up the sauce.

Coquilles Bretonne

Scallops Poached in Wine and Cream

This delicate creamy sauce can provide the base for many variations, all of which complement scallops beautifully. Mushrooms can be added, and the whole dish sprinkled with grated cheese and browned; aromatic herbs may be added; saffron, garlic or tomato purée will give a Provençale flavour; some chefs sauté the scallops in butter and then flambé them in brandy before adding the stock and cream; some garnish them with seedless white grapes and serve the dish chilled — the list is endless! This basic recipe will give imaginative cooks a wealth of dishes at their fingertips.

Imperial (Metric)	American
8 fresh scallops	8 fresh scallops
2 oz (50g) butter	¼ cup butter
2 shallots, finely chopped	2 shallots, finely chopped
6 fl oz (180ml) Muscadet	¾ cup Muscadet
3 fl oz (90ml) fish stock (page 170)	⅓ cup fish stock (page 170)
Sea salt and freshly ground black pepper	Sea salt and freshly ground black pepper
Pinch cayenne	Pinch cayenne
½ level teaspoon cornflour	½ level teaspoon cornstarch
2 egg yolks	2 egg yolks
4 fl oz (120ml) sour cream	½ cup sour cream
Pinch ground thyme	Pinch ground thyme
Juice of ¼ lemon	Juice of ¼ lemon
2 oz (50g) dry wholemeal breadcrumbs (optional)	¾ cup dry whole wheat breadcrumbs (optional)
1 tablespoon fresh chopped parsley	1 tablespoon fresh chopped parsley

1 Rinse and drain the scallops, separate the whites from the corals and cut the white meal in half laterally.

2 Heat the butter in a shallow pan and sauté the shallots for 2 minutes without browning. Add the scallop pieces, wine, stock and seasoning and poach the scallops for 3 minutes without allowing the liquid to boil. Drain the scallops and place in clean, warm scallop shells or shell-shaped dishes and keep warm.

3 In a bowl, beat together the cornflour (cornstarch), egg yolks, cream and thyme. Strain the wine and fish stock into a clean pan and bring to the boil. Stir in the cream mixture and cook, stirring, for 4 minutes to produce a thin, smooth sauce. Check the seasoning and add lemon juice to taste.

4 Pour the sauce over the scallops and place under a hot grill (broiler) to glaze. Serve at once, sprinkled with chopped parsley. Alternatively, sprinkle with breadcrumbs before placing under the grill (broiler).

Note: For a traditional and decorative touch — which also ensures a neat border to your scallop shells — pipe a ribbon of *duchesse* (page 88) potato around the edge of each shell, and dry out a little under the grill (broiler) before adding the scallops and sauce.

Mouclade aux Crevettes sur un Nid de Nouilles Vertes

Mussels and Prawns (Shrimp) on a Bed of Green Noodles

You will find, along the coast of France, many ways of preparing mussels. As well as the basic *Moules Marinières*, cooked in white wine with a hint of vinegar, there is the creamy mixture favoured in Normandy and Brittany which makes use of the wonderful dairy produce of these regions, and the rich flavours of the South of France marrying mussels with tomatoes, garlic and saffron — and many other styles and variations are to be found between these two extremes! In this recipe we will stay in the South by adding plump Mediterranean prawns (jumbo shrimp) to the dish, and by serving it on a bed of green pasta, reflecting the Italian influence on the cooking of that region. But we will tip our hats to the North by enriching our recipes with cream, good butter, and Gruyère cheese. The resulting harmony of flavours and influences is a sheer delight.

Imperial (Metric)	American
4 pints (2 litres) mussels	2 quarts mussels
1 medium onion, chopped	1 medium onion, chopped
1 small carrot, chopped	1 small carrot, chopped
4 fl oz (120ml) white Bordeaux	½ cup white Bordeaux
4 fl oz (120ml) fish stock (page 170)	½ cup fish stock (page 170)
1 sprig thyme	1 sprig thyme
4 sprigs tarragon	4 sprigs tarragon
2 cloves garlic, chopped	2 cloves garlic, chopped
Sea salt and freshly ground black pepper	Sea salt and freshly ground black pepper
5 oz (125g) sliced button mushrooms	2½ cups sliced button mushrooms
½ teaspoon cornflour	½ teaspoon cornstarch
3 fl oz (90ml) double cream	⅓ cup heavy cream
1 teaspoon curry power	1 teaspoon curry power
8 oz (225g) flat green noodles	4 cups flat green noodles
2 oz (50g) butter	¼ cup butter
2 oz (50g) grated Gruyère cheese	½ cup grated Gruyère cheese
12 Mediterranean prawns, shelled	12 jumbo shrimp, shelled
1 tablespoon chopped parsley	1 tablespoon chopped parsley

1 Wash the mussels in several changes of water, removing any seaweed attached to the shells.

2 Place the onion, carrot and cleaned mussels in a pan and cover with half the wine and all the fish stock. Add the thyme, tarragon, garlic and seasoning. Marinate the mushrooms in the remaining wine.

3 Bring the liquid to a boil and simmer for 5 minutes. All the mussels should have opened by this time, so discard any which are still shut.

4 Strain the liquid through a fine cloth into a clean saucepan. Remove one shell from each mussel and keep them warm while you prepare the rest of the dish.

5 Boil the stock for 10 minutes. In a bowl, blend together the cornflour (cornstarch) and cream, then stir this gradually into the liquid to make a creamy sauce. Simmer this sauce for 4 minutes, so that the starch is completely cooked. Season to taste, and add curry powder.

6 While the sauce is cooking, bring a large pan of salted water to the boil and cook the noodles until tender. Drain and toss with butter and grated cheese.

7 Place a portion of noodles on four warmed serving plates and decorate attractively with mussels and prawns. Drizzle a little sauce over each portion and serve the rest separately.

8 Decorate each dish with a few of the marinated mushrooms and their marinade, and sprinkle with chopped parsley. Serve at once.

Variations:
An alternative presentation would be to toss the mushrooms in the pasta, contrasting hot and cold appealingly. Place the noodles in the centre of a serving dish, drizzle a ribbon of sauce around the edge and decorate this with mussels and prawns. Sprinkle each mussel with parsley.

Palourdes Frites aux Noisettes
Clams in a Crisp Nut Coating

Here is a recipe using another member of the clam family — the previous clam recipe made use of the 'warty venus' clam (*Venus verrucosa*) whereas here we are using the 'smooth venus' (*Callista chione*), which is slightly larger and thus better suited to this type of dish. When coated in a nutty outer layer and fried, and served with a piquant sauce in which to dip them, they make a delicious appetizer. Be sure to heat the oil in a deep pan, so there is no chance of spilling or splashing — and ensure that it is heated to 350°F/180°C so that your clams are crisply coated while the insides remain succulent.

Imperial (Metric)	American
36 shelled clams	36 shucked clams
2 oz (50g) seasoned wholemeal flour	½ cup seasoned whole wheat flour
2 eggs, beaten	2 eggs, beaten
2 oz (50g) fresh wholemeal breadcrumbs	1 cup fresh whole wheat breadcrumbs
2 oz (50g) crushed mixed nuts	½ cup crushed mixed nuts
Vegetable oil for frying	Vegetable oil for frying
1 crisp lettuce, washed	1 crisp lettuce, washed
1 lemon, quartered	1 lemon, quartered
4 tomatoes, quartered	4 tomatoes, quartered
1 recipe Cressonnière sauce (page 184)	1 recipe Cressonnière sauce (page 184)

1 Dust the clams in seasoned flour.
2 Dip in beaten egg, then toss in the mixed breadcrumbs and nuts.
3 Heat the oil in a large pan (*friture*) and fry the clams for 4 to 5 minutes, until golden-brown outside and tender within. Drain on paper towels.
4 Serve on a bed of lettuce, garnished with lemon and tomato, and with a bowl of sauce in which to dip the clams.

Variation:
Sauce Rouille (page 181) could be served as a second or alternative sauce.

Coquilles Saint-Jacques Charentaise
Nutty Scallops in a Garlic and Pernod Butter

Fresh scallops are visually most appealing, with their white flesh and orange roes nestling in fluted, pinkish-brown shells. These shells are so decorative that they give their shape to the traditional lace hats worn by the fishwives of Boulogne on ceremonial occasions. Not only that, but they serve as an attractive base on which to present many fish dishes — and indeed fine porcelain works of art now imitate life in shape, if not in colouring.

Imperial (Metric)	American
4 fresh scallops	4 fresh scallops
Seasoned wholemeal flour	Seasoned whole wheat flour
1 egg, beaten	1 egg, beaten
2 oz (50g) wholemeal breadcrumbs	1 cup whole wheat breadcrumbs
2 oz (50g) crushed walnuts and peanuts	½ cup crushed walnuts and peanuts
2 oz (50g) butter	¼ cup butter
2 tablespoons vegetable oil	2 tablespoons vegetable oil
1 clove garlic, roughly chopped	1 clove garlic, roughly chopped
2 tablespoons Pernod	2 tablespoons Pernod
2 tablespoons lemon juice	2 tablespoons lemon juice
Chopped fresh parsley to garnish	Chopped fresh parsley to garnish

1 Open and clean the scallops. Reserve the 4 deep shells. Separate the white flesh and the corals. Slice the white parts.
2 Dust the pieces of scallop in seasoned flour, coat in beaten egg and then in the mixed nuts and breadcrumbs.
3 Heat the butter and oil together in a large pan. Sauté the garlic gently for 1 minute.
4 Toss the scallops in the butter and oil for 2 minutes, until golden and sizzling.
5 Just before serving, stir in the Pernod and lemon juice, cook for 1 minute, then check the seasoning.
6 Pile the mixture into the scallop shells and sprinkle with parsley. Serve at once.

9

Les Crustaces:
'Princes de l'Océan'

Crustacean Dishes

What a wealth of choice can be found in the nets and lobster pots of the Normandy coast. It is hard to imagine, watching the fishermen of this region going about their work in a way unchanged for centuries, that things have ever been different, yet this is a coastline that has seen brutal times — from the setting forth of the boats of William the Conqueror to the landing of the great Allied Invasion force in 1944. The towns themselves bear the scars — many have been almost entirely rebuilt since World War II — but the sea shows no wounds and the way of life it supports has healed as if it had never been interrupted.

Fish and shellfish of many kinds flourish along the hundreds of kilometres of coast, but not for nothing are those delicious crustaceans langoustines known widely as *demoiselles de Caën* or *de Cherbourg* — the 'young ladies' of the towns — since the fairest and most tender surely come from this region of France, as is true of many other crustaceans.

We should perhaps pause here in an attempt to clarify a situation which can be confusing, regarding the names of the seafood we shall be covering in this chapter.

Langouste is the French name for *Palinurus elephas*, which is known in Brtain as crawfish, and in America as rock lobster. It is also sometimes called spiny lobster, and this is perhaps the best description of this creature, which is lobster-like in size but has spiny growths at the head instead of claws. We shall be referring to it as langouste for British readers and rock lobster for American cooks.

Langoustine has a variety of different names throughout the world. In America it is known as crayfish. Its Latin name of *Nephrops norvegicus* might give you the clue that it is often called Norwegian lobster, but it is also known as Dublin Bay prawn or — usually in peeled form — as scampi, though experts will tell you that the *scampo* of the Adriatic is a slightly different species. Langoustines look like large prawns with long claws which are seldom eaten — only the tail meat is used. We have used the term langoustine (or crayfish for Amcrican readers) to indicate the whole crustacean or scampi to indicate the peeled tail meat if ready-bought.

Ecrevisse is what we in France call *Astacus astacus*, and which is known in both Britain and America as crayfish, to confuse matters. This looks like a miniature lobster, but is a freshwater crustacean. It is sometimes called crawdad in America, but we shall use the term crayfish throughout. American cooks uncertain of the fish in question should look at the French recipe title.

Crevettes are prawns or shrimps in France, their size being indicated by the following word *Mediterranée* for king prawns, *rose* for ordinary prawns and *grise* for shrimps. The American terminology ignores the differentiation of size by calling all this type

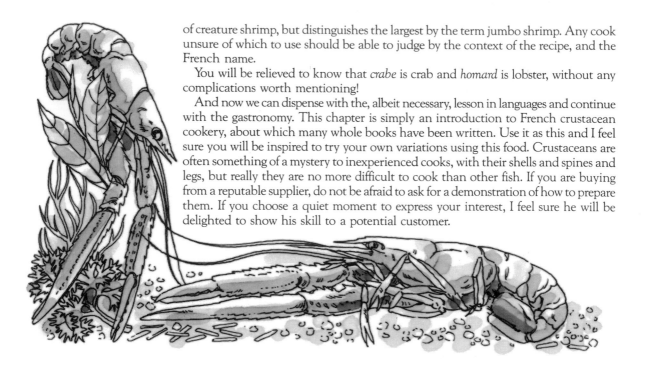

of creature shrimp, but distinguishes the largest by the term jumbo shrimp. Any cook unsure of which to use should be able to judge by the context of the recipe, and the French name.

You will be relieved to know that *crabe* is crab and *homard* is lobster, without any complications worth mentioning!

And now we can dispense with the, albeit necessary, lesson in languages and continue with the gastronomy. This chapter is simply an introduction to French crustacean cookery, about which many whole books have been written. Use it as this and I feel sure you will be inspired to try your own variations using this food. Crustaceans are often something of a mystery to inexperienced cooks, with their shells and spines and legs, but really they are no more difficult to cook than other fish. If you are buying from a reputable supplier, do not be afraid to ask for a demonstration of how to prepare them. If you choose a quiet moment to express your interest, I feel sure he will be delighted to show his skill to a potential customer.

Langoustines au Pastis
Langoustines (Crayfish) in Pastis

As we have seen, langoustines have a variety of names, depending on where they are found, and their method of presentation. But whether they are to be enjoyed as Norwegian lobsters as their Latin name *Nephrops norvegicus* suggests, or as Dublin Bay prawns, or ready peeled as scampi, they are always a delicious and luxurious food to be cooked and enjoyed with care and respect. This recipe teams their delicate texture and flavour with a hint of aniseed and a swirl of cream, for a most appealing appetizer.

Imperial (Metric)	American
1 lb (450g) peeled langoustine tails (scampi)	2 cups peeled crayfish tails (scampi)
2 oz (50g) seasoned wholemeal flour	½ cup seasoned whole wheat flour
2 oz (50g) butter	¼ cup butter
1 small shallot, chopped	1 small shallot, chopped
2 tablespoons pastis (Ricard *or* Pernod)	2 tablespoons pastis (Ricard *or* Pernod)
¼ pint (150ml) fish stock (page 170)	⅔ cup fish stock (page 170)
1 teaspoon aniseeds	1 teaspoon aniseeds
1 small sprig dill	1 small sprig dill
3 fl oz (90ml) cream	6 tablespoons cream
Juice of ¼ lemon	Juice of ¼ lemon
Sea salt	Sea salt
Pinch cayenne pepper	Pinch cayenne pepper
4 langoustine heads, to garnish (if fresh have been used)	4 crayfish heads, to garnish (if fresh have been used)
4 slices kiwi fruit	4 slices kiwi fruit
4 slices fresh strawberry	4 slices fresh strawberry

1 Toss the scampi in seasoned flour, shaking off any excess.
2 Heat the butter in a shallow pan and sauté the scampi for 1 minute. Add the chopped shallot and cook for a further 30 seconds, tossing and stirring.
3 Pour on the pastis and set alight. Immediately add the fish stock to extinguish the flame.
4 Simmer the mixture for 2 minutes then remove the scampi with a slotted spoon and keep warm.
5 Add the aniseed and dill to the pan and simmer for 10 minutes to reduce.
6 Stir in the cream and lemon juice, check the seasoning and add a pinch of cayenne. Strain the sauce.
7 Pour 3 tablespoons of sauce onto each warm serving plate and decorate with scampi and the garnishes.

Note: If fresh scampi (langoustines/crayfish) are used, allow 8 ounces (225g) per portion.

Les Crevettes Méditerranée aux Graines de Sésame
Honeyed King Prawns (Jumbo Shrimp) with Sesame Seeds

King prawns (jumbo shrimp) are a favourite appetizer in most top restaurants, but are so easily spoiled by overcooking or careless presentation that many people never get the chance to taste them at their best. This dish is quite perfect when prepared with fresh prawns (shrimp), and can equally make the more easily obtained frozen varieties into a gourmet treat.

Imperial (Metric)	American
1½ lb (700g) whole king prawns, *or* 1 lb (450g) peeled	1½ pounds whole jumbo shrimp, *or* 1 pound peeled
1 tablespoon cornflour	1 tablespoon cornstarch
5 oz (125g) seasoned self-raising wholemeal flour	1¼ cups seasoned self-rising whole wheat flour
Large pinch ground ginger	Large pinch ground ginger
½ pint (300ml) water	1⅓ cups water
1 egg, beaten	1 egg, beaten
Vegetable oil for deep frying	Vegetable oil for deep frying
1 tablespoon walnut oil	1 tablespoon walnut oil
2 tablespoons clear honey	2 tablespoons clear honey
2 oz (50g) toasted sesame seeds	⅓ cup toasted sesame seeds

1 If the prawns (shrimp) are whole, peel carefully and remove the vein from along the back. Toss them in cornflour (cornstarch).
2 In a bowl beat together the seasoned flour, ginger, water and beaten egg to form a smooth batter.
3 Heat the oil in a deep pan to approximately 400°F/200°C.
4 Dip the prawns in batter a few at a time and fry them for just 2 minutes. Drain on kitchen paper towels and keep warm until all the batches are cooked.
5 Heat the walnut oil in a small pan, add the honey and cook for 1 minute to a syrupy consistency. Toss the prawns (shrimp) in this mixture to coat them, then roll them in sesame seeds.
6 Serve with lemon wedges. A bowl of sweet and sour sauce makes a good accompaniment — provide cocktail sticks on which to spear the prawns (shrimp) before dipping in the sauce.

Roulade de Crabe Avocadine Tropicale
Crab and Avocado Roulade

Illustrated opposite page 161.

This dish is as exotic in flavour as it is beautiful to look at. It takes a little while to prepare, but can be made in advance and is a wonderful appetizer for an important dinner party. The flavours of the rosé Martini and the mango enhance that of the crab, and the contrasting pink and green mousses are quite delightful. You could use this dish to set the theme for your meal — pale pink and pale green make a charming colour scheme for a summer evening's meal. Choose other foods to continue the effect, and select linen, china, candles and flowers in the same scheme. Your guests will be enchanted!

Imperial (Metric)	American
For the crab mousse:	For the crab mousse:
1 oz (25g) butter	2 tablespoons butter
1 oz (25g) vegetable oil	2 tablespoons vegetable oil
1 shallot, chopped	1 shallot, chopped
1 clove garlic, crushed	1 clove garlic, crushed
2 tablespoons tomato purée	2 tablespoons tomato paste
4 strands saffron, finely crushed	4 strands saffron, finely crushed
1 oz (25g) wholemeal flour	¼ cup whole wheat flour
¼ oz (7g) agar-agar powder	1 tablespoon agar-agar powder
3 fl oz (90ml) boiling water *or* fish stock	⅓ cup boiling water *or* fish stock
4 fl oz (120ml) rosé Martini	½ cup rosé Martini
3 oz (75g) fresh mango pulp	½ cup fresh mango pulp
Sea salt and freshly ground black pepper	Sea salt and freshly ground black pepper
½ teaspoon curry powder	½ teaspoon curry powder
2 fl oz (60ml) natural yogurt	¼ cup plain yogurt
5 oz (125g) cooked brown crab meat	1¼ cups cooked brown crab meat
4 oz (100g) cooked white crab meat	1 cup cooked white crab meat
2 fl oz (60ml) double cream, whipped	¼ cup heavy cream, whipped
For the avocado mousse:	For the avocado mousse:
Flesh from 2 medium avocados, mashed	Flesh from 2 medium avocados, mashed
2 fl oz (60ml) natural yogurt	¼ cup plain yogurt
Sea salt and freshly ground black pepper	Sea salt and freshly ground black pepper
Pinch cayenne pepper	Pinch cayenne pepper
1 oz (25g) dry spinach purée	¼ cup dry spinach purée
Juice and finely grated rind of 1 lime	Juice and finely grated rind of 1 lime
½ oz (15g) agar-agar powder	2 tablespoons agar-agar powder
3 fl oz (90ml) boiling water *or* fish stock	⅓ cup boiling water *or* fish stock
3 fl oz (90ml) double cream, whipped	⅓ cup heavy cream, whipped
For decoration:	For decoration:
1 avocado	1 avocado
8 crab claws	8 crab claws
1 lime	1 lime
1 mango	1 mango

1 Heat the butter and oil in a pan and sauté the shallot and garlic for 2 minutes without browning.

2 Add the tomato purée (paste) and cook gently for 4 minutes, then stir in the saffron. Sprinkle on the flour and stir to absorb any surplus fat. Cook for 2 minutes over a low heat.

3 Boil the agar-agar in the water for 5 minutes, then stir this into the sauce. Add the Martini and stir well.

4 Add the mango to the mixture, season with salt, pepper and curry powder, then remove from the heat.

5 Stir in the yogurt and the crab. Blend in a food processor or blender and refrigerate. When the mixture is quite cold, fold in the whipped cream.

6 In a bowl, mix the mashed avocado with the yogurt. Season. Stir in the spinach purée and the lime juice and rind.

7 Dissolve the agar-agar in the boiling water or fish stock, then stir this into the avocado mixture, beating well to distribute the setting agent evenly. Allow the mixture to cool, then fold in the whipped cream.

8 To assemble the roulade, spread the crab mixture on a sheet of greaseproof (parchment) paper into an oblong shape, approx. 14×8 inches (35×20cm). Place in the freezer for 10 minutes.

9 Spread the avocado mixture onto another sheet of greaseproof (parchment) paper into an oblong shape, approx. 14×3 inches (35×8cm). With the help of the paper, roll this oblong widthways into a solid sausage shape as tightly as possible. Chill in the freezer for 10 minutes.

10 Remove the mousses from the freezer, place the avocado 'sausage' in the centre of the crab mousse and mould the crab mixture around it to form a large sausage shape. Neaten the ends, then wrap in greaseproof (parchment) paper or foil and refrigerate until completely set.

11 To serve, peel off the wrapping and cut the roulade into slices about ½-inch (1cm) thick. Arrange on individual plates with peeled avocado slices, cracked crab claws, twists of lime and slices of mango. Serve with a dill or mint flavoured yogurt dressing.

Crevettes au Poivre Vert

King Prawns (Jumbo Shrimp) in a Peppercorn Sauce

This is a light and tasty dish which could be served as an entrée or as a simple supper with the addition of rice or couscous to make it more complete. You might think that a mere eight green peppercorns would be too little, but these delicious little items have a wonderful flavour which permeates the sauce as soon as they are added, and eight is quite sufficient. They are expensive to buy, so it is comforting to know that a little goes a long way.

Imperial (Metric)	American
1 lb (450g) king prawns	1 pound jumbo shrimp
1 oz (25g) butter	2 tablespoons butter
1 fl oz (30ml) olive oil	2 tablespoons olive oil
1 small onion, sliced	1 small onion, sliced
1 small carrot, sliced	1 small carrot, sliced
1 stick celery, chopped	1 stalk celery, chopped
2 cloves garlic, crushed	2 cloves garlic, crushed
2 tablespoons dry white wine *or* white port	2 tablespoons dry white wine *or* white port
¼ pint (150ml) water	⅔ cup water
2 oz (50g) tomato purée	¼ cup tomato paste
Pinch saffron	Pinch saffron
1 teaspoon cornflour	1 teaspoon cornstarch
4 fl oz (120ml) double cream	½ cup heavy cream
Sea salt	Sea salt
8 tinned green peppercorns	8 canned green peppercorns
Cucumber to garnish	Cucumber to garnish

1 Peel the prawns (shrimp). Heat the butter and oil in a pan and toss the prawns (shrimp) for 2 minutes. Remove with a slotted spoon and keep warm while making the sauce.

2 In the same pan sauté the vegetables and garlic for 5 minutes. Stir in the wine or port, water, tomato purée (paste) and saffron. Bring to the boil and cook for 6 minutes to reduce and thicken the sauce slightly.

3 Beat the cornflour (cornstarch) into the cream and stir this slowly into the sauce. Bring back to the boil and simmer for a further 3 minutes.

4 Strain the sauce into a clean pan and reheat. Add sea salt and the peppercorns.

5 To serve, arrange 2 tablespoons of sauce on each warmed serving plate and place the prawns decoratively onto this. Trim the cucumber into fan-shapes or simply slice, and serve with rice or couscous if wished.

Civet de Langouste au Martini Rosé

Langouste (Rock Lobster) Casserole with Wild Rice

Serves 6
Illustrated opposite page 128.

This is a rich and substantial dish, using the crustacean *langouste* which the British sometimes call crawfish and the Americans rock or spiny lobster. Langouste can reach a large size — up to 14 pounds (6 to 8 kilos) — but the flesh of these large ones is often tough. A smaller one is often a better buy, and in a dish such as this one a little goes a long way by being combined with other complementary ingredients. You can use crawfish (rock lobster) in any dish which calls for lobster, since the two are so closely related.

Imperial (Metric)	American
1 freshly cooked langouste (approx. 2¼ lb/1 kilo)	1 freshly cooked rock lobster (approx. 2¼ pounds)
2 fl oz (60ml) olive oil	¼ cup olive oil
1 large red onion, chopped	1 large red onion, chopped
2 shallots, chopped	2 shallots, chopped
2 large carrots, diced small	2 large carrots, diced small
1 tablespoon tomato purée	1 tablespoon tomato paste
1 sprig tarragon	1 sprig tarragon
1 red and 1 green chilli, sliced	1 red and 1 green chili, sliced
1 lb (450g) button mushrooms	1 pound button mushrooms
½ pint (300ml) fish stock (page 170)	1⅓ cups fish stock (page 170)
¼ pint (150ml) rosé Martini	⅔ cup rosé Martini
2 oz (50g) butter	¼ cup butter
1 oz (25g) wholemeal flour	¼ cup whole wheat flour
5 tomatoes, skinned, seeded and diced	5 tomatoes, skinned, seeded and diced
10 oz (300g) cooked *Uncle Ben's* wild rice	3⅓ cups cooked *Uncle Ben's* wild rice

1 Separate the langouste (rock lobster) head from the tail. Remove the tail meat in one piece and slice across into rounds. Split the head and remove the coral and tomalley (liver) and reserve. Discard the sac of gravel.

2 Chop the shell into small pieces. Heat the oil in a sauté pan and fry the shell pieces for a few minutes. This adds a wonderful flavour to the sauce. Add the onion, shallot and carrots to the pan and sauté for 8 minutes.

3 Stir in the tomato purée (paste), herbs, chillies and the stalks of the mushrooms. Add the fish stock and Martini and boil for 15 minutes.

4 Strain this liquid into a clean pan and reboil.

5 Cream together the butter, flour, coral and tomalley until you have a smooth paste. Add this to the liquid, little by little, to produce a smooth sauce. Boil for 4 minutes, then strain again.

6 To this sauce add the mushroom caps and the diced tomatoes. Check seasoning.

7 Spoon a ribbon of sauce onto one side of each individual serving platter and arrange the medallions of langouste (rock lobster) along this. Garnish with wild rice and vegetables of your choice and serve at once.

Crabe à la Conil
Two Contrasting Crab Pâtés

Illustrated opposite page 161.

Dressed crab served hot or cold was one of the most famous specialities at my father's fish restaurant. In the style of those days it was served in the shell, but I prefer to present the meat in pâté form, prettily arranged on a plate with a simple garnish. For this recipe I have used pawpaw (papaya) as a decoration, but it also serves to make the crab more digestible due to the enzyme it contains.

Imperial (Metric)	American
For the light pâté:	For the light pâté:
¼ pint (150ml) low-fat yogurt	⅔ cup low-fat yogurt
2 tablespoons mayonnaise	2 tablespoons mayonnaise
Sea salt and freshly ground black pepper	Sea salt and freshly ground black pepper
1 lb (450g) white crab meat	1 pound white crab meat
For the dark pâté:	For the dark pâté:
8 oz (225g) brown crab meat	1 cup brown crab meat
2 oz (50g) wholemeal breadcrumbs	1 cup whole wheat breadcrumbs
¼ pint (150ml) mayonnaise	⅔ cup mayonnaise
2 tablespoons peanut oil	2 tablespoons peanut oil
1 small shallot, finely chopped	1 small shallot, finely chopped
1 teaspoon curry powder	1 teaspoon curry powder
1 tablespoon white port	1 tablespoon white port
2 hard-boiled eggs	2 hard-cooked eggs
For the garnish:	For the garnish:
2 small pawpaws, peeled, seeded and sliced	2 small papayas, peeled, seeded and sliced
4 sprigs corn salad	4 sprigs corn salad
4 cracked crab claws (optional)	4 cracked crab claws (optional)

1 In a bowl, beat together the yogurt and mayonnaise. Season, then pound in the white crab meat. Chill for 30 minutes.

2 In a second bowl, beat together the brown crab meat and the breadcrumbs. Stir in the mayonnaise.

3 Heat the oil in a pan and sauté the chopped shallot for 2 minutes. Sprinkle on the curry powder and cook briefly to develop the flavour.

4 Add the port and simmer for 1 minute.

5 Place the peeled eggs in a blender with one-quarter of the dark crab mixture and all of the curried shallot mixture. Blend until smooth, then beat into the remaining crab mixture. Chill for 15 minutes or until needed.

6 Place egg-shaped spoonfuls of each mixture onto four plates and garnish with slices of pawpaw (papaya), corn salad and crab claws if used. A few seeds from the fruit could be sprinkled on for contrast, if wished.

Crevettes de la Méditerranée, Flambées au Cognac

Mediterranean Prawns (Shrimp), Flamed in Cognac

This is a dish to create a sensation at your dinner table! For many people, flamed dishes are limited to crêpes Suzette or Chrismas pudding, but a savoury flambé can be equally good, and is certainly original. This dish is very simple to prepare, yet the presentation — and of course the flavour — make it both memorable and fun.

Imperial (Metric)	American
2 lb (900g) raw king prawns	2 pounds raw jumbo shrimp
2 teaspoons cornflour	2 teaspoons cornstarch
Sea salt	Sea salt
1 egg white, beaten	1 egg white, beaten
4 fl oz (120ml) safflower oil	½ cup safflower oil
2 spring onions, sliced	2 scallions, sliced
1 green chilli, seeded and sliced	1 green chili, seeded and sliced
4 fl oz (120ml) dry white wine	½ cup dry white wine
4 fl oz (120ml) double cream	½ cup heavy cream
1 teaspoon clear honey	1 teaspoon clear honey
Freshly ground black pepper	Freshly ground black pepper
2 oz (50g) sliced button mushrooms	1 cup button mushrooms, sliced
½ small red pepper, thinly sliced	½ small red pepper, thinly sliced
Lettuce leaves	Lettuce leaves
4 fl oz (120ml) warmed cognac	½ cup warmed cognac

1 Peel the prawns (shrimp), remove the vein and slice along the back, but do not cut in half. Rinse and pat dry.

2 In a bowl, beat together the cornflour (cornstarch), salt and egg white. Add the prawns (shrimp), stir well and leave for 1 hour.

3 Heat the oil in a sauté pan and stir-fry the prawns (shrimp), a few at a time, for 2 minutes. Remove from the pan with a slotted spoon and drain well.

4 Drain off the oil from the pan except for about 2 tablespoons. Sauté the onions and chilli for 3 minutes.

5 Add the wine, cream and honey and bring to the boil. Add the prawns, mushrooms and pepper to the sauce and cook for about another minute to heat everything well.

6 Place lettuce leaves all around the edge of a large serving dish and spoon the prawns over them. Place a small metal bowl in the centre and pour in the warmed cognac. Set it alight so that each guest can spear a prawn on a cocktail stick and pass it through the flame before eating it with the lettuce and sauce — alternatively, heat the brandy in a pan and set it alight before pouring it over a lettuce-lined serving dish filled with the prawn mixture. As the flames die away, your guests can help themselves.

Paella Biarritz
Seafood Paella

Illustrated opposite.

The Basque influence is very much in evidence all along the French coast from Biarritz to Bordeaux. Equally, a French approach to cooking can be seen in the cuisine of the Spanish Pyrenees, especially its fish dishes. Being something of a purist I don't accept the mixture of meat and poultry with fish. It seems to me that there is such a wealth of seafood available that a simply splendid paella can be made without it becoming a jumble of different foods by staying with fish and seafood as a unifying ingredient. Of course, fish is not necessary to a good paella — increase the vegetables and add others of your choice, plus perhaps a few toasted cashew nuts, to make a delicious and nourishing vegetarian meal.

Imperial (Metric)	American
6 fl oz (180ml) olive oil	¾ cup olive oil
1 large onion, chopped	1 large onion, chopped
6 oz (150g) *Uncle Ben's* wholegrain rice	1 cup *Uncle Ben's* wholegrain rice
1 pint (600ml) fish stock (page 170)	2½ cups fish stock (page 170)
1 squid, cleaned and sliced into rings	1 squid, cleaned and sliced into rings
1 oz (25g) seasoned wholemeal flour	¼ cup seasoned whole wheat flour
2 small sprigs thyme	2 small sprigs thyme
2 large pinches saffron threads	2 large pinches saffron threads
2 cloves garlic, chopped	2 cloves garlic, chopped
1 pint (600ml) mussels, cleaned	3 cups mussels, cleaned
¼ pint (150ml) red *or* white wine	⅔ cup red *or* white wine
1 shallot, chopped	1 shallot, chopped
1 lb (500g) shelled raw scampi	2 cups shelled raw scampi
2 oz (50g) cooked peas	⅓ cup cooked peas
2 oz (50g) cooked red kidney beans	⅓ cup cooked red kidney beans
2 oz (50g) blanched, diced red pepper	⅓ cup blanched, diced red pepper
2 oz (50g) blanchd almonds	⅓ cup blanched almonds
6 whole, cooked langoustines	6 whole, cooked crayfish

1 Heat half the oil in a large pan and sauté the chopped onion for a few seconds to soften, then stir in the rice and mix well, so that each grain is impregnated with oil. Add the fish stock and bring slowly to the boil.

2 Toss the squid rings in seasoned flour, reserving any excess.

3 Heat the remaining oil in a frying pan and sauté the squid for 3 minutes, then drain well, reserving the oil.

4 When the rice has been boiling for 5 minutes, stir in the squid, a sprig of thyme, a pinch of saffron, and the garlic. Transfer the mixture to a shallow metal dish (a paella dish if you have one) and place in a preheated oven at 400°F/200°C (Gas Mark 6). Bake for 15 to 20 minutes, by which time almost all the liquid should have been absorbed.

5 Meanwhile, poach the mussels in the wine, along with the chopped shallot, a sprig of thyme and a pinch of saffron. After 5 minutes, strain off the juices into a bowl.

6 Reserve 6 mussels for garnish and remove the rest from their shells.

7 Toss the scampi in the remaining seasoned flour, heat the oil which was used to sauté the squid, and stir-fry the scampi in it for 2 minutes.

8 Five minutes before the rice is finished cooking, stir in the mussel juices, along with the vegetables,

nuts, mussels, squid and scampi. Stir well and return to the oven to finish cooking and warm through completely.

9 Serve straight from the oven, decorated with the mussels in their shells and the cooked langoustines. Offer slices of lemon to squeeze over the paella.

Brochettes de Fruits de Mer Vieille Bretagne
Seafood Kebabs

This simple dish is redolent of summer days and fresh sea air. Simply cooked over hot coals it is unbeatable outdoor fare, but even if cooked indoors under a hot grill (broiler) it will bring memories of holidays back to you. Served with a brown rice salad if you are eating al fresco, or freshly cooked hot brown rice if you have access to a full-scale stove, it makes a nourishing as well as delicious meal. A green salad is the only other accompaniment needed, except perhaps for a chilled glass of Blanc de Blancs to wash it all down with.

Imperial (Metric)	American
2 lb (900g) cooked lobster *or* langouste	2 pound cooked lobster
8 oz (225g) cooked prawns *or* shrimps	2 cups cooked shrimp
8 oz (225g) fresh, shelled scallops	1⅓ cups fresh, shucked scallops
2 oz (50g) butter	¼ cup butter
2 tablespoons lemon juice	2 tablespoons lemon juice
8-12 cherry tomatoes	8-12 cherry tomatoes
Sea salt and freshly ground black pepper	Sea salt and freshly ground black pepper
2 tablespoons finely chopped parsley	2 tablespoons finely chopped parsley

1 Remove the tail meat from the lobster and cut into chunks.
2 Shell the shrimps.
3 Poach the scallops for 2 minutes in the melted butter and lemon juice, then remove with a slotted spoon and keep the lemon butter for basting.
4 Onto four skewers, thread alternate pieces of lobster, shrimps, scallops and tomatoes. Season and brush with lemon butter.
5 Barbecue over hot coals (or cook under the grill/broiler) for about 5 to 6 minutes, turning and basting frequently. Sprinkle with parsley and serve.

Note:
Uncle Ben's long grain and wild rice blend goes well with this dish, and adds an exotic touch to the meal.

Opposite: *Crabe à la Conil* (page 158); *Roulade de Crabe Avocadine Tropicale* (page 154).

Homard à la Pomme d'Amour
Lobster with a Tomato and Sour Cream Sauce

Serves 2

Size is no indication of quality in a lobster — indeed, many gourmets now prefer the smaller lobster, taking it to be more tender than its older and large relations. However, part of this new-found tenderness is as a result of a new approach to cooking on the part of chefs. In old cookery books, cooking times for lobsters will be given at around 15 minutes per pound, but we now find that when they are boiled for 2 to 5 minutes only, before being left in the hot stock away from the heat for a further 15 minutes, they remain tender and delicate. For this recipe, choose a hen lobster with eggs under the tail. These can be removed before cooking for use later to enrich the sauce in which the lobster meat will be served.

Pomme d'amour was the ancient name for the tomato. Its meaning is 'apple of love' as it was thought to be an aphrodisiac; very appropriate, for this romantic dinner *à deux*!

Imperial (Metric)	American
1 hen lobster, well-washed	1 hen lobster, well-washed
3 pints (1.8 litres) court bouillon (page 170)	7½ cups court bouillon (page 170)
Lobster eggs	Lobster eggs
1 teaspoon white wine vinegar	1 teaspoon white wine vinegar
2 oz (50g) softened butter	¼ cup softened butter
1 oz (25g) wholemeal flour	¼ cup whole wheat flour
2 fl oz (60ml) vegetable oil	¼ cup vegetable oil
1 onion, chopped	1 onion, chopped
2 cloves garlic, crushed	2 cloves garlic, crushed
1 red pepper, seeded and chopped	1 red pepper, seeded and chopped
1 red chilli, seeded and diced	1 red chili, seeded and diced
2 oz (50g) tomato purée	4 tablespoons tomato paste
½ pint (300ml) fish stock (page 170)	1⅓ cups fish stock (page 170)
1 fl oz (30ml) brandy	2 tablespoons brandy
Sea salt and freshly ground black pepper	Sea salt and freshly ground black pepper
4 fl oz (120ml) sour cream	½ cup sour cream
4 tomatoes, skinned, seeded and diced	4 tomatoes, skinned, seeded and diced
4 sprigs tarragon, snipped	4 sprigs tarragon, snipped
4 basil leaves	4 basil leaves

1 Plunge the lobster into the boiling court bouillon and boil for 5 minutes. Simmer for a further 5 minutes, then remove from the heat and allow to cool in the liquid. The cooling can be speeded up by placing the pan in a bowl of ice cubes.

2 Place the lobster eggs in the vinegar — this improves their colour. Pound them with the butter and flour to make a *beurre d'homard*.

3 Remove the cold lobster from the stock and remove the tail meat with a fork.

4 Remove the coral and tomalley (the greenish liver) from the lobster and beat these into the *beurre d'homard*.

5 Crack the claws and remove the flesh carefully from them. Dry the shell of the lobster in a warm oven for 20 minutes, then crush it.

6 In a deep pan, heat the oil and stir-fry the crushed shell with the onion for 4 minutes. Then add the garlic, red pepper, chilli, tomato purée (paste) and stock. Bring to the boil and simmer for 20 minutes, then strain the liquid into a clean pan. Reheat to boiling point.

7 Beat the brandy into the *beurre d'homard*, then gradually add this to the sauce, stirring constantly. This will add colour, flavour and thickness to the sauce. Simmer for 5 minutes before straining once more.

8 Check the seasoning, then stir in the sour cream. Stir well, bring back to a simmer. Stir in half the diced tomato and all the herbs.

9 Cut the lobster flesh into slices and reheat for 3 minutes in some of the court bouillon.

10 Spoon some sauce onto each plate and arrange slices of tail and claw meat over this. Decorate with a little diced tomato and serve with brown or wild rice.

Bouquet de Tahiti à l'Ananas

Pineapple and Crab Cocktail

The combination of fresh pineapple and seafood is quite delightful, and the fruit is especially useful for those people who find shellfish indigestible, since it contains an enzyme which aids the digestion of protein — it must be fresh pineapple, however, since the canning process kills the valuable enzyme. This refreshing and piquant dish makes an ideal luncheon dish, and can be varied by the substitution of other seafood for the crab — prawns (shrimp) are very good, but you will need more of them. About 1 pound (450g) unshelled weight would be about right by the time they have been peeled.

Imperial (Metric)	American
4 slices fresh pineapple	4 slices fresh pineapple
1 tablespoon whisky *or* rum	1 tablespoon whisky *or* rum
4 oz (100g) sliced white mushrooms	1½ cups sliced white mushrooms
2 tablespoons fresh pineapple juice	2 tablespoons fresh pineapple juice
6 oz (150g) crab meat	1 cup crab meat
2 oz (50g) cream *or* low-fat cheese	¼ cup cream *or* low-fat cheese
1 small shallot, very finely chopped	1 small shallot, very finely chopped
1 teaspoon French mustard	1 teaspoon French mustard
Sea salt	Sea salt
Pinch cayenne pepper	Pinch cayenne pepper
1 small piece preserved ginger, cut into *julienne*	1 small piece preserved ginger, cut into *julienne*
Salad leaves to garnish	Salad leaves to garnish

1 Cut the slices of pineapple to your preferred thickness, trim the tough exterior and core. Place a slice on each serving plate and sprinkle with the whisky. Reserve 2 tablespoons of the juice.

2 Place the sliced mushrooms in a bowl and toss with the juice. Leave to marinate for 10 minutes.

3 In another bowl, flake the crab meat and mix with the cheese. Stir in the chopped shallot and the mustard. Season to taste.

4 Spoon the crab mixture into the cored centres of the pineapple.

5 Decorate the plate with little heaps of marinated mushrooms sprinkled with strips of ginger and garnish with salad. A cracked crab claw makes a pleasant garnish, too, and adds a little more substance to a light dish.

Panier de Crevettes Mediterranée Surprise

Sweet-sour King Prawns (Jumbo Shrimp) Served in a Potato Basket

Serves 1
Illustrated opposite page 16.

The delightful presentation is the keynote to this dish — along with a harmonious combination of flavours, of course. The potato basket makes a charming container in which to serve all manner of light, crisp appetizers. 'Scampi in the Basket' is a perennial favourite on pub menus, here in Britain where I live; how much more fun it is when you can eat the basket too!

Imperial (Metric)	American
2 tablespoons clear honey	2 tablespoons clear honey
1 tablespoon white wine vinegar	1 tablespoon white wine vinegar
1 crushed clove garlic	1 crushed clove garlic
1 tablespoon natural soya sauce	1 tablespoon natural soy sauce
1 tablespoon pineapple juice	1 tablespoon pineapple juice
½-inch (1cm) cube peeled fresh ginger	½-inch cube (1cm) peeled fresh ginger
Sea salt and freshly ground black pepper	Sea salt and freshly ground black pepper
6 large king prawns *or* scampi, peeled	6 large jumbo shrimp *or* scampi, peeled
1 oz (25g) seasoned wholemeal flour	¼ cup seasoned whole wheat flour
Vegetable oil for frying	Vegetable oil for frying
8 oz (225g) peeled and coarsely grated potato	1⅓ cups peeled and coarsely grated potato
1 tablespoon cornflour	1 tablespoon cornstarch
4 button mushrooms, sliced	4 button mushrooms, sliced
3 spring onions, trimmed	3 scallions, trimmed

1 Place the honey, vinegar, garlic, soya sauce, pineapple juice, ginger and seasoning in a blender and reduce to a smooth sauce. Marinate the prawns (shrimp) in this for 30 minutes.

2 Drain the marinade into a small pan, bring to the boil and cook for 4 minutes. Set aside to serve as a sauce with the finished dish.

3 Pass the drained prawns (shrimp) in seasoned flour. Heat a little oil in a sauté pan and toss the fish in this for 2 minutes. Drain and set aside on kitchen paper towels to cool.

4 To make the potato basket, take two wire sieves (strainers) which fit inside one another. Heat a deep pan, one-third full of oil and dip the sieves (strainers) in this. Remove them, and line one with grated potato to form a nest.

5 Sprinkle the potato with a little cornflour, then place the other sieve (Strainer) over the potato, pressing it down firmly. Place the sieves (strainers) in the hot oil and cook the basket for 2 minutes, until golden-brown and crisp. Remove from the oil, drain on kitchen paper towels and set aside to cool.

6 When ready to serve, quickly sauté the mushrooms in a little oil, drain and place in the basket along with the prawns (shrimp) and the spring onions (scallions) trimmed and chilled to form feathery shapes. Serve the sauce separately, to drizzle over or use as a dip.

Note: You can buy special baskets from kitchen supplies stores, which are specially designed for making potato or noodle 'nests'. You can also buy serrated graters which can be used to make latticed potatoes such as we have chosen for our potato basket illustrated opposite page 16. Run the potato over the serrated cutter, and then turn the cut edge 90 degrees and repeat. You will have a pretty latticed slice of raw potato which you may find easier to use in lining your basket. It looks most attractive, too, as you can see.

Crevettes à la Tonkinoise
Deep-fried Shrimp Fritters

When I was younger, one of the fasionable songs of the day was about a 'Tonkinoise who was left behind'. This referred, I suppose, to the days when the French Empire stretched across the whole of Vietnam, a region of which was the Tonkin. Years later I became great friends in Paris with an exceptional Vietnamese chef, and we shared many secrets of our national cuisines, often creating new dishes for special functions which in some way amalgamated the two styles of cooking. Here is just one such dish, which I hope you will enjoy.

Imperial (Metric)	American
For the dough:	For the dough:
1 lb (450g) self-raising wholemeal flour	4 cups self-rising whole wheat flour
½ teaspoon sea salt	½ teaspoon sea salt
1 egg, beaten	1 egg, beaten
½ pint (300ml) water	1⅓ cups water
For the filling:	For the filling:
8 oz (225g) skinned and filleted whiting *or* cod, *or* other white fish	1⅓ cups skinned fillets of whiting *or* cod, *or* other white fish
5 oz (125g) peeled shrimps	1 cup peeled shrimp
1 shallot, very finely chopped	1 shallot, very finely chopped
3 oz (75g) flaked almonds, crushed	½ cup slivered almonds, crushed
4 oz (100g) mushrooms, finely chopped	2 cups mushrooms, finely chopped
1 tablespoon dry sherry *or* saké	1 tablespoon dry sherry *or* saké
1 tablespoon natural soya sauce	1 tablespoon natural soy sauce
½ oz (15g) fresh ginger, peeled and chopped	½ tablespoon fresh ginger, peeled and chopped
1 egg, beaten	1 egg, beaten
Sea salt and freshly ground black pepper	Sea salt and freshly ground black pepper
Vegetable oil for deep frying	Vegetable oil for deep frying

1 In a bowl, beat together the flour, salt, beaten egg and water to form a smooth, firm but pliable dough. Gather it into a ball, cover and leave to rest for 5 minutes.

2 In another bowl, beat together the fish, shallot, almonds and mushrooms. Add the sherry or saké, soya sauce and ginger, then bind everything together with the beaten egg. Season. The mixture should be stiff, but should hold together well.

3 Roll out the dough into an oblong ⅛ inch (3mm) thick. Roll the fish filling into a sausage about ¾ inch (2cm) in diameter. Lay a piece of this along one edge of the pastry and fold the dough over it as if making sausage rolls.

4 Moisten the edges and seal down, then cut the strip off of the remaining dough. Cut this strip into chunks about 1 inch (2.5cm) long and shape into small balls with the filling enclosed in the dough.

5 Repeat until all the dough and filling has been used.

6 Heat the oil in a deep pan and fry the balls until golden-brown — about 3 minutes. Serve with a choice of sauces to dip in, or a simple stir-fry of fresh vegetables.

Feuilletandine de Crabe aux Epinards
Crab in Puff Pastry with Spinach and a Ginger Sauce

The famous Canadian Snow Crab is exported to many countries around the world, including France. The leg flesh is a very versatile seafood and is well worth asking for. My eminent colleague, Joseph Rostang, owner of the three-star restaurant La Bonne Auberge, features several *specialités* using this ingredient, but here is a simpler dish for you to try, which is equally good.

Imperial (Metric)	American
1 lb (450g) wholemeal puff pastry (page 58)	1 pound whole wheat puff pastry (page 58)
1 egg, beaten	1 egg, beaten
1 lb (450g) cooked snow crab meat	2 cups cooked snow crab meat
Juice of ½ a lemon	Juice of ½ a lemon
5 oz (125g) cooked leaf spinach	1 cup cooked leaf spinach
Sea salt and freshly ground black pepper	Sea salt and freshly ground black pepper
For the sauce:	For the sauce:
⅓ oz (10g) preserved ginger	1 teaspoon preserved ginger
1 fl oz (30ml) ginger syrup	2 tablespoons ginger syrup
2 rinsed anchovy fillets	2 rinsed anchovy fillets
1 clove garlic, chopped	1 clove garlic, chopped
2 leaves fresh basil	2 leaves fresh basil
¼ pint (150ml) mayonnaise (page 179)	⅔ cup mayonnaise (page 179)
¼ pint (150ml) natural yogurt	⅔ cup plain yogurt
Sea salt and freshly ground black pepper	Sea salt and freshly ground black pepper

1 Roll out the pastry to ¼ inch (5mm) thick and cut four equal oblongs, 2×3 inches (5×8cm). Using a sharp knife, cut a border (taking care not to cut right through the pastry) ½ inch (1cm) wide around each side. Using the back of a knife gently mark a pattern of criss-cross lines across the pastry.

2 Place these pastry oblongs on a greased baking tray. Leave for 1 hour at room temperature, then brush with beaten egg and bake at 400°F/200°C (Gas Mark 6) for 15 minutes, when they should be well risen and golden. Remove the central 'lid'.

3 In one bowl, place the crab meat, season and sprinkle with a little lemon juice.

4 In another bowl, season the cooked spinach and add a little lemon juice to that, too.

5 Place the ginger, syrup, anchovies, garlic, basil and mayonnaise in a blender and purée together. Stir in the yogurt and season to taste.

6 Pour a little sauce onto each serving plate. Lay a pastry case on this, spoon in some spinach and then top with crab meat. Top each case with a pastry lid and serve.

Omelette aux Crevettes à la Boulonnaise

Fisherman's Shrimp Omelette

To end this chapter, here is a simple, quick and inexpensive country dish which makes a tasty supper at the end of a long, hard day. You can vary the vegetables according to your taste or supplies, but I find this combination very good. Served with crusty French bread and a jug of cider it is an unbeatable meal for restoring the spirits and ensuring a good night's rest.

Imperial (Metric)	American
2 fl oz (60ml) olive oil	¼ cup olive oil
1 small onion, chopped	1 small onion, chopped
1 diced, cold, boiled potato	1 diced, cold, boiled potato
4 oz (100g) peeled cooked shrimps	⅔ cup peeled cooked shrimp
1 oz (25g) cooked green peas	2 tablespoons cooked green peas
1 tablespoon chopped parsley	1 tablespoon chopped parsley
12 eggs, beaten	12 eggs, beaten
Sea salt and freshly ground black pepper	Sea salt and freshly ground black pepper
2 fl oz (60ml) vegetable oil, for frying	¼ cup vegetable oil, for frying
4 oz (100g) butter, for frying	½ cup butter, for frying

1 In a frying pan, heat the olive oil and sauté the onion until soft, then add the potato, shrimps, peas and parsley. Cook, stirring, until just starting to brown. Remove the pan from the heat.

2 Season the beaten eggs with salt and pepper.

3 Condition a 6-inch (15cm) omelette pan by heating a little vegetable oil in it, then wiping round with kitchen paper towels.

4 Heat a quarter of the oil and butter in the pan. Pour in a quarter of the beaten egg. Cook gently until the eggs are half set, then spoon on a quarter of the filling mixture and spread out evenly. Either toss the omelette like a pancake, or place under a hot grill (broiler) to finish cooking, then slip the omelette out flat onto a warm plate.

5 Make the other three omelettes in the same way. Serve piping hot.

Variations:
A little grated Gruyère or mature Cheddar could be sprinkled onto the omelette before browning, if wished. Tiny shelled mussels make a delicious substitute for some, or all, of the shrimps.

10 *Les Sauces Nouvelles*

New-Style Sauces

A sauce should always serve to enhance a dish, in both a visual and a culinary way. To a chef, the sauce is comparable to fine jewellery on a well-dressed woman, or carefully chosen accessories on a smart man — an impression is being created by the person with the clothes they wear, and the final touches should be just enough to enhance. They should not dazzle or swamp but neither should they be ignored as unimportant. Be they classic pearls or austere, modern cufflinks they are a part of the whole, and the discerning eye will view them as such.

Just so, the gourmet regards the sauce as the final touch to the carefully devised, cooked and presented dish — he expects the chef or cook to devote as much care to that aspect of the meal as to any other part. From a classic *Beurre Blanc* to a modern yogurt-based creation, the rule should always be to match the sauce carefully with the food it accompanies, to take as much trouble with the ingredients used and their preparation, and to serve just enough to bring out hidden qualities in the dish rather than to smother everything until the meal tastes only of the sauce.

Picardy has a small coastline by comparison to, say, the long sweep of Aquitaine or the rugged outcrop of Brittany, but its little harbours are as teeming with fishing boats and their catch as those of its neighbours Normandy and the Pas-de-Calais, and a clue to the importance of the sea in the lives of its people can be found in the fishermen's chapel at Saint-Valery, which is hung with model ships that have been offered as thanks for a safe return to the shore. Like its neighbours, its harvest of fish is complemented by the bounty of the countryside inland, and Picardy's green pastures provide good grazing for dairy herds — ironic that land which had been torn by such battles as Crécy and the Somme should now stretch smoothly to the horizon as a home for these placid, gentle beasts.

The cream, butter and cheese from the dairy farms of the region are, of course, fundamental to the classic French sauce, but now more and more farms are using the abundant milk to make delicious French yogurt, too, free from unnecessary additives, vivid colours and strong flavours but full of character and goodness. What chef could resist using this delicious product to offer his clients (and readers) an alternative to the richness of the 'special occasion' sauce?

French wine plays an important part in a great many of these recipes, but the piquancy this provides the sauce can be achieved in other ways, if you prefer. Lemon juice adds a delicate flavour that is especially suited to sauces for fish — 3 tablespoons per pint of liquid is about right when making a sauce. Sherry or wine vinegar can be added in a ratio of 1 tablespoon per pint of sauce. Dry French vermouth is often used by chefs, as it provides a ready-made balance of herbs and wine which is aromatic yet

subtle. But most recipes will be just as good if simple wine is used — just remember to taste the sauce before serving to ensure it is flavoured to your liking. Sauces using sour cream or yogurt are already piquant, of course, and are good just as they are. The same is true of mayonnaise and the hollandaise-type sauce. Try to experiment with making sauces from all the types in this chapter, and you will soon discover the flavourings and styles you like best.

The chapter has been divided into seven different 'families' of sauce, from the most basic stock and court bouillon to more complex mayonnaise and coulis. From these groupings have been chosen over forty variations, to give you a wealth of choice in complementing your fish dish. Each recipe has been especially chosen or adapted to blend harmoniously with all sorts of fish cuisine, but some are especially suited to particular types of fish and these happy partnerships are always noted — a piquant sauce, for example, will offset an oily fish and bring out its flavours; a light, mild sauce will be a better choice for the delicate flavour and texture of fresh salmon or plaice.

Other 'marriages' are to be found in this chapter — that of East and West which has come about through the French love of Vietnamese cuisine and which is reflected in the use of a sweet-sour balance in some sauces, or the use of oriental bean curd (tofu) in others. And classic French mayonnaise can be united with low-fat yogurt to create a sauce which encompasses the best of both approaches with a creamy fullness yet a light tang. This feeling of harmony links charmingly with the region of Picardy which in itself brings together so many aspects of French cuisine — the flowing cornucopia of the lands of Northern France, the fine wines of Champagne on its inland border, the full nets and pots of the fishermen along the coast. And, coincidentally, at Senlis near the border of the Ile-de-France, is the castle where Henry V of England married Catherine of France — one of many royal marriages between the country of my birth and the country I have made my home. The love-hate relationship between France and Britain has always existed and will no doubt always continue, but at its base is always a mutual admiration for the very things that makes us different — *vive la différence*!

Court Bouillon

Poaching Liquid for Fish

This stock can be used to poach all sorts of fish, such as trout, mackerel, salmon, herrings or any kind of crustacean. The stock must always be prepared before the fish is added. Small pieces of fish, such as steaks, should be immersed in hot stock, but whole fish must be placed in cold bouillon and heated gently to poach, as hot stock would cause the fish to crack open.

Imperial (Metric)	American
1¾ pint (1 litre) water	4½ cups water
¼ pint (150ml) white wine *or* other alcohol, as recipe indicates	⅔ cup white wine *or* other alcohol, as recipe indicates
1 fl oz (30ml) distilled white vinegar	2 tablespoons distilled white vinegar
1 carrot, grooved and sliced	1 carrot, grooved and sliced
1 stick celery, sliced	1 stalk celery, sliced
1 stick fennel, sliced	1 stalk fennel, sliced
1 small onion, sliced in rings *or* left whole and studded with 2 cloves	1 small onion, sliced in rings *or* left whole and studded with 2 cloves
1 small sprig thyme	1 small sprig thyme
6 black peppercorns, crushed	6 black peppercorns, crushed
2 teaspoons sea salt	2 teaspoons sea salt

1 Place all the ingredients in a large pan. Bring to a boil and simmer for 30 minutes. The stock is now ready to use in your recipe. It may be frozen for later use.

Note: This quantity is sufficient to cook a 2 pound (1 kilo) fish. A large fish of 5 to 7 pounds (2 to 3 kilos) should be poached for 15 minutes, a 14 pound salmon (6 kilos) will need about 20 minutes. Fish steaks of around 8 ounces (225g) need only 5 to 8 minutes. Never allow the stock to boil — poaching temperature is 194°F/90°C.

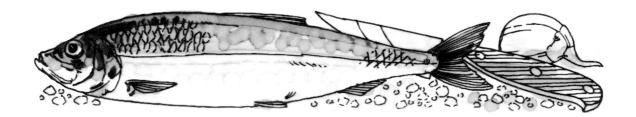

Fumet de Poisson

Fish Stock

This stock is the basis for many of the recipes in this book, and will vary according to individual recipe requirements. You can buy fish bones especially to make a batch of stock or, if time allows, use the bones or shells from the fish or crustaceans you will later be cooking. The only type of fish bones which cannot be used are those from oily fish such as herring or mackerel.

This stock also forms the basis for a number of sauces to complement your fish dishes, a selection of which follow the master recipe.

Imperial (Metric)	American
1 oz (25g) butter	2 tablespoons butter
1 fl oz (30ml) vegetable oil	2 tablespoons vegetable oil
1 large onion, sliced into rings	1 large onion, sliced into rings
1 stick celery, sliced	1 stalk celery, sliced
1 stick fennel, sliced	1 stalk fennel, sliced
About 2 lb (1 kilo) white fish bones, heads and trimmings *or* crustacean shells	About 2 pounds white fish bones, heads and trimmings *or* crustacean shells
3½ pints (2 litres) water	8½ cups water
¼ pint (150ml) dry white wine such as Chablis *or* Muscadet	⅔ cup dry white wine such as Chablis *or* Muscadet
Juice of 1 lemon	Juice of 1 lemon
6 black peppercorns, crushed	6 black peppercorns, crushed
1 sprig thyme	1 sprig thyme

1 In a large pan, heat the butter and oil. Add the vegetables and fish bones and sauté together for about 5 minutes. This is best done with the pan tightly covered, by shaking it frequently to prevent the ingredients sticking and browning.

2 After 5 minutes add all the liquids, the peppercorns and thyme, bring to the boil and simmer for 20 minutes. Pass the liquid through a fine strainer. The stock is now ready for use in soups or sauces, or for baking fish.

Variations:
Clear Fish Stock/Consommé

Imperial (Metric)	American
8 oz (225g) minced white fish	1 cup minced white fish
2 oz (50g) finely chopped leeks	⅓ cup finely chopped leeks
2 oz (50g) finely chopped carrot	⅓ cup finely chopped carrot
2 oz (50g) finely chopped onion	⅓ cup finely chopped onion
2 oz (50g) finely chopped celery	⅓ cup finely chopped celery
1 egg white	1 egg white
1 quantity fish stock (above)	1 quantity fish stock (above)

1 In a bowl, combine the minced fish and vegetables with the egg white.

2 Gradually stir in the cold fish stock, then transfer the mixture to a large pan and heat gently to boiling point but not beyond.

3 Simmer the mixture very gently for about 20 minutes. The solids will coagulate and most can be skimmed off with a slotted spoon. To remove all remaining trace, pass the stock through a fine strainer lined with a muslin cloth (cheesecloth). The broth should now be perfectly clear and can be served hot or cold as fish consommé, or used for sauces or poaching.

Fish Glaze

To produce a glaze of concentrated fish stock, boil the stock (it is not necessary to clarify it first, but this may be done, according to the proposed use of the glaze) until it is one-tenth of its original volume. When cold it will form a jelly which can be frozen for later use. This is especially useful if frozen in ice cube trays or bags, as a cube or two can be used to replace the usual fish stock cube in recipes and has all the goodness and flavour of fish with no risk of suspect additives.

Sauces Based on a Fish Fumet

Sauce Palavasienne

A Rich Vegetable Sauce from the Languedoc

Imperial (Metric)	American
2 fl oz (60ml) olive oil	¼ cup olive oil
1 small onion, chopped	1 small onion, chopped
1 small courgette, diced	1 small zucchini, diced
1 small aubergine, diced	1 small eggplant, diced
2 cloves garlic, crushed	2 cloves garlic, crushed
½ pint (300ml) fish stock made with red wine (page 170)	1⅓ cups fish stock made with red wine (page 170)
2 oz (50g) tomato purée	4 tablespoons tomato paste
Sea salt and freshly ground black pepper	Sea salt and freshly ground black pepper
1 teaspoon cornflour (optional)	1 teaspoon cornstarch (optional)
3 fl oz (90ml) water (optional)	⅓ cup water (optional)

For the garnish:	For the garnish:
1 hard-boiled egg, finely chopped	1 hard-cooked egg, finely chopped
4 black olives, stoned and diced	4 black olives, pitted and diced
1 red pepper, seeded, diced and blanched	1 red pepper, seeded, diced and blanched
2 oz (50g) diced cucumber	⅓ cup diced cucumber
1 tablespoon chopped parsley	1 tablespoon chopped parsley
1 teaspoon chopped basil	1 teaspoon chopped basil

1 Heat the oil in a large pan and sauté the vegetables and garlic for about 5 minutes, until soft but not browned.

2 Stir in the fish stock and the tomato purée (paste). Bring to the boil and simmer for 15 minutes.

3 Purée the sauce in a blender, return to the pan and reheat. The mixture may be thickened with a slurry of cornflour (cornstarch) and water, if wished. Add the garnish when serving your chosen fish with this sauce.

Note: Serve with monkfish, mullet or poached or grilled white fish.

Sauce de Carottes au Miel

Carrot and Madeira Sauce with Honey

Imperial (Metric)	American
8 oz (225g) cooked carrots	1⅓ cups cooked carrots
1 tablespoon honey	1 tablespoon honey
½ pint (300ml) fish stock (page 170)	1⅓ cups fish stock (page 170)
3 leaves fresh mint	3 leaves fresh mint
2 fl oz (60ml) dry Madeira wine	¼ cup dry Madeira wine
Juice of ½ an orange	Juice of ½ an orange
Juice of ½ a lemon	Juice of ½ a lemon
Sea salt and freshly ground black pepper	Sea salt and freshly ground black pepper
2 fl oz (60ml) natural yogurt, whipped	¼ cup plain yogurt, whipped

1 Place the carrots, honey and stock in a blender with the mint leaves and blend to a smooth purée.
2 Place the purée in a pan with the Madeira and fruit juice and reheat gently. Season and serve hot, or serve cold with the whipped yogurt stirred in when the sauce is cool.

Note: Serve with poached hake, cod, turbot or haddock.

Sauce au Fenouil

Fennel Sauce

Imperial (Metric)	American
4 oz (100g) thinly sliced fennel	1 cup thinly sliced fennel
½ pint (300ml) fish stock (page 170)	1⅓ cups fish stock (page 170)
Sea salt and freshly ground black pepper	Sea salt and freshly ground black pepper
2 fl oz (60ml) natural yogurt, whipped	¼ cup plain yogurt, whipped

1 Place the fennel in a pan with the stock, bring to the boil and simmer for 12 minutes, until tender.
2 Place the fennel and stock in a blender and reduce to a smooth purée. Turn into a bowl and beat in the yogurt.

Note: Serve as an ideal accompaniment to herrings, mackerel or trout.

Sauce Féroce

Fiery Vegetable Sauce

Imperial (Metric)	American
2 oz (50g) diced onion	⅓ cup diced onion
2 oz (50g) diced carrot	⅓ cup diced carrot
2 oz (50g) chopped celery	⅓ cup chopped celery
1 fl oz (30ml) olive oil	2 tablespoons olive oil
2 tablespoons tomato purée	2 tablespoons tomato paste
2 cloves garlic, crushed	2 cloves garlic, crushed
1 red chilli, seeded and chopped	1 red chili, seeded and chopped
½ pint (300ml) fish stock (page 170)	1⅓ cups fish stock (page 170)

1 Sauté all the chopped vegetables in the oil for about 4 minutes, until tender but not browned.
2 Stir in the tomato purée (paste), garlic and chilli and mix well, then add the fish stock.
3 Place all the ingredients in a blender and purée to a smooth sauce. Reheat to boiling point.

Note: Serve with grilled red mullet (snapper), mackerel, or any barbecued fish.

Sauce au Vert

Herb Sauce

Imperial (Metric)	American
2 oz (50g) mixture of the following chopped fresh herbs: basil, mint, chervil, rosemary, sage, sorrel and marjoram	⅔ cup mixture of the following chopped fresh herbs: basil, mint, chervil, rosemary, sage, sorrel and marjoram
2 oz (50g) chopped fresh spinach	1 cup chopped fresh spinach
½ pint (300ml) fish stock (page 000)	1⅓ cups fish stock (page 000)
3 fl oz (90ml) yogurt *or* sour cream	⅓ cup yogurt *or* sour cream
Sea salt and freshly ground black pepper	Sea salt and freshly ground black pepper

1 Liquidize all the ingredients together (add seasoning last, tasting before you add extra salt).

Note: This sauce is delicious served with jellied or smoked eel fillets. Serve the fillets on a bed of lettuce with lemon wedges and freshly fried croûtons. Serve the sauce separately as it is quite strong.

Sauce aux Huitres

Oyster Sauce

Imperial (Metric)	American
2 oz (50g) butter	¼ cup butter
2 shallots, finely chopped	2 shallots, finely chopped
¼ pint (150ml) fish stock (page 170) *or* dry white wine	⅔ cup fish stock (page 170) *or* dry white wine
1 sprig thyme	1 sprig thyme
8 shelled oysters, with their strained juice	8 shelled oysters, with their strained juice
Juice of ½ a lemon	Juice of ½ a lemon
2 tablespoons sour cream *or* yogurt	2 tablespoons sour cream *or* yogurt
Sea salt and freshly ground black pepper	Sea salt and freshly ground black pepper
A dash of Tabasco	A dash of Tabasco
1 tablespoon chopped fresh parsley	1 tablespoon chopped fresh parsley

1 Melt the butter in a pan and sauté the shallot for 1 minute without browning.
2 Stir in the stock or wine, add the thyme and boil for 3 minutes.
3 Remove the thyme and add the oysters, their juice and that of the lemon. Poach the oysters for 2 minutes without boiling.
4 Place the contents of the pan in a blender and purée the sauce until quite smooth. Stir in the cream or yogurt.
5 Warm the sauce gently without boiling, and season to taste. Add a dash of Tabasco, and stir in the parsley just before serving.

Note: This sauce is excellent with a delicate steamed fish.

Beurre Blanc

White Butter Sauce

Imperial (Metric)	American
3 large tablespoons fish stock glaze (page 171)	3 large tablespoons fish stock glaze (page 171)
1 teaspoon lime juice	1 teaspoon lime juice
1 tablespoon *Noilly Prat* vermouth	1 tablespoon *Noilly Prat* vermouth
1 tablespoon chopped shallot	1 tablespoon chopped shallot
8 oz (225g) unsalted farm butter	1 cup unsalted farm butter
Sea salt and freshly ground black pepper	Sea salt and freshly ground black pepper

1 Boil together all the ingredients except the butter and seasoning for 5 minutes, to reduce the volume by half.
2 Bit by bit, add the butter to the hot sauce, whisking it to form a creamy emulsion. Check the seasoning and then pour at once over poached or baked fish. Serve immediately, sprinkled with fresh chopped herbs of your choice, if wished.

Note: My version of this classic sauce ends this section, and demonstrates the use of concentrated fish glaze in a sauce. *Cabillaud au Beurre Blanc* (Cod in Butter Sauce) is an almost unbeatable combination, but try this sauce with any of your favourite white fish.
For a thicker and more stable sauce, beat in 1 egg yolk and 1 tablespoon creamy mashed potato before serving.

Velouté de Poisson Nouveau
Basic White Fish Sauce

This simple white sauce forms the basis for an endless range of complementary fish sauces, from those flavoured with just a few herbs or spices, to more luxurious and heavier ones enriched with cream, or piquant sauces made with the addition of yogurt or acidulated with lemon or lime juice, vermouth or wine. It also acts as a base for almost any vegetable or other fish such as prawns or anchovies. Here we have the basic recipe, followed by two ways of enriching it, and then just a sample of the many recipes which stem from this velouté, to give you an idea of its versatility.

Imperial (Metric)	American
1 oz (25g) butter	2 tablespoons butter
1 oz (25g) wholemeal flour *or* unbleached white flour	¼ cup whole wheat flour *or* unbleached white flour
1 pint (600ml) fish stock (page 170)	2½ cups fish stock (page 170)
Sea salt and freshly ground black pepper	Sea salt and freshly ground black pepper

1 Melt the butter in a pan, add the flour and cook gently for just less than a minute. Stir constantly to avoid the mixture browning. It should come to resemble wet sand — this is called a roux.
2 Gradually whisk in the cold stock and bring to the boil, whisking all the time. Cook the sauce gently for about 5 minutes, so that it thickens to a smooth cream. Strain and use in your chosen recipe.

Note: This amount will be sufficient for up to 8 portions, depending on its use, and contains only a few calories per portion.

Variations:
Enrichment (a) Sabayon
Beat together 3 egg yolks and 1 whole egg with 2 tablespoons *Noilly Prat* vermouth and 2 tablespoons water in a metal bowl. Place over a pan of hot water and whisk until the mixture resembles a thick, frothy custard. Add this to the basic velouté when cooking a fish dish which is to be covered with a sauce and glazed under the grill (broiler) as it gives an excellent finish to the dish.

Enrichment (b) Cream and Egg Yolk Liaison
Blend together 2 egg yolks and 2½ fl oz (75ml/⅓ cup) cream and beat this mixture into the velouté at the last minute, taking care it does not boil fiercely afterwards. This rich sauce is especially good when the velouté is to be used as the basis for a creamy fish soup.

Brown Fish Velouté
This is made by adding 2 oz (50g/⅓ cup) sliced carrots and the same amount of tomato purée (paste) to the basic fish stock and replacing the *Noilly Prat* with Martini Rosso, Madeira or port. This makes the basic sauce much darker, and the carrots add a rich, sweet flavour. For a stronger velouté, add 1 oz (25g/2 tablespoons) puréed anchovy — this can be bought in tubes or made at home.

Opposite: *Pot-Pourri de Saint Jacques à la Conil* (page 144).
Overleaf: *Aiguillettes de Truite Marinée au Vinaigre de Framboise* (page 27).

Sauces Based on a Velouté de Poisson

Sauce Normande Nouvelle
New-Style Normandy Sauce

Imperial (Metric)	American
1 oz (25g) sliced button mushrooms	⅓ cup sliced button mushrooms
2 oysters, shelled	2 oysters, shucked
2 fl oz (60ml) dry white wine	¼ cup dry white wine
1 pint (600ml) fish velouté (page 176)	2½ cups fish velouté (page 176)
2 fl oz (60ml) double *or* sour cream	¼ cup heavy *or* sour cream
Juice of ½ a lemon	Juice of ½ a lemon

1 Poach the mushrooms and oysters in the wine for 2 minutes. Purée in a blender until smooth.
2 Stir into the basic velouté the cream, lemon juice and oyster purée. Heat gently and serve as required.

Variations:
Garnish with shrimps and mussels for a *Sauce Dieppoise*, or with chopped fresh chives and mint and finely chopped hard-boiled egg for a *Sauce Havraise*.

Sauce à l'Estragon
Tarragon Sauce

Imperial (Metric)	American
12 fresh tarragon leaves, chopped	12 fresh tarragon leaves, chopped
1 pint (600ml) fish velouté (page 176)	2½ cups fish velouté (page 176)
2 fl oz (60ml) mayonnaise (page 179)	½ cup mayonnaise (page 179)

1 Place the tarragon in a blender with the velouté and blend together until smooth.
2 Allow the velouté to cool completely, then whisk in the mayonnaise.

Note: Serve with cold poached turbot, haddock or hake, or with prawns.

Sauce aux Poireaux
Leek Sauce

Imperial (Metric)	American
8 oz (225g) leeks, trimmed	8 ounces trimmed leeks
2 oz (50g) butter	¼ cup butter
½ pint (300ml) fish velouté (page 176)	1⅓ cups fish velouté (page 176)

1 Cut the leeks into *julienne* and sauté in the melted butter for 3 minutes.
2 Stir in the fish velouté, then transfer the mixture to a blender and purée to a smooth sauce. Reheat gently and serve, or allow to cool before serving.

Note: Serve hot or cold with mackerel, sole (flounder), plaice or the white fish of your choice.

Sauce Antiboise
Anchovy and Madeira Sauce

Imperial (Metric)	American
3 cloves garlic, chopped	3 cloves garlic, chopped
4 fl oz (120ml) Madeira	½ cup Madeira
4 rinsed anchovy fillets	4 rinsed anchovy fillets
4 black olives, stoned	4 black olives, pitted
½ pint (300ml) fish velouté (page 176)	1⅓ cups fish velouté (page 176)

1 Boil the garlic in the Madeira for 1 minute. Place in a blender with the anchovies and olives, and blend until smooth.
2 Beat this mixture into the velouté, and reheat before serving.

Note: Serve with grilled or barbecued fish of all types.

Sauce Raifort
Creamy Horseradish Sauce

Imperial (Metric)	American
½ pint (300ml) fish velouté (page 176)	1⅓ cups fish velouté (page 176)
3 fl oz (90ml) cream	⅓ cup cream
1 oz (25g) horseradish cream	2 tablespoons horseradish cream
1 teaspoon Dijon mustard	1 teaspoon Dijon *or* French mustard

1 Heat the velouté gently and add all the other ingredients. Stir until smooth and creamy. Serve hot or cold.

Note: Serve with oily fish such as mackerel or herrings, or cold with smoked fish such as eels.

Sauce Basquaise
Rich Onion and Pepper Sauce

Imperial (Metric)	American
2 fl oz (60ml) olive oil	¼ cup olive oil
2 oz (50g) chopped onion	⅓ cup chopped onion
2 oz (50g) chopped red and green pepper	⅓ cup chopped red and green pepper
¼ pint (150ml) ruby port	⅔ cup ruby port
1 oz (25g) tomato purée	2 tablespoons tomato paste
½ pint (300ml) fish velouté (page 176)	1⅓ cups fish velouté (page 176)

1 Heat the oil and sauté the onion and peppers for 3 minutes, stirring to avoid browning.
2 Add the ruby port and tomato purée (paste) and simmer for another minute.

3 Purée this mixture in a blender, then return to the pan, stir in the fish velouté and reheat the mixture to boiling. Simmer for 5 minutes and serve.

Note: Serve with any white fish fillets, or fresh tuna or mackerel.

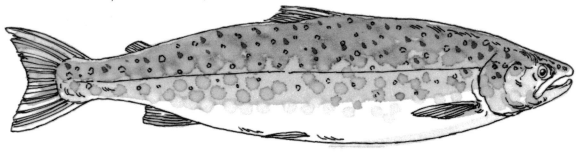

Mayonnaise
Basic Mayonnaise

There is still an air of mystery about mayonnaise-making — like soufflés it has a reputation of being difficult to make yet, just as with soufflés, if you follow the instructions and learn the rules, it is really very simple and successful. Mayonnaise is an emulsion — that is, two liquids which cannot completely mix are whisked together so that one is suspended in the other. With mayonnaise the mixing is rather special, however, because the whisking increases the volume, and the egg yolks can miraculously absorb far more than their own volume in oil, thus binding and thickening the emulsion to enable it to remain thickened once it is made. A vinaigrette dressing, for example, although the oil and vinegar are whisked together, will eventually separate in a way that mayonnaise does not. Mayonnaise is always a cold sauce — heating will cook the eggs, ruining the emulsion — but equally it cannot be frozen as the emulsion will break down when thawed.

I have devised a slight variation upon a standard mayonnaise for this book, especially created to complement fish of all kinds due to its piquancy, and it is followed with just a few of the many variations which lend themselves to accompanying fish dishes.

Imperial (Metric)	American
4 egg yolks	4 egg yolks
1 teaspoon Dijon mustard	1 teaspoon Dijon or French mustard
½ teaspoon sea salt	½ teaspoon sea salt
Large pinch freshly ground pepper	Large pinch freshly ground pepper
½ pint (300ml) walnut or olive oil	1⅓ cups walnut or olive oil
Juice of 2 limes	Juice of 2 limes
2 tablespoons Noilly Prat vermouth, warmed	2 tabelspoons Noilly Prat vermouth, warmed

1 Place the egg yolks, mustard, salt and pepper in a basin, and start to whisk gently in one direction (clockwise or anti-clockwise) only — do not change.
2 When the mixture starts to thicken, begin beating in the oil a drop at a time. As the mixture thickens further, the oil can be added in a very thin stream until it has all been absorbed and the sauce is extremely thick.
3 Finally, whisk in the lime juice and warm vermouth — this gives the sauce a good consistency.

Variations:
Mayonnaise can be thinned down or lightened by the addition of whipped cream or, preferably, whisked yogurt. Grainy mustard gives a pleasant texture. Olive oil is traditionally used, and can be substituted if walnut is unavailable, but do try to obtain the latter, which is quite delicious and perfect with fish.

Sauces Based on Mayonnaise

Sauce au Basil
Basil Sauce

To the basic mayonaise add 1 teaspoon tomato purée (paste), 8 finely chopped leaves of basil, 1 crushed clove of garlic and 2 large tablespoons of yogurt. Mix well and serve.

Sauce Avocatine
Avocado Sauce

To the basic mayonnaise add 6 oz (150g/¾ cup) smoothly mashed avocado pulp, 2 fl oz (60ml/¼ cup) low-fat yogurt and a good pinch of cayenne pepper. Check the salt content and add more if necessary, and serve.

Sauce Paloise
Mint Sauce

Blend the basic mayonnaise with 8 fresh mint leaves and 3 fl oz (90ml/⅓ cup) yogurt. Serve.

Sauce Mousseline
Whipped Cream Mayonnaise

Beat 4 fl oz (120ml/½ cup) double (heavy) cream and 1 egg white separately until light and fluffy. Fold both into the basic mayonnaise, check seasoning and serve.

Sauce Orangine
Brandied Orange Sauce

To the basic mayonnaise add the juice of half a blood orange and 2 tablespoons of Cognac. Serve.

Sauce Royale
Exotic Sauce for Shellfish

Place the basic mayonnaise in a blender with 1 oz (25g/¼ cup) pineapple flesh, 1 teaspoon of preserved ginger in its syrup, 1 chilli with its seeds removed, 2 tablespoons of tomato purée (paste), 1 teaspoon of clear honey and 2 tablespoons of either vodka or Marc de Bourgogne. Blend to a smooth sauce, check the seasoning and serve with lobster, crab or prawns, or shellfish of your choice.

Sauce au Saffran Méridional
Saffron Sauce

Brew 5 threads of saffron in 4 tablespoons of hot Martini Rosso or Saint Raphaël aperitif for 5 minutes. Liquidize and beat the liquid into the basic mayonnaise along with ½ teaspoon of turmeric powder. Serve.

Sauce Albigenoise
Piquant Green Sauce

Finely chop 1 ounce (25g) of the following: capers, pickled cucumber, rinsed anchovy fillets, fresh mint leaves, tender spinach leaves. Finely chop 1 hard-boiled egg, and crush 1 clove of garlic. Beat all these ingredients into the basic mayonnaise. Lastly stir in 3 fl oz (90ml/⅓ cup) whipped yogurt and serve.

Sauce Rouille
Provençale Garlic Sauce

Place the basic mayonnaise in a blender with 4 chopped cloves of garlic, 2 small sprigs of basil, 2 teaspoons of tomato purée (paste), 1 seeded red or green chilli and a few threads of saffron. Blend to a smooth purée. Place this sauce in a bowl and beat in 3 oz (75g/⅓ cup) hot creamy mashed potato. Use as a garnish for fish soups or stews. One sieved hard-boiled egg could also be added, or you could follow the Provençal custom of puréeing the yellow meat from a sea urchin with the other ingredients.

Variations:
This sauce is sometimes made by beating garlicy mashed potato (about 8 oz/225g/1 cup) in a bowl with 3 sieved hard-boiled eggs. It will then emulsify with at least ½ pint (300ml/1⅓ cups) olive oil to make a type of mayonnaise. Season well and serve as for rouille.

A nother variation, from Marseilles, makes a sort of emulsion from breadcrumbs and flavoured oil. One seeded and chopped red chilli is placed in a blender with 2 peeled and chopped cloves of garlic. These are puréed, and 3 fl oz (90ml/⅓ cup) olive oil is drizzled in as for mayonnaise. This mixture is then added to 3 oz (75g/1½ cups) wholemeal (whole wheat) breadcrumbs, to form a stiff purée. Smoked cod's roe, or other roe, can be added (about 1 oz/25g/2 tablespoons) or 1 egg yolk could be beaten in, as can sea urchin meat, as mentioned above.

Sauce Conil
Piquant Mint Mayonnaise

Beat together ¼ pint (150ml/⅓ cup) basic mayonnaise with an equal amount of whipped cream. Stir in 2 tablespoons dry French vermouth and 1 tablespoon of French gin. Add 1 tablespoon chopped fresh mint and season generously. This sauce is used to dip the flesh of prawns (shrimp) and *écrevisses*, but is so good it could just as well be spread on crusty French bread.

Les Sauce aux Oeufs
Egg-based Sauces

I have chosen not to give a definitive master recipe for this section, although the two which follow are both, in their way, definitive examples of the principle. In fact, hot egg-based sauces of the type most people know best as Hollandaise are to a certain extent a variation on the principle of mayonnaise, in that they rely upon the seemingly magical ability of eggs to absorb large volumes of oil to thicken and emulsify the sauce. For these hot sauces, the acidulating ingredients are added early in the recipe, and the oil from the mayonnaise is replaced by butter, added in tiny pieces just as the oil was poured in drop by drop. Great care must be taken to keep the temperature of the eggs low since, as is quite obvious, too much heat will result in scrambled — albeit tasty — eggs! This first sauce, from the town where *Noilly Prat* vermouth is made, is very similar to a Bearnaise and epitomizes the principle of this type of egg-thickened sauce. The second sauce is a delightful variation on the theme.

Sauce Marseillan
Egg Sauce with Vermouth

Imperial (Metric)	American
3 fl oz (90ml) *Noilly Prat* vermouth	6 tablespoons *Noilly Prat* vermouth
1 fl oz (30ml) white wine vinegar	2 tablespoons white wine vinegar
2 oz (50g) chopped shallot *or* red onion	1/3 cup chopped shallot *or* red onion
1 teaspoon sea salt	1 teaspoon sea salt
1 teaspoon crushed peppercorns	1 teaspoon crushed peppercorns
6 egg yolks	6 egg yolks
8 oz (225g) unsalted farm butter	1 cup sweet farm butter

1 Place the vermouth and vinegar in a pan with the shallots, salt and pepper. Boil the liquid to reduce to just 3 tablespoons. Cool and strain the liquid.

2 In a clean pan, or the top of a double boiler, beat together the egg yolks and the reduced vermouth. Place over another pan (or the base of the double boiler) containing simmering water and whisk until the mixture turns pale and thickens to a light custard consistency.

3 Add the butter bit by bit — you may find it easiest to cut it into about 24 equal cubes before beginning to cook. Beat each piece in well before adding the next. The sauce will thicken and increase in volume to become a creamy, rich and smooth sauce resembling a hot mayonnaise. Check throughout cooking that the water below the pan does not boil as that would cook the eggs, and do not stop whisking while the eggs are over the hot water. Remove the pan from the heat if you are at all worried. Serve as soon as the last of the butter has been added and beaten in.

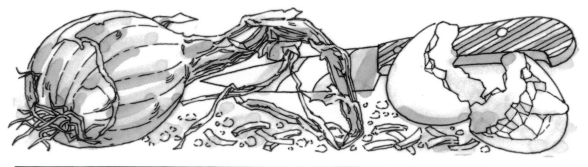

Sauce à l'Oseille et Rameaux de Salicorne

Egg Sauce with Sorrel and Samphire

Imperial (Metric)	American
4 oz (100g) tender sorrel leaves	1 cup tender sorrel leaves
2 oz (50g) fresh samphire	½ cup fresh samphire
5 leaves fresh mint	5 leaves fresh mint
¼ pint (150ml) dry white wine	⅔ cup dry white wine
Sea salt and freshly ground black pepper	Sea salt and freshly ground black pepper
1 teaspoon clear honey	1 teaspoon clear honey
4 egg yolks	4 egg yolks
8 oz (225g) unsalted farm butter	1 cup sweet farm butter
1 tablespoon fresh chopped herbs (mint, sorrel and chervil), to garnish	1 tablespoon fresh chopped herbs (mint, sorrel and chervil), to garnish

1 Clean and pick over the sorrel and samphire. Drain well.

2 Place the sorrel and samphire in a blender with the wine, seasoning and honey (do not add too much salt at this stage as the samphire can be quite salty — it is better to check the seasoning later and add more if necessary at that stage). Blend to a smooth purée.

3 Place this mixture in a pan and bring to the boil. Boil for about 5 minutes, or until reduced by about one-third. Remove from the heat and allow to cool somewhat.

4 Beat in the eggs. Place the pan over another pan half-filled with hot water and whisk constantly until the mixture starts to lighten and thicken — taking care not to over-cook and thus scramble the eggs.

5 Beat in the butter bit by bit, letting each piece be absorbed before adding the next. The sauce will become thick and glossy, with a wonderful colour and flavour.

6 Check the seasoning and serve the sauce warm, sprinkled with fresh herbs.

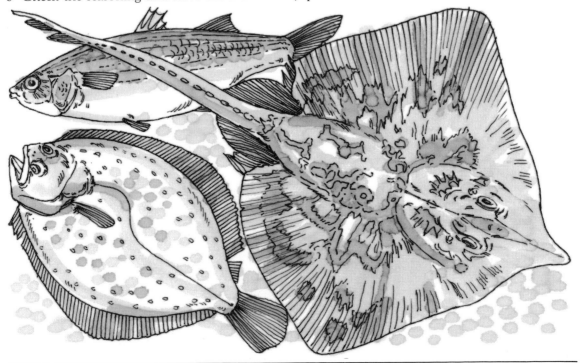

Les Sauces au Yaourt
Yogurt-based Sauces

Once again, there is no master recipe for this section — rather, the unifying factor is the already prepared base of natural, low-fat yogurt to which a wide range of flavours and textures can be added. The result is always a piquant, appetizing sauce which marries well with the mellow flavours of fresh fish and with a fresh tang which cuts through the richness of the oilier types. These sauces are becoming more and more popular with health-conscious diners, surpassing in some cases the more traditional sauces we have already met in this chapter. Not so surprising, really, since so many people are turning to fish from red meat because of its health aspects — what could be more logical than to accompany it with a sauce which reflects the same approach. Still, I am all for variety, and feel that if you approach food sensibly, you can enjoy a taste of both the richer, egg-based sauces with your fresh, healthy fish, and sample these new-style yogurt ones as well.

All these sauces have as their base ¼ pint (150ml/⅔ cup) plain, low-fat yogurt, whipped.

La Cressonière
Watercress Sauce

Melt 1 oz (25g/2 tablespoons) butter in a pan. In this sauté 1 small chopped shallot, 3 oz (75g/½ cup) watercress leaves and 1 small chopped leek. Stir in 3 fl oz (90ml/⅓ cup) fish velouté (page 176) and simmer for 3 minutes. Cool the mixture and blend it to a purée. Stir this purée into the yogurt, season with salt and cayenne pepper and serve.

La Florentine
Spinach Sauce

In a blender place 5 oz (125g/¾ cup) cooked, drained, spinach, 1 chopped clove for garlic, 2 rinsed anchovy fillets, 2 stoned (pitted) black olives, the juice of a lemon and the grated rind of one-quarter of it. Blend to a smooth purée and stir this into the yogurt. Season and serve with white fish.

La Sauce aux Noix
Walnut Sauce

In a blender place 3 oz (75g/½ cup) shelled walnuts, 2 leaves of basil and 3 fl oz (75ml/⅓ cup) white port. Blend to a smooth paste and stir this into the yogurt. Season and serve with simple poached salmon or trout.

La Ciboulette
Leek Sauce

Melt 2 oz (50g/¼ cup) butter in a pan and sauté 4 oz (100g) of chopped white leek for 3 minutes. Place this in a blender with the yogurt and purée to a smooth sauce. Before serving, season and stir in a small bunch of snipped chives. Serve with grilled red mullet (snapper) or plaice.

La Sauce au Caviar
Caviar Sauce

To the yogurt base simply add 1 teaspoon of finely chopped shallot, the juice of ½ a lemon and 1 oz (25g/2 tablespoons) of fresh caviar of the best quality you can afford.

La Groseillaise
Gooseberry Sauce

Blend 5 oz (125g/1 cup) ripe gooseberries, 1 teaspoon of clear honey and 2 fresh mint leaves to a purée. Stir this into the yogurt, season and serve with grilled mackerel, trout or salmon

La Délicieuse
Heavenly Apple Sauce

To the yogurt base add 5 oz (125g/1 scant cup) stewed cooking apple purée and 2 tablespoons of strong (hard) cider. Season and serve with oily fish. If you find the sauce too sharp, add 1 teaspoon of clear honey or blend the sauce with 1 chopped hard-boiled egg.

La Cantaloupaise
Spiced Melon Sauce

Place 6 oz (150g/1 cup) of melon flesh — preferably a very scented type such as cantaloupe or musk melon — in a blender with 1 tablespoon of preserved ginger in syrup. Purée and stir into the yogurt. Season with a pinch of cayenne pepper and serve with any grilled (broiled) or barbecued fish, especially trout.

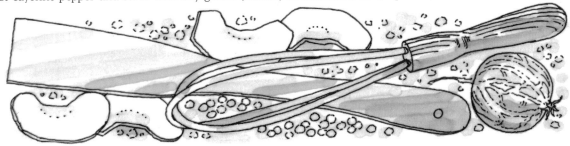

Les Sauces Piquantes aux Légumes et Fruits
Piquant Vegetable- and Fruit-based Sauces

This last collection is quite eclectic, reflecting a general theme of emphasis on fresh fruits and vegetables to give savour and interest to the sauce. Some are thickened very lightly with a slurry of cornflour (cornstarch) and water, others rely on the thickness of the ingredients when puréed, and we finish this section with a trio of recipes which are unusual in different ways — the first because it uses the silken bean curd tofu, which is catching on fast in France as a result of our love-affair with Vietnamese cooking; the second because it is a jellied sauce which is served in attractive cubes or diamonds as a garnish; the last because it is a marinade which has become so popular that it has achieved the status of a sauce — the aromatic and distinctive raspberry vinegar which, when used badly, becomes a *bête noire* for the discerning palate yet, when used with discretion can stimulate the tastebuds and augment a dish in a very special way

Sauce à l'Ananas Aigre-Doux
Sweet-Sour Pineapple Sauce

Imperial (Metric)	American
¼ pint (150ml) cider vinegar	⅔ cup cider vinegar
4 oz (100g) fresh pineapple flesh	⅔ cup fresh pineapple flesh
½ oz (15g) fresh ginger, peeled and chopped	1 small piece fresh ginger, peeled and chopped
½ pint (300ml) unsweetened pineapple juice	1⅓ cups unsweetened pineapple juice
1 tablespoon tomato purée	1 tablespoon tomato paste
1 tablespoon natural soya sauce	1 tablespoon natural soy sauce
2 cloves garlic, chopped	2 cloves garlic, chopped
2 fl oz (60ml) clear honey	2 tablespoons clear honey
1 green chilli, seeded and chopped	1 green chili, seeded and chopped
½ tablespoon cornflour	½ tablespoon cornstarch
4 fl oz (120ml) water	½ cup water
For the garnish:	For the garnish:
1 slice pineapple, cubed	1 slice pineapple, cubed
1 red pepper, seeded and diced	1 red pepper, seeded and diced
1 stick celery, chopped	1 stalk celery, chopped
2 spring onions, thinly sliced	2 scallions, thinly sliced
1 fl oz (30ml) vegetable oil	2 tablespoons vegetable oil

1 Place all the ingredients except the cornflour (cornstarch), water, and garnish ingredients, into a blender and purée to a smooth sauce.

2 Pour the sauce into a pan and heat to boiling pount. Mix the cornflour (cornstarch) with the water and stir this slowly into the sauce, stirring.

3 Let the sauce simmer for 4 minutes to thicken the sauce and clear the starch.

4 Meanwhile, sauté all the garnish vegetables very briefly in the hot oil.

5 Check the seasoning of the sauce — a pinch of cayenne may be added for a more fiery taste — and serve garnished with sizzling vegetables. This sauce is very good for barbecued fish and shellfish.

Coulis de Tomates au Poivron Rouge

Tomato and Red Pepper Sauce

Imperial (Metric)	American
2 fl oz (60ml) olive oil	¼ cup olive oil
1 red onion, chopped	1 red onion, chopped
3 cloves garlic, chopped	3 cloves garlic, chopped
1 red pepper, seeded and diced	1 red pepper, seeded and diced
1 red chilli, seeded and chopped	1 red chili, seeded and chopped
6 leaves fresh basil	6 leaves fresh basil
1 lb (450g) large ribbed tomatoes, skinned and chopped	1 pound large ribbed tomatoes, skinned and chopped
¼ pint (150ml) dry white wine	⅔ cup dry white wine
Juice of 1 orange	Juice of 1 orange
1 teaspoon clear honey	1 teaspoon clear honey
1 teaspoon paprika	1 teaspoon paprika
Sea salt and freshly ground black pepper	Sea salt and freshly ground black pepper
1 tablespoon toasted sesame seeds	1 tablespoon toasted sesame seeds

1 Heat the oil in a large pan and sauté the onion for 2 minutes, then add the garlic, red pepper, chilli and basil. Sauté gently for 5 minutes, stirring, then add the fresh tomatoes, wine, orange juice, honey, paprika and seasoning.

2 Bring the sauce to the boil and simmer for 15 minutes until thick and rich. Place in a blender and purée.

3 This sauce is best served cold, although it can be served hot. Serve with barbecued or grilled fish or shellfish, sprinkling sesame seeds as a decoration before serving.

Sauce Escabèche Mediterranée

Spicy Pickling Sauce

Imperial (Metric)	American
¼ pint (150ml) *Noilly Prat* vermouth *or* dry white wine	⅔ cup *Noilly Prat* vermouth *or* dry white wine
3 fl oz (90ml) fresh lime juice	⅓ cup fresh lime juice
3 fl oz (90ml) cognac	⅓ cup cognac
1 dried chilli pepper, crushed	1 dried chili pepper, crushed
1 sprig dill	1 sprig dill
1 red onion, cut into thin rings	1 red onion, cut into thin rings
1 fresh red chilli, seeded and chopped	1 fresh red chili, seeded and chopped
2 tablespoons olive oil	2 tablespoons olive oil
1 teaspoon sea salt	1 teaspoon sea salt

1 Place all the ingredients in a blender, purée and use as a pickling sauce — marinate thin fillets of fish in the sauce for 36 hours, refrigerated.

Sauce Victoire aux Prunes Rouges

Plum Sauce with Black Beans

Imperial (Metric)	American
2 fl oz (50ml) cider vinegar	¼ cup cider vinegar
4 oz (100g) fresh red *or* black plums	4 ounces fresh red *or* black plums
1 red chilli, seeded and chopped	1 red chili, seeded and chopped
4 fl oz (120ml) clear honey	⅓ cup clear honey
4 fl oz (120ml) water	½ cup water
4 oz (100g) cooked black *or* red beans	½ cup cooked black *or* red beans
2 tablespoons natural soya sauce	2 tablespoons natural soy sauce
¼ teaspoon each of ground ginger, cinnamon and paprika	¼ teaspoon each of ground ginger, cinnamon and paprika
½ teaspoon sea salt	½ teaspoon sea salt
½ oz (15g) cornflour	½ tablespoon cornstarch
3 fl oz (90ml) cold water	⅓ cup cold water
For the garnish:	For the garnish:
2 sticks celery, chopped	2 stalks celery, chopped
4 oz (100g) diced fresh firm plums	⅔ cup diced fresh firm plums
2 tablespoons vegetable oil	2 tablespoons vegetable oil

1 Place in a blender all the ingredients except for the cornflour (cornstarch), water and garnish ingredients.

2 Purée the sauce ingredients, then heat them in a pan until the sauce is simmering.

3 Blend together the cornflour (cornstarch) and water, stir this into the sauce and simmer for 4 minutes to allow the sauce to thicken and clear.

4 Meanwhile sauté the celery for 4 minutes in the hot oil then add the plums and cook just until crisp and sizzling. Serve the sauce garnished with the hot vegetables. It is delicious with grilled prawns (shrimp) or white fish fillets.

Gelée de Raifort à la Citronelle

Horseradish Jelly with Lime

Imperial (Metric)	American
½ pint (300ml) double cream	1⅓ cups heavy cream
1 oz (25g) horseradish cream	2 tablespoons horseradish cream
Juice and grated rind of 1 lime	Juice and grated rind of 1 lime
1 tablespoon agar-agar	1 tablespoon agar-agar
Sea salt and freshly ground black pepper	Sea salt and freshly ground black pepper

1 Beat together the cream, horseradish and lime juice and rind.

2 Boil the agar-agar in a little water for 2 minutes, then beat into the cream mixture. Season to taste.

3 Pour the mixture into an ice cube tray and leave to set. When firm cut into squares or diamonds — the mixture has a marshmallow or Turkish Delight consistency — and serve as a garnish to marinated trout or salmon.

Sauce Exotique à la Mangue

Mango Sauce

Imperial (Metric)	American
3 fl oz (90ml) mayonnaise (page 179)	⅓ cup mayonnaise (page 179)
3 fl oz (90ml) natural yogurt	⅓ cup plain yogurt
3 oz (75g) silken tofu	⅓ cup silken tofu
2 oz (50g) mango chutney	¼ cup mango chutney
1 ripe mango, peeled and stoned	1 ripe mango, peeled and pitted
1 small green chilli, seeded and chopped	1 small green chili, seeded and chopped
¼ red pepper, seeded and diced	¼ red pepper, seeded and diced
Juice of ½ a lemon	Juice of ½ a lemon
2 teaspoons honey *or* ginger syrup	2 teaspoons honey *or* ginger syrup
Sea salt and freshly ground black pepper	Sea salt and freshly ground black pepper

1   Place all the ingredients in a blender and purée to a smooth sauce.

Vinaigre de Framboises

Raspberry Vinegar

Imperial (Metric)	American
3 lb (1.3 kilos) fresh raspberries	3 pounds fresh raspberries
1 pint (600ml) distilled white vinegar	2½ cups white distilled vinegar
3 fl oz (90ml) clear honey	¼ cup clear honey
¼ pint (150ml) red wine	⅔ cup red wine
½ pint (300ml) cooking brandy	1⅓ cups cooking brandy

1   In an earthenware jar, macerate two-thirds of the raspberries in the vinegar and honey. Leave for 24 hours, covered, in the refrigerator.

2   Pass the vinegar and raspberries through a nylon sieve (strainer), discarding the pulp.

3   Blend the remaining raspberries with the red wine, sieve (strain) and discard the pulp.

4   In a tall container, stir together the two liquids. Place the container in a bain-marie or saucepan half-filled with hot water. Heat gently for 1 hour. The vinegar should not be allowed to get too hot — 200°F/90°C is about right.

5   Cool the vinegar and then add the brandy. Transfer the vinegar to a corked bottle and use sparingly.

Variation:
Other soft fruits can be used in place of the raspberries — such as strawberries, blackberries or blackcurrants.

Index